Samuel Greene Wheeler Benjamin

The Atlantic Islands as Resorts of Health and Pleasure

Samuel Greene Wheeler Benjamin

The Atlantic Islands as Resorts of Health and Pleasure

ISBN/EAN: 9783743321892

Manufactured in Europe, USA, Canada, Australia, Japa

Cover: Foto ©ninafisch / pixelio.de

Manufactured and distributed by brebook publishing software
(www.brebook.com)

Samuel Greene Wheeler Benjamin

The Atlantic Islands as Resorts of Health and Pleasure

THE ATLANTIC ISLANDS

AS RESORTS OF

HEALTH AND PLEASURE.

By S. G. W. BENJAMIN,

AUTHOR OF "CONTEMPORARY ART IN EUROPE," ETC.

ILLUSTRATED.

"Summer isles of Eden lying in dark purple spheres of sea."—TENNYSON.
"O, health! health!—the blessing of the rich, the riches of the poor! who can buy thee at too dear a rate, since there is no enjoying this world without thee."—JONSON.

NEW YORK:
HARPER & BROTHERS, PUBLISHERS,
FRANKLIN SQUARE.
1878.

PREFACE.

THIS work on the islands of the North Atlantic has been prepared with the hope that it will meet a growing want of the travelling public. These islands, for the best reasons in the world, are becoming more and more the resort of the invalid and the pleasure-seeker. But, up to this time, no guide-book has existed giving a comparative and comprehensive statement of the advantages of such islands, whether as summer or winter resorts.

No islands are included in these pages except such as are free from the visitations of yellow fever or persistent malarial and zymotic epidemics. Great care has also been taken to obtain the fullest and most correct sanitary statistics on the subject, in which the author has perhaps been assisted by his interest in medical topics. Official documents and data have been consulted, and the opinions of the ablest resident physicians have been received and compared. And in every instance, regarding all points of information, the writer has gathered his facts from careful personal observation or from the highest authorities.

As all of these islands have been recently visited by him, he has thought fit to leave the description of them in their original narrative form, as he saw all the important places mentioned, while the book may thus perhaps be rendered more attractive to the general reader by the introduction of incidents of travel and adventure.

The Appendix, although placed at the end, really contains the pith of the book. It is intended to convey copious information regarding the attractions of each island for both invalids and sportsmen, sanitary statistics, the means for reaching these resorts, and the hotels and expenses of living. The islands are there distinctly classified in the order of their respective advantages, without bias or prejudice. It may be that one or two well-known resorts receive less indiscriminate praise than has hitherto been awarded to them, while other less known resorts come in for a share of credit that may surprise some who are ignorant of their merits. But the writer can honestly say that he has stated the facts as they appeared to the best of his judgment.

The author avails himself of this opportunity to express his hearty acknowledgments for the genial hospitality, the many kind attentions, and the uniform courtesy he has met in his rambles among the Atlantic Isles, whether from the officials of the local governments, the consuls of the United States and other countries, or from private citizens.

CONTENTS.

CHAPTER I.
The Bahamas.. 13

CHAPTER II.
The Azores... 33

CHAPTER III.
The Channel Islands... 57

CHAPTER IV.
The Magdalen Islands.. 78

CHAPTER V.
Madeira... 94

CHAPTER VI.
Teneriffe... 121

CHAPTER VII.
Newfoundland.. 146

CHAPTER VIII.
The Bermudas.. 161

CHAPTER IX.
Belleisle-en-Mer.. 179

CHAPTER X.
Prince Edward Island.. 188

CHAPTER XI.
Isles of Shoals... 205

CHAPTER XII.
Cape Breton Island.. 222

CHAPTER XIII.
The Isle of Wight... 234

Appendix.. 257

ILLUSTRATIONS.

	PAGE
GRÈVE AU LANÇON	*Frontispiece.*
HOPETOWN HARBOR, ABACO	13
GOVERNMENT HOUSE	15
OLD GUNNYBAGS	16
SPONGE YARD	17
ENTRANCE TO PORT NASSAU	19
BLACKBEARD, THE PIRATE	20
FORT FINCASTLE, NASSAU	21
THE HERMITAGE, COUNTRY-SEAT OF LORD DUNMORE, AT NASSAU	21
ROYAL VICTORIA HOTEL	23
PUBLIC LIBRARY, NASSAU	24
SILK-COTTON-TREE, NASSAU	26
DUNMORE TOWN	28
GLASS WINDOWS	30
STREET IN NASSAU	32
AZORES, OR WESTERN ISLES	34
FLORES CART AND PEASANT HUT	37
PICO, FROM FAYAL	38
PICO PEAK, FROM FAYAL	39
THE PICO FERRY	41
MARKET-DAY IN FAYAL	47
HOSPITAL OF VILLAFRANCA DO CAMPO	49
JETTY OF PONTA DELGADA, ST. MICHAEL	51
A ST. MICHAEL WAGON	53
THE CHANNEL ISLANDS	57
ST. PETER'S PORT, GUERNSEY	58
MONUMENT TO PRINCE ALBERT, GUERNSEY	59
MARKET-PLACE AT ST. PETER'S PORT, GUERNSEY	60
CHILDREN BEGGING FOR "DOUBLES"	61
DOLMEN AND MARTELLO TOWER, GUERNSEY	62
HAUTEVILLE, VICTOR HUGO'S LATE RESIDENCE IN GUERNSEY	64
GUARD-HOUSE DESCRIBED IN "TOILERS OF THE SEA"	65
THE CORBIÈRE AND LIGHT-HOUSE, JERSEY	66
MOUNT ORGUEIL CASTLE, JERSEY	68
THE PINNACLE, JERSEY	69

	PAGE
ST. BRELADE'S CHURCH, JERSEY	70
VRAICKING	71
CREUX HARBOR, SARK	72
ENTRANCE TO THE CREUX LANDING-PLACE, SARK	73
THE AUTELETS, SARK	74
CREUX DU DERRIBLE, SARK	75
NATURAL BRIDGE, PONT-DU-MOULIN, SARK	76
SEIGNEUR'S HOUSE, SARK	77
SAND DUNES AND WRECKS BETWEEN AMHERST AND GRINDSTONE ISLANDS	79
THE MAGDALEN ISLANDS	80
AMHERST, LOOKING TOWARD DEMOISELLE HILL	81
LANDING ON ENTRY ISLAND	82
OLD MAN AND OLD WOMAN	83
DRAGGING THE HULL OF A SCHOONER TO THE BEACH	85
THROUGH THE SURF	86
PORT AND VILLAGE OF ÉTANG DU NORD, GRINDSTONE ISLAND	87
CAP AU MEULE AND WRECK, GRINDSTONE ISLAND	89
PART OF CAPE ALRIGHT	90
THE SERENE JOSEPH	91
THE MADEIRA ISLANDS	95
FUNCHAL HARBOR AND BRAZEN HEAD	96
LOO ROCK	97
THE SLEDGE-BACK	99
THE MOUNTAIN SLED	101
CHURCH OF NOSTRA SENHORA DO MONTE	103
HAMMOCK-RIDING IN MADEIRA	107
VILLAGE OF CAMA DO LOBOS	109
A THRESHING-FLOOR	110
A GRIST-MILL	111
PEASANTS' HUT AND PEASANTS	115
PENHA D'AGUA	117
PLAZA DE LA CONSTITUCION, SANTA CRUZ	121
THE CANARY ISLANDS	122

ILLUSTRATIONS.

	Page
Teneriffe	123
Spanish Señorita	124
The Postigo	125
Milk-venders	126
Camels and Cochineal-carriers	128
Group of Chuzas, or Huts, near Laguna	129
Teneriffe Costume	130
Guanche Mummies at Tacaronte	131
City of San Juan, Orotava	133
Dragon-tree as it was	134
Botanic Gardens, Orotava	135
View of the Peak from Orotava	137
Peasant Spinning	138
A Peasant-woman of Icod	139
Peak of Teneriffe, as seen on approaching the Large Crater	141
Costume of Peasant	144
The Spout off Cape Broyle	147
Entrance to the Harbor of St. Johns	149
Ascent to a "Flake"	151
Cape Bay.—Telegraph House	153
St. Johns, from Signal Hill	155
Cleaning Fish	157
The Bermudas	161
Cuba and the Bahama Islands	162
Hamilton, Bermudas	163
Floating-dock	165
Trinity Church, Hamilton	166
Moore's Calabash-tree	167
View from Light-house	168
Cottage and Garden in Hamilton	169
A Street Scene in Hamilton — The Wharf	170
A Street Scene in St. George's	171
The Devil's Hole	172
Caves on the Coast	173
Ravine on South Shore, Bermuda	174
Pitts Bay	175
India-rubber-tree	177
Fish-women of the Morbihan	179
Cæsar's Table, or Table of the Merchants, Locmariaquer	180
Le Palais, Belleisle	182
Peasant-girl, Belleisle	186
Sambro' Light.—Entrance to Halifax Harbor	188
Entrance to Strait of Canso	189
Halifax, from the Citadel	190
Light-house.—Entrance to Pictou Port	191
Government House, Charlottetown	192
Methodist Church and Part of Charlottetown—East River in the Distance	193

	Page
Avenue leading to Government House	194
Market Building, Charlottetown	195
Carrying the Mails across Northumberland Strait in Winter	197
Scene on Hunter River	198
Fish-house and Stage, and Fishing-boats, Rustico	199
Fishing-boats beating into Rustico Harbor, between the Bar and the Spit: Bathing-house in the Foreground	200
Fishing Party	201
Shag and Mingo Rocks, Duck Island	205
Isles of Shoals	206
Whale's-back Light	208
Duck Island, from Appledore	210
Laighton's Grave	211
South-east End of Appledore, looking South	212
Haley's Dock and Homestead	213
Ledge of Rocks, Haley's Island	214
Smutty Nose	215
Old Church, Star Island	216
Captain John Smith's Monument, Star Island	217
Gorge, Star Island	218
White Island Light	218
Cliffs, White Island	219
Covered Walk and Light-house, White Island	220
Londoner, from Star Island	221
Fishermen Cruising	223
Tall Fishing	225
Riding out a North-easter	227
The Micmac Indians	228
One of the Fisherman's Perils	229
Taking a Sight	232
Isle of Wight	234
Ryde	235
Grave of the Young Cottager	237
Legh Richmond	238
John Wilkes	239
Shanklin Chine	240
Ventnor, from Pulpit Rock	241
The Natural Enemy	243
Bonchurch	244
The Well of St. Lawrence	245
A Crab-stoner	246
Black Gang Chine	247
Faringford, the Residence of Alfred Tennyson	248
Scratchell's Bay	249
Tomb of the Princess Elizabeth	251
Carisbrooke Castle	252
Osborne	254

THE ATLANTIC ISLANDS;

AS RESORTS FOR

HEALTH AND PLEASURE.

CHAPTER I.

THE BAHAMAS.

WE had been heading southward in the steamer *City of Merida* for two days, followed by raw northerly winds, when the wind suddenly shifted to the south. The change in the temperature was magical. Overcoats were thrown aside at once, and all hands were called aft to spread the awning; the waves went down, the clouds disappeared, the cold gray color of the sea turned to azure, and every breath of the "sweet south" seemed to sing a welcome to enchanted isles where reigns perpetual summer. On the fourth night we passed the Elbow Light, on the north-east angle of Abaco, and sighted Hole-in-the-Wall at midnight. Many of us also now saw for the first time the Southern Cross gleaming over the bow, while the North Star and the Bear were still visible on the quarter. At dawn a long, low line of green keys lay abeam, and soon we saw the graceful groves of cocoa and the spires of Nassau gleaming in the sun, now rising in a cloudless sky. The vessel drew too much water to go over the bar, and therefore came to anchor outside of the light-house at the western end of Hog Island, a beautiful coral islet three miles long, which, by furnishing a breakwater cheaper and safer than that of Plymouth or Cherbourg, enables Nassau to claim the best port in the Bahamas. Boats of all descriptions darted from the shore, manned by negroes, presenting sometimes a diverting variety of raggedness in the slender wardrobe prescribed by conventional propriety rather than by any need of protection against the weather. As we rowed in over the bar the first object to attract our attention was the absolute clearness of the water—hyaline, as a poet might truthfully call it—which enables the eye to see everything on the white sand bottom, and the vivid, almost dazzling, green hue of the surface, mottled with varied tints of the same color, giving exactly the appearance of polished malachite. On landing, amidst a hubbub of negroes, we found the streets of almost snowy whiteness, intensified by the glare of the white walls, so that straw hats and shade umbrellas were at once called into requisition. One very soon gets accustomed to this, however, and the effect could be greatly modified if the worthy citizens would only content themselves with lower walls around their gardens, or would color those they have with some sober gray. This is evident when one rides out beyond the city, where the roads are of precisely the same character, but much more tolerable, because lined with verdure instead of staring white walls.

It was a charming transition from the glare of the streets to the cool, spacious verandas of the Royal Victoria Hotel, which occupies noble grounds on an elevated position commanding a superb prospect over the city, the harbor, and the ocean beyond; and a breakfast of turtle steak, chocolate, and tropical fruits freshly plucked, reminded us again that for a while at least we were free from the furnace-heated prison-houses of the North, and the icy, capricious, penetrating winds of our Northern spring, if it is not a misnomer to call it spring.

Nassau is not only the chief town of the island of New Providence, but also the capital of the Bahamas. There the Legislature meets and the governor resides. The Government House is pleasantly situated, and the approach to it is appropriately adorned by a colossal statue of Christopher Columbus. The Legislature is elected once in seven years, and generally includes several colored members. The black population largely predominates, for not only did the early settlers own slaves, but many cargoes of captured slavers were taken to Nassau and left there to shift for themselves. The aboriginal race of the Bahamas is now entirely extinct. The negroes are generally tall and well formed, and very civil in their demeanor, and great crimes are uncommon among them. Theft and licentiousness are their chief "irregularities." It is creditable to the people that the spacious and handsome prison recently constructed at high cost is half empty, which gave the jailer a curious uneasiness, because, as he said to me, he had a piece of road-mending to be done in the broiling sun of mid-day, and the number of criminals under his charge was not equal to completing it within a given time! The old prison, a rather picturesque building resembling a mosque, is now turned into a public library; the cells, once filled with pirates and boozy blockade-runners, now form the alcoves of a very well-arranged library, stocked with some six thousand volumes, generally well selected, and open to the use of the

GOVERNMENT HOUSE.

public. As this institution is near the hotel, it is of great advantage to strangers sojourning on the island.

Some of the mulattoes display considerable talent as artisans. The shell-work they produce shows exquisite taste and skill; and Bethel, the best ship-builder of the group—and a very clever man he is, too—is of the colored persuasion. Captain Stuart, who commands the light-house and revenue schooner, is a man of commanding appearance and marked intelligence, and is regarded by the negroes of Nassau as "a sort of god round heah," as they phrase it, because he foretold the great hurricane of 1866. The colored people of Nassau are much addicted to church-going, and it is pleasant of a calm evening to hear the singing from the churches all over the town. Poppy Rumer, as he is familiarly called, a quaint, unique character, is their most noted preacher, and many of his curious sayings and eccentricities are current. He is, in addition, a man possessed of intellectual power, and is thoroughly in earnest. Old Gunnybags is another noted character of Nassau, a modern Diogenes, who takes up his residence in Grantstown, the suburb affected by the black gentry. The old fellow, not to speak disrespectfully of him, was crossed in love in his earlier days, it is said, since which melancholy event he has worn a suit of gunny bags of a fashion not borrowed from Paris, and has slept in a hogshead laid on its side under a wall by the wayside: owing to the narrowness of his quarters and the heat of the climate, he cooks his meals in the open air. A little beyond Grantstown are the places called Jericho and Jericho-beyond-Jordan, which show what thrift the negro can display on occasion.

OLD GUNNYBAGS.

As a class, however, the negroes of the Bahamas are far more superstitious than religious. They are great cowards at night, shutting up their cabins tight as a drum to keep out the wandering powers of darkness. Although the fact is resented by many of the most intelligent colored residents, there is no doubt that the more ignorant negroes of these islands entertain an almost incredible belief in fetichism. The obeah men drive a thriving business, and it is seldom a sponging-boat goes to sea without first enlisting the valuable aid of the man-witch or warlock. They are said to be lazy, and certainly they seem to take life very easily, lying on the ground sometimes for hours under the full blaze of the noonday sun, chewing the end of a sugar-cane, or brawling in grandiloquent and often meaningless rodomontade at the street corners. But there is little need

of exertion when it takes so little to supply their immediate wants. A
recent pastoral of one of the ritualistic priests, giving directions for the
observance of Lent, created "inextinguishable laughter" in Nassau, for,
among other ordinances, it forbade the eating of sugar. As sugar-cane
forms a staple article of food with the negroes, a strict observance of
his directions would have been followed by lamentable results. But I
think the charge of laziness unfounded, if one but considers the severe
labor the negroes often accomplish, as, for example, in the sponge fishery,
which gives employment to the owners and crews of five hundred licensed
craft of ten to twenty-five tons burden, and is carried on with some risk
from the weather, and much hardship, for the sponges are two or three
fathoms below the surface, and must be torn from the rocks with hooks
attached to long poles. The position of the sponges is ascertained by
means of a water-glass, which is a simple oblong box a foot square, open
at the upper end, and containing a pane of glass at the other; on holding
this perpendicularly over the water one can see everything through it as
clearly as in an aquarium—fish, sponges, coral, or shells. The Bahama

SPONGE YARD.

sponges are chiefly of four sorts—sheep-wool (which is the most valuable),
reef, velvet, and glove; and, although inferior to the finest Mediterranean
sponges, are very strong, and serviceable for washing carriages, surgery,
and the like. The sponge-boats usually get in on Saturday, and the

sponges are assorted in the markets, each boat-load and variety by itself. On Monday they are disposed of at auction, only members of the sponge guild and those making genuine offers being permitted to bid, which is done by written tenders.

Talking aloud to themselves is another trait peculiar to the negroes of the Bahamas. As a proof of their love for large-sounding phrases alluded to above, which are often used without the slightest idea of their meaning, I give here a copy of a letter written by a soldier of one of the native regiments, addressed to his physician, who kindly placed it at my disposal, selecting it at random from a number of similar precious documents he had received:

"Feb. 23, 187-.

"Sir,—I thy most worthy servant, have the honour, at this time, to implore and beseeche thee, this 2d time to Pore this thy patient and impenitent hand Maid, for although it has pleased the Almighty to deal thus with her, as she at present is, still i trust that it may please him also to release her, out of her present pains and sufferings, to her former position again. And we trust that his Never failing providence may and will support thee to listen to the Tortures and cries of the Afflicted, for his mercies sake. Sir the present positions of thy penitent hand Maid is thus, a severe and Protruberance pain in the back, and a cough in proportion to the pain in the back, and a pain in the stomach in proportion to the cough, and a standing weakness, and a stubborn faintiness, with restlessness day and night, and Sir she stands at present in need of a good proportion of blood, for Sir she loose a good set, before she came to thee the first time. For Sir, she was losing it from Sunday to Sunday, which was eight days, and it began to abate on the ninth day. And Sir by the help of God and thy assistance, I implore thee to try for her for

"I am thy humble Servant."

Wrecking is another branch of business for which the Bahamas have long been famous, owing to their intricate navigation. At one time this was very lucrative, but it has been falling off of late years. Formerly everything saved from a wreck was sold at auction in Nassau; now all goods not of a perishable nature, and undamaged, are reshipped to the port of destination. Collusion between ship-masters and the pilots was also frequent; but increased vigilance on the part of the insurance companies has interfered with this nefarious business, while the numerous light-houses recently erected by the Government, with noble self-sacrifice, have operated in the same direction. The uncertainties attending money-making in this precarious way have their effect on the character of the people, as is the case when the element of chance enters largely into business; the prizes in the lottery are few, but are occasionally so large as to excite undue expectations, and thus unfit many for any pursuit more steady but less exciting. For months they will cruise around, watching and hoping, and barely kept alive on a scant supply of sugar-cane and conchs; then they fall in with a wreck, and make enough from it, perhaps, to keep them going another year. It is not a healthy or desirable state of affairs.

One Sunday morning a commotion arose quite unusual in the uncom-

ENTRANCE TO PORT NASSAU.

monly quiet and orderly streets of Nassau. There was hurrying to and fro, and the sound of voices shrill and rapid indicated some sudden and extraordinary excitement. The wharves of the little port were thronged and positively black with eager negroes, and great activity was noticeable among the sloops and schooners. Some were discharging their cargoes of sponges, shells, fish, and cattle in hot haste; others were provisioning or setting up their rigging; others again were expeditiously hoisting their sails and heaving up their anchors; while the crews, black and white, sung songs in merry chorus, as if under the influence of great and good tidings. What could it all mean? It meant this: another vein in the Bahama gold mines had been struck, another lead discovered, and the miners were off to develop it, each hoping to be the lucky one to turn out the largest nugget, and to retire on it for life. In other words, news had just been brought of the wreck of a Spanish vessel on the Lavadeiros Shoal, one hundred and fifty miles away. She was none of your wretched colliers or fruiters, with a cargo valueless to wreckers, but a ship whose hold from keelson to deck beams was packed with a thousand tons of choice silks and stuffs for the black-eyed brunettes of Havana, just enough damaged to oblige them to be sold at auction in Nassau, where all goods wrecked in that archipelago must be brought for adjudication. Verily, we thought, "it's an ill wind that blows nobody any good;" the misfortune which has wrung the soul and perhaps ruined the happiness of two or three in far-off lands has made glad the hearts of several thousand darkies, mulattoes, and whites in the Bahamas. Here is a text for La Rochefoucauld, the modern cynic.

The manufacture and exportation of salt have also been among the most lucrative pursuits of the islands. With the single exception of Andros Island, which seems to be still in a formative state, there is not a fresh-water lake or stream in the whole group; but lakes of some size, containing more or less salt, are found on many of the islands. Vast quantities of salt have been made at Exuma, Long Island, Rose Island, Inagua, and Turk's Island. The latter is now under the jurisdiction of Jamaica, and the production of salt at the other islands is at present in a very languishing condition, the result of the high duties imposed by our Government on the article, which act in two ways, like a two-edged sword, forcing our people to pay a higher price than they otherwise would for what salt they consume, and effectually crippling one of the most important trades of the West Indies.

BLACKBEARD, THE PIRATE.

But the branches of business which in past years have brought most wealth into Nassau have been buccaneering, privateering, and blockade-running. The buccaneers were at one time in high feather there; they bought up or captured the governors, toasted and roasted the people when recalcitrant, and, hiding behind the low keys in their little vessels, sprung out, spider-like, on any unwary trader quietly sailing by. Blackbeard, who is represented in the cut given above, from an old print, was the most celebrated of the ruffian chiefs who at various times ruled over these islands. An immense silk-cotton-tree stood until within a few years on

Bay Street, in Nassau, under the broad branches of which he administered high-handed justice, and caroused with his harridan dames. He was finally killed off the coast of South Carolina in a desperate fight, and the land had rest for certain years, the escutcheon of the colony bearing since that time the significant legend, "*Expulsis piratis, restituta commercia.*"

After the pirates came the privateers of the Revolution. Fincastle (Lord Dunmore), when he left Virginia, settled in the Bahamas, of which he was appointed governor, and he was followed by many Tories. Although not a great man, his is one of the most noted names connected with the history of the Bahamas. Traces of his administration still exist in many

FORT FINCASTLE, NASSAU.

places. There is a quaint fort named Fincastle behind the Victoria Hotel, curiously resembling a paddle-box steamer; and the country-seat where he resided, now called the Hermitage, is still standing by the water, admirably situated, surrounded by a noble grove of oaks and cocoa-palms. Royal Island, having a snug little harbor easy of access, was a rendezvous where arms and stores were concealed, and royalist privateers made it a common resort during the American Revolution. An old stone house still remains there which has doubtless witnessed many wild, mysterious scenes in days gone by.

THE HERMITAGE, COUNTRY-SEAT OF LORD DUNMORE, AT NASSAU.

We may add, in passing, that one of the most noted characters who ever figured in Nassau was Blennerhasset, notorious for his relations with Aaron Burr. It will be remembered that after the excitement produced by the trial had blown over, Blennerhasset passed off the scene; but Blennerhasset still lived. There is excellent authority for stating that the Bahamas, a refuge for so many rovers and adventurers, gave him a shelter during some of the remaining years of his life. Leaving his wife (whom the classic oration of Wirt has made famous) to care for herself, he there assumed the name of Carr, and received the position of Attorney-general. The secret was known to but few. Another wife consoled him for the absence of Mrs. Blennerhasset, who once discovered his retreat, but was spirited out of the island, and maintained elsewhere on a separate allowance. Those were roistering days, when gentlemen drank hard, played high, and fought duels like devils—days now fortunately passed, it is hoped, forever, at least in Nassau—and Blennerhasset acted his *rôle* well, by no means a looker-on in Vienna.

And now we come to the most remarkable episode in the history of the Bahamas, the part they played in the Southern rebellion, about which a volume of entertaining information could be written. On the 5th of December, 1861, the first Confederate vessel arrived from Charleston, with 144 bales of cotton; and between that time and the close of the war 397 vessels entered Nassau from Confederate ports, and 588 sailed thence for Southern ports. Of these the steamers were to the sailing vessels in the ratio of three to one. Of the clearances 432 were ostensibly for St. John, New Brunswick, and of the total number only thirty-two carried the Confederate flag—a pretty fair indication of the amount of complicity practised about that time by Her Majesty's subjects and officials in Nassau, and of the value of the British capital engaged in this questionable traffic. In nothing was this connivance on the part of a neutral power more evident than in the case of the *Florida*, or *Oreto*, which was three times seized by the commander of the British man-of-war *Bull-dog*, and three times released by the decision of the insular Admiralty Court on grounds afterward wisely disavowed by the Home Government.

During the Confederate years the little town actually swarmed with Southern refugees, the captains and crews of blockade-runners, cotton-brokers, rum-sellers, Jews and Gentiles of high and low degree, coining money and squandering it as if they owned the secret of the transmutation of metals. They played toss-penny in the verandas of the Royal Victoria Hotel with gold eagles! The shops were packed to the ceilings; the streets were crowded with bales, boxes, and barrels—cotton coming in,

Confederate uniforms and pills of lead and quinine, to pepper patriots and patients, going out. Semmes and his bold boys twisted their mustaches at every corner, danced involuntary reels and hornpipes from groggery to groggery, and from the waxed floors of the Government House, where they were always sure of a cordial reception, to the decks of the *Banshee* and *Alabama*, or brandished their revolvers in the faces of Union men, whose lives were too uncertain to insure thereabouts in those rollicking days. A spicy little paper called the *Young Punch*, edited by a witty Confederate in Nassau, under the sobriquet of "The Can't Get Away Club," gives a glimpse of the state of things then existing, and shows that there was some real fun connected with blockade-running. A

ROYAL VICTORIA HOTEL.

rather grim joke was played at the expense of the rebels *via* Nassau. A large invoice of prayer-books was brought from England and reshipped to Charleston, with the express understanding that they were suited to the devotional wants of the Confederacy. Quite a number had been distributed before it was discovered that the prayers for the President and Congress of the United States had not been altered!

It is not a creditable fact that some of the goods smuggled into the

PUBLIC LIBRARY, NASSAU.

Confederacy by way of Nassau were from Northern ports, as, for example, ship-loads of pistols brought from Boston in barrels of lard. On the other hand, there are many instances of noble patriotism on record. The name of Timothy Darling, Esq., is deserving the honor and respect of every true American. A native of Maine, but long a resident of Nassau, a British subject, and one of the principal merchants and politicians of the Bahamas, he was more than once offered the agency of the Confederacy, and always firmly declined—a proposal which, as the event proved, would have been worth several hundred thousand dollars to him.

During the continuance of the war the weather was exceptionally fine even for the West Indies; no hurricanes, and but few gales of any violence, occurred. Everything went on merry as a marriage-bell, and the policies of vessels clearing for Nassau might well have omitted the words "wind and weather permitting." But in the year succeeding the fall of Richmond, 1866, occurred the most terrible hurricane experienced in those waters during this century. The ocean rolled completely over Hog Island into the harbor in surges so enormous that the crest was even with the gallery of the light-house, sixty feet above the sea. Houses and forests went down before the wind like reeds; many which withstood its force when it blew from north-east collapsed when it shifted to south-west. In twenty-four hours the city was like a town sacked and burned by the enemy, and a large part of the wealth accumulated during the war had disappeared into thin air. The island has never entirely recovered from the blow. Those who are inclined to believe in special providences may find food for reflection in the circumstance that no Union man had his house wrecked, or suffered any considerable loss. This is, at least, a curious coincidence. It is not to be supposed, however, that violent weather or hurricanes are frequent in the Bahamas. Formerly they occurred once in two or three years, in August to October, but now blow at much longer intervals. There has been no hurricane in that archipelago since the one of 1866. The prevailing winds are north to south, round by east, taking the form of trade-winds from the eastward during a large part of the year, and it is rarely that the heat of mid-day is not cooled by a breeze from the sea. The facilities for yachting and fishing at Nassau are admirable, fast yachts being always on hand, while the neighboring keys present attractive resorts for picnic parties, and the variety, beauty, and savage character of many of the fish render fishing a sport of more than ordinary interest. The beautiful Lakes of Killarney, in the interior of New Providence, abound with wild-duck, and those who care to cruise as far as Green Key may find lots of pigeon-shooting.

The drives around Nassau are also very charming, often leading by the sea-side. There are few scenes more replete with quiet but exquisite and satisfying beauty than the drive to Fort Montague toward sunset; on one side, groves of palms, lithe and graceful as nymphs, gently swaying their undulating plumage in the evening wind; on the other side, the sea murmuring on the yellow sand; in the distance, the city and the port limned against a sky ablaze with the glory of the tropics. The roads are always excellent, and of such a nature that the horses, when shod at all, are only shod on the fore-feet. With a few exceptions, they are small and meagre to a degree that renders Rosinante corpulent in comparison, being fed chiefly on sugar-cane stalks. It is curious that on islands generally the equine race, while exceptionally hardy, has a tendency to dwindle in size. But although appearances would lead one to expect a similar condition in the vegetation of the Bahamas, the reverse seems to hold good. With but one or two exceptions, the islands are low calcareous rocks, probably the summits of peaks once rising far above the sea, and enlarged and re-elevated by coral insects since their submergence. The limestone is gray, and so hard as to strike fire when exposed to the weather, but soft enough below to be shaped with saw and hatchet, while the layer of soil scattered over it is so thin as to make it impossible to understand how anything but scrub and goats could flourish upon it. Any Yankee so enterprising or hare-brained as to introduce the latest improved plough into Nassau would be considered a fit candidate for the Insane Asylum behind the bishop's residence. And yet there is not a plant of the tropics that may not be made to grow there, and many of the temperate zone. The mahogany is common, chiefly on Andros Island, and might become a lucrative branch of commerce if there were roads to transport it to the sea.

SILK-COTTON-TREE, NASSAU.

The variety called the horse-flesh is exceedingly durable, and is exclusively used for the frames of Bahama vessels. It seems to rival oak for this purpose. The pine reaches a good size in the interior of New Providence, where the palmetto is so intermingled with it as to present a suggestive blending of the vegetation of two zones. The wild pineapple, or air-plant, which lives in the branches of forest trees, holding sometimes a quart of dew in its silver-gray bowl of spiky leaves, is also an interesting object. The satinwood, lignumvitæ, yellow-wood, fustic, and cedar grow everywhere, and cocoa and date palms abound, together with the *Ficus Indicus*, a species of banyan. Of the East Indian banyan a very perfect specimen exists near Fort Montague. The banana, tamarind, sapodilla, mango, coffee-plant, guava, custard-apple, orange, sugar-cane, mammee, and almost every vegetable production of the tropics, grow more or less in the Bahamas. The oranges of San Salvador or Watling's Island are exceptionally sweet. How such vegetation can thrive on a mere basis of rock is a perpetual mystery. I visited an orange plantation outside of Nassau where the gray rock was completely honey-combed with depressions called cave-holes. On the bottom of these was a little soil, and there the trees grew and flourished in clumps of eight or ten. The grape fruit is a species of large orange, the color of a citron, and with a thick rind and a pleasant flavor. Why it should be called the grape fruit seems difficult to understand. A gentleman from the Bahamas saw some of them in a fruit-vender's stall in New York labelled California oranges, their size seeming in accordance with the usual exaggerated character of the productions of that ambitious State. "My friend," said he to the fruit-vender, "those are not California oranges; they are Bahama grape fruit."

"I guess you'd better move on," was the vender's reply, in an unmistakable tone of asperity.

One of the most singular trees in the Bahamas is the silk-cotton, which attains a large size, not only reaching a good height, but spreading laterally over a wide surface, and buttressed at the base like a Gothic tower, evidently an adaptation by nature to support it in the absence of any perpendicular hold it might have in a deeper soil. The roots also extend to a great distance, creeping over the rock like vast anacondas, and clinging to every crevice. The bolls are full of a soft brown cotton, resembling floss silk, but not adhesive enough for use. One of the most remarkable specimens of this tree is the one behind the Government House. Its roots extend nearly the eighth of a mile, and then shoot up into another magnificent specimen in the grounds of the Royal Victoria Hotel, in whose branches a large platform has been constructed.

The cactus and aloe are, of course, common, and especially the Sisal aloe, from which manilla rope might very well be manufactured with a little enterprise, as might also be added regarding the production of castor-oil, as the plant grows abundantly on the islands. The pineapple flourishes in San Salvador and Eleuthera; the chief supplies of that delicious fruit which reach our markets are from the latter island.

The cruise to Harbor Island and Eleuthera is one of the most interesting within easy distance of Nassau. It can be made in a yacht or in one of the many little schooners constantly plying to and fro; keys are always in sight, and a lee can be made at any time; while one can return by way of Abaco, where a cruise in the sounds on either side of that island, and a visit to the curious little settlement called Hopetown, inhabited by descendants of the buccaneers, present various attractions. Spanish Wells, on the island of that name, is a most singular place. Planted on the low beach, the houses are huddled together in inconceivable disorder, and built on posts to raise them above the sea waves, and also to keep them free from the incursions of the hermit-crabs, which live in the rocks in vast numbers, and often come out at night and prowl over the land. Before every house is an oven—it was baking-day when we touched there—and the smell of fresh bread could be observed before we got to land. It was also ironing-day, and before every cabin flat-irons were ranged on coals.

DUNMORE TOWN.

The women wear the peculiar oblong pasteboard sun-bonnet which was common years ago in our rural districts, called in some places "rantamskoots," and their appearance is not especially attractive; but then I did not see them in their best bibs and tuckers, and dress does make a difference. The school-house is thatched with palm leaves, and is a quaint little building. The school-master told me they lived on conchs and fish, and he had not tasted meat for two months. If fish makes brain, the Bahamians ought to be intellectual to a degree; but facts do sometimes conflict with theories. Many of the fish in those waters are poisonous at times, especially the barracuda, which is a very savage fish, three to five feet long. The cause for the noxious character of the West India fish is not yet fully explained. The symptoms of poisoning by the barracuda are great itching, pain in the joints, and baldness, lasting sometimes for years. The first hint of poison is a violent sickness of the stomach, attended with vomiting within half an hour after eating the fish. The white people of the Bahamas generally induce the negro fish-sellers to eat of the fish first, and, if it prove harmless, then partake of it themselves. We caught a large barracuda, on the way to Harbor Island, and it was cooked. Ignorant of its dangerous qualities, I ate freely of it. After I had satisfied my appetite, I was told of the possible symptoms that might soon follow. It being too late to avoid the mischief, I gave the matter no further thought, and happily suffered no ill effects.

From Spanish Wells the track lies over a succession of coral reefs, through which the passage is of the most intricate character; one of the worst places, a long zigzag reef, is called the Devil's Backbone. Were it not for the extraordinary clearness and vivid malachite tints of the water, and that wherever a reef rises near the surface it is indicated by a reddish spot, the complementary color of green, it would be next to impossible for a vessel to work into the port. The brilliance of this hue at mid-day also causes the deep water beyond to appear purple, while the sky is actually flushed with rose to the zenith on a bright day. The port of Harbor Island is spacious, and so protected by reefs and bars at each entrance as to be the safest in the world for vessels not drawing over nine feet of water, after they once get inside of it. It is formed by a low island stretching across a bight at the north-eastern end of Eleuthera. On the inner slope of this isle is situated Dunmore Town, containing twenty-five hundred inhabitants, next to Nassau the largest settlement in the Bahamas. A very pleasing little place it is, encircled by beautiful cocoa-nut groves, and dreaming by the green water in an air of solitude and peace which is very bewitching to one who is weary of the rush and giddy whirl of the nineteenth century, while the cool trade-winds always moderate the heat. On the ocean side of Harbor Island is the finest beach I have seen, of very fine, delicate pinkish sand, hard as a floor, a glorious galloping ground for the half-dozen ponies in the place. The people depend for fresh water chiefly on wells sunk in the drifted sand immediately back of the beach. When the well is dug, it is protected from falling in by three or four barrels, one over the other, and the rude curb is guarded with a padlock. The sea-water filters through the sand into these wells, and becomes sweet as ordinary spring-water. A gale of wind destroys the wells once in three or four years, and excavating new ones is a dangerous process. The inhabitants gain a livelihood cultivating pineapples on Eleuthera. A fleet of two hundred boats is owned in the settlement. Every morning at sunrise this little fleet spreads its wings to the trade-wind, and wafts eight hundred men and boys, black and white, to the lovely beach and cocoa-nut groves on Eleuthera, two miles away; every night they return. The pineapples begin to ripen in April, and only grow to advantage on a peculiar red soil that is always thin, and is found in but few districts. The plantations are on undulating ground, the highest in the Bahamas, and are skirted by mahogany, logwood, and cocoa-nut groves, overgrown with the brown love vine, and abounding in scarlet-flowered hop, clitoria or wild pea, and various other flowers, while the song of the brown thrush resounds in every thicket. A pine field, when

GLASS WINDOWS.

the pines are ripe, looks as if it were on fire, the scarlet of the spiked leaves forming a flame-color with the vivid orange-yellow of the fruit. There are two principal varieties of the pineapple, the scarlet and the sugar-loaf, the latter of which is the best. It is almost needless to add that pineapples such as those of Eleuthera, eaten perfectly ripe on the spot, are infinitely superior to the pineapples sold in our markets. The same may be said of the cocoa-nut. For a penny a negro urchin would climb up a tree and fetch me a pair of what are called jelly cocoa-nuts, the fruit being plucked before the pulp has hardened, so that it can be eaten with a spoon. The flavor is very delicate, while the milk is cool even at mid-day.

and furnishes a thoroughly healthy, mildly astringent drink, preferable to water or the brandy-and-water in which the residents too often indulge for a warm climate.

Some charming excursions may be made from Harbor Island. The bay is one of the most beautiful sheets of water ever marked by the keel of a yacht, fringed by cocoa-nut groves, and protected from the surges of ocean by the silver-flashing barrier of the bar. The walk from Bottom Cove to the arch called the Glass Windows is remarkable for the suggestive beauty of the land forms, the effect being heightened by the stately stalks of the aloe rising here and there, like solitary bronze columns, lifting a massy coronal of golden flowers against the sky; while on one side, owing to the narrowness of Eleuthera at that spot, the green water of the coral reefs is close at hand, and on the other actually blue water, for Eleuthera is on the extreme edge of the Banks, serving for some seventy miles as a breakwater for the rest of the group against the vast waves of the Atlantic, which rise there suddenly sometimes without any wind, and last for several hours. The natives call these windless risings of the sea "rages;" they are probably caused by a heavy storm blowing at a distance. In 1872 an extraordinary tidal wave rose without warning at the Glass Windows, washing under the arch and entirely over the island, carrying away several young people who were enjoying a picnic there. The account of the rescue of one of them is a thrilling and remarkable story, too long for narration here; but those who visit Harbor Island will find Mr. Cole, the intelligent and courteous school-master, quite willing to repeat the narrative of an adventure of which he was himself an eye-witness. The arch is of limestone, eighty-five feet above the sea. A line can be dropped plumb down to the water. It is split entirely across at the centre, and as one stands over the crack fancy readily suggests the consequences if the arch should fall in at that moment. Near Gregory's Harbor is a cave extending eleven hundred feet underground, enriched with stalactites of a brilliant brown hue. It is really worth visiting. There is also a large cave at Long Island.

South by east of Eleuthera is Cat Island, or Guanahani, celebrated as the land first seen by Columbus, and called by him San Salvador. The reader must here be prepared, however, for a surprise, when it is stated that in all probability it was not Cat Island which Columbus named San Salvador, but Watling's Island—a smaller isle a little more to the southward and eastward. The facts in the case are these: contrary, probably, to the general opinion, it has never been definitely known which was the island entitled to the honor; but about fifty years ago, when historians were busy with the voyage of Columbus, they undertook to settle the question by comparing his journal with the imperfect charts of the Bahamas then existing. Navarette fixed on Turk's Island, which later investigation has proved to be erroneous; while Irving, supported by the strong authority of Humboldt, argued for Cat Island, and since then this has been generally accepted as San Salvador, and it is so designated on our charts to this day. But the English reversed their opinion some time ago, and transferred the name of San Salvador to Wat-

STREET IN NASSAU.

ling's Island, and it will be so found on their latest charts. The reasons for this change seem conclusive. Lieutenant Beecher, of the English navy, proves beyond question that Cat Island cannot be San Salvador, and that Watling's Island answers the conditions required better than any other island lying in the track of Columbus. His two strongest reasons against Cat Island are that Columbus states that he rowed around the northern end in one day. The size of Cat Island makes this physically impossible there, while it is quite feasible at the other island. He also speaks of a large lake in the interior. There is no such water on Cat Island, while such a lake does exist on Watling's Island.

CHAPTER II.

THE AZORES.

IT was on the 23d of July that the A 1 clipper-bark *John* sailed from Boston for Fayal and a market, in ballast. She had in the steerage thirty-one Portuguese, who were returning home, and the object of the voyage was ostensibly to secure a charter for an early cargo of oranges in November, but really to obtain, clandestinely, a haul of Azorean passengers flying the islands in face of the stringent prohibitory laws against emigration. There is in the Portuguese dominions a strict system of conscription, under which every man, on reaching twenty-one, must incur the chance of being drawn for the army; and in consequence no one can leave the Azores who has not yet had his name shaken in the lot, unless he gives bonds in three hundred dollars that he will return and serve, if drawn, the money to be forfeited if he fails to respond; and this regulation applies even to mere lads scarce weaned. It is evident that the great poverty of the people makes this a pretty effectual bar to emigration. It is true that passports are with some reluctance granted to those who do not come within the application of this law, yet those wishing to emigrate are principally young and enterprising males. But for years they have found means to evade the observation of the Government, escaping on passing whalers, whose crews are largely composed of Portuguese, or on English and American traders, which have occasionally cruised among the islands for the purpose of "stealing Portuguese," as the business is called. The *John* was at the time the only American vessel then depending for its profits on this curious and hazardous traffic, the other packets plying between this country and the Azores being partly owned by residents there, who do not dare to trespass on the laws of the land.

Mannel, the second mate, and all the crew were Portuguese; he was very handsome, black-bearded, eagle-eyed, and with a herculean frame. We had baffling winds, with calms and fogs, until we got near whaling ground. The Azores are an important rendezvous for whalers, who can provision there more cheaply than at home, and for that purpose touch there even when bound around the Horn. The waters in that vicinity are also good for cruising, although whales are less abundant than formerly. On the 5th of August we took a sou'-wester, and the *John* flew toward Flores with every stitch of canvas set and all drawing, making a thousand miles in four days, galloping away with the wind abaft the beam, and carrying sail until it blew away. An observation on the 8th showed that we had passed Flores, which had been hidden in mist, at midnight, when we should have been abreast of the island. Captain Brown had thought of lying to the previous night, but had unwisely concluded to

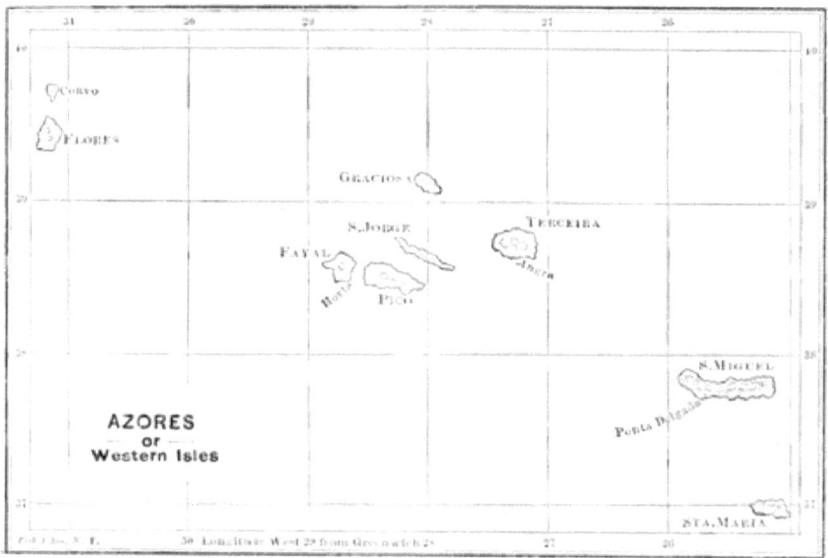

keep on, and we now had to beat to windward sixty miles. We were not the first who had found the Western Islands elusive as the Flying Dutchman or St. Brandon's Isle. Lying far apart as they do, it is quite easy, when the weather is at all thick, to miss them, or come foul of them with a fatal crash, for they are all so precipitous that a ship may almost anywhere butt her bowsprit against the cliffs before grounding or finding anchorage. The Azores (so called from the *açor*, a hawk peculiar to those islands) were discovered early in the fifteenth century by Cabral, and the Formigas, a reef near St. Mary, were the first seen. St. Michael and St. Mary were the first to be settled, about 1431, sixty years before the voyage of Columbus; who on his return, in pursuance of a vow made during a great storm, landed half his crew, who went barefoot to the Chapel of the

Virgin to offer thanksgiving. He was about to follow with the remainder of the crew, but was hindered by the unfriendly conduct of the governor.

It was a fine morning in August when we reached Flores—the Isle of Flowers—and with a fresh leading wind stood close along the shore, enjoying a good view of the jagged volcanic peaks and well-cultivated slopes. We hove to at breakfast-time off Santa Cruz, the chief place on the island. A boat soon came off with the health officer, and after getting *pratique*, I went ashore with the captain. The boats of Flores are made for out-at-sea work, deep and broad, more like a small ship than a row-boat, and the oars are very clumsy, and constructed of two or three pieces, crooked boughs, fastened together with marline, and turning on the gunwale by a broad slab through which the thole-pin passes: it requires two or three men to pull them. We reached the port—and what a port! Riding in on the top of a roller, through a gauntlet of black lava rocks, hoary with roaring foam, and scarce thirty yards apart, we entered a haven about an acre and a half in extent, surrounded by perpendicular cliffs, on whose edges the houses are perched, and with a beach to match, affording scant room for a dozen boats. The boatmen took us off the boat on their shoulders, and landed us high and dry amidst a throng of eager men, women, and children, who occupied every spare foothold from which the new arrivals could be seen. Closely they gathered around us, the young and the old, the halt and the maimed, the rich and the poor, the latter in large majority; some to welcome us, others to gaze, others to badger and barter, and still others to beg. A public fountain near the landing, emptying its musical stream into a stone trough, and surrounded by a group of barefooted, black-eyed, olive-hued girls in white mantles, filling earthen jars, was the first object to fix my attention, vividly reminding me that, although yet in the Atlantic, I had again come within the magic influence which lends an indescribable charm to the shores of the Mediterranean.

The people of Flores are good-looking, many of the young girls and youths having a piquant beauty that is very attractive. But the aged often have the parchment-like, deeply wrinkled skin common the world over to the peasantry when advanced in years. The women of Flores generally wear a shawl or white cloth over their heads. Excepting the few of the upper class, both sexes of all ages go barefoot. When they attend mass they carry their shoes with them, and put them on before entering the church.

Convents for both sexes were abolished throughout the group by Dom Pedro I., but the Franciscan convent of Santa Cruz still stands. The dormitories are let to tenants, but the chapel belonging to it is a fair specimen of the Renaissance-Italian style as seen in colonial churches, adapted, by its profuse and rather tawdrily gilded ornamentation, to impress an ignorant populace. The church of Santa Cruz occupies a commanding position, and is externally one of the best in the Azores. It is flanked by two towers surmounted by Saracenic domes; but the interior is cold and naked. Both church and convent are about three centuries old.

The formation of Flores and the neighboring island of Corvo, which is merely a crater whose sides are cultivated by a small colony of Moriscos not a thousand in number, is in some respects different from that of the remainder of the group; that they are distinct is partially proved by the circumstance that earthquake-shocks felt in the other islands are not experienced in these two, which have shocks entirely their own. Figs, yams, potatoes, corn, wheat, bananas, apples, peaches, and almost any vegetable production of both spheres, grow, or can be made to grow, on these islands, so mild is the average temperature, extremes being unknown. But to bring many of them to perfection, a more intelligent culture is necessary than they receive at these islands. It never freezes, even during the rainy season, except on the mountains, nor does the mercury often rise above 85° in summer. Excellent figs I tasted, yet by no means comparable to the fig of the Levant; the apples are far inferior to ours; and the grapes are only tolerable. It is but fair to add that for eighteen years a blight has cursed the Azorean vineyards, as in the Madeiras, and both grapes and wine are scarcer, and possibly poorer, than formerly. The indications now are that the blight is about over.

There are several villages in Flores, and agriculture is prosecuted with much industry, women also laboring in the fields, and the implements are of a patriarchal character. Donkeys and horses are scarce, and the means of transportation are the human head and small carts drawn by diminutive cattle; the wheels are solid, turning on an axle of chestnut-wood, selected especially on account of the infernal squeak it gives out. The peasants find this a congenial music on the lonely roads; it can be heard a great distance, and is so modulated as to produce alternately a squeak and a groan! The cattle become accustomed to work to this doleful accompaniment, and the drivers maintain that it is essential to their own happiness; each cart-owner is, in fact, boastful of the peculiar tune creaked by his own vehicle.

Having landed some of our passengers, and engaged provisions against our return, we sailed for Fayal. Two days' sail took us close to Castello Branco, or White Castle, a bold headland at the southern end of the island, four hundred feet high, and resembling a huge fortress, connected with the land by a slender natural causeway. But night came on before we could weather this headland, and we stood out to sea again to avoid being becalmed and sucked against the rocks by the swift, treacherous currents. Vessels overtaken by calms sometimes have very narrow escapes in those waters. On the following morning we beat into the roadstead of Horta, the town of Fayal, the latter name being often incorrectly used for both. The name Fayal is derived from the *faya*, a small evergreen tree, found, however, more on Pico than on the island to which its name is given. The harbor is the best in the group, affording tolerable anchorage and shelter from westerly winds, Pico, four miles distant, presenting a magnificent breakwater to east winds; but against gales from the north-

FLORES CART AND PEASANT HUT.

east and south-east there is no shelter, and vessels have then to cut and run, or incur great risk of going ashore. They always ride at heavy moorings, and sometimes in a gale all hands seek refuge on land.

We threw the topsail aback, and waited for the port-boat, which soon came out, followed closely by the revenue and several other boats. The officers very carefully examined our captain as to the number on board, causing all hands to be mustered along the rail to count noses. As we had several who had come without passports, and therefore could not pass muster, some sharp practice resulted, after which everything was, with some hesitation, pronounced satisfactory. Two guards, one more than usual, owing to the doubtful character of the *Jehu*, were detailed to remain on board during her stay. Very particular are these Portuguese martinets in all the punctilios of revenue law, on the principle that the smaller the State the more necessary is it to maintain its dignity with fuss and feathers. So strict are the revenue laws that even a mere sail-boat cannot leave one island district for another without a clearance. A person cannot go

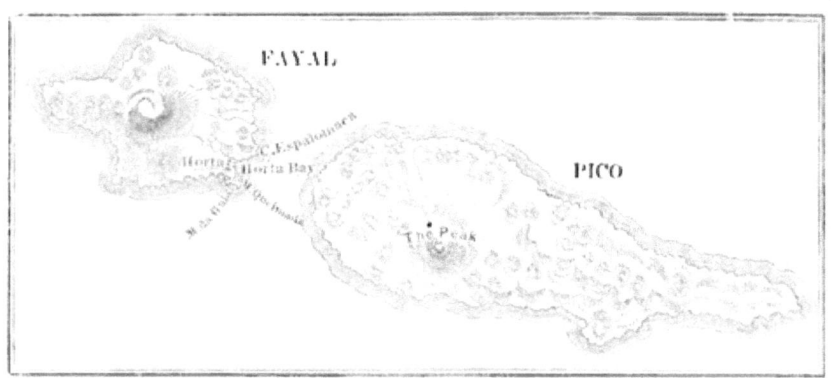

PICO FROM FAYAL.

from Pico, in the Fayal district, to St. George, only sixteen miles off, but in the Terceira district, except with a passport; and if caught without one, he is permitted to meditate on his sins in jail.

The captain of a Yankee whaler played a good joke on the port authorities of Horta. While cruising in the neighboring waters, one of his crew fell from aloft and broke his leg. Accordingly, the vessel put into Fayal to land the poor fellow.

"Where are you last from?" asked the port officer.

"From Barbadoes."

He looked over his instructions, and found Barbadoes to be a suspected island, so nothing would do but that the whaler must proceed seven hundred miles to Lisbon, the capital of Portugal, and go into quarantine there, before she could land the man. What does our sharp Yankee do but sail to the island of Terceira, only seventy miles distant.

"Where are you last from?" asked the port officer of Terceira.

"From Fayal," replied the American.

So they gave him *pratique*. Then he sailed back to Fayal.

"Where are you last from?" again asks the port officer there.

"From Terceira."

"Ah, very good."

They could do nothing else but give him *pratique*, and the man with a broken leg was at last landed, and sent to the hospital at Fayal. Possibly this is not the only instance of sharp practice winked at in Fayal.

The *Jehu* was now sent in charge of the mate to St. George to land the remaining steerage passengers, while Captain Brown stayed at Fayal to negotiate for a charter. On landing, I called at the town residence of the Dabneys, where I was politely received and treated to fine blackberries and figs, and Pico wine, a mild tipple suggesting sherry, although decidedly inferior to it in flavor and quality. The house, built by the late Mr. Dabney, for many years United States consul, is surrounded by extensive grounds, admirably laid out and stocked with choice exotics. We took up our quarters at the hotel kept by Mr. Edwards. The afternoon was pleasantly spent in a stroll to Porto Pim, an excellent little haven adjoining the main port, if it were not exposed to the full sweep of westerly gales. The town on that side is protected by old fortifications, erected in former ages as a defense against the descents of corsairs, and is entered by a picturesque mediaeval gate.

Pico began to show his head in the afternoon, indicating good weather. He is the barometer of the Azores: when his head is muffled, the weather will be dubious; but when the peak is visible, all will be propitious. The mountain stands at the western end of the Pico island, and towers 7613 feet above the sea, an isolated volcanic cone, surrounded at its base by

PICO PEAK, FROM FAYAL.

many smaller craters. Later in the day I visited the fort by the jetty, and there saw "Long Tom," a gun which belonged to the privateer *General Armstrong*, in the war of 1812. The defense of this vessel, on the 26th of September, 1814, is one of the most gallant exploits in the history of American naval warfare. Captain Reid and his officers were at a ball when it was reported that an English fleet was off the port. He hurried on board, and moored his ship under protection of the fort. He had only seven guns and ninety men, but repulsed three attacks of flotillas sent in by an English squadron, destroying many boats, and inflicting on the enemy a loss of three hundred men. Finding that he must eventually be overpowered, Captain Reid caused the muzzle of "Long Tom" to be pointed into the hold, and fired, thus scuttling the vessel, and escaping to the shore with his crew. "Long Tom" was afterward fished up and mounted in the fort.*

On the day following I sallied out before breakfast, strolling along the water-street which skirts the shore and is protected by a parapeted seawall. I was in season to see the Pico ferry-boats landing their passengers and cargoes, which were carried through the surf on the heads or shoulders of barelegged boatmen. The boats carry two lateen-sails, and are made to stand heavy weather. In the early morning they come from Magdalena and Larga, villages of Pico, deeply laden with passengers, wood, charcoal, fruits, and other commodities, and, after discharging, reload and return. So soon as the goods were landed, peasant women, barefooted and nut-brown, but pleasant-featured, raised the heavy baskets or jars to their heads, and wended their way to the market-place, which is entered through a high gate from the Rua de Collegio. It is a square enclosure, with a row of booths running entirely around, and within these meat and provision stalls. On the pavement in front sat the countrywomen, displaying panniers of fruit and vegetables. In the centre of the quadrangle is a large well shaded by fine trees. There is a picturesqueness quite Oriental about the whole scene.

The remainder of the day was agreeably passed in rambling about the city, which has five thousand inhabitants, and is well laid out, on a slope, containing some elegant residences and gardens, and several churches, which, however, present no architectural points worthy of note. The large buildings formerly erected for a Jesuit college, convent, and church are now occupied as barracks.

The freemasons have two lodges in Horta, and the order has some strength in the islands. The shops of Horta, as throughout the Azores,

---

* It is not generally known that the English fleet which thus attacked Captain Reid in a neutral port was carrying re-enforcements to General Packenham at New Orleans. The losses it sustained in the fight detained them so long at Fayal that they did not reach New Orleans until after the battle at that place had been lost.

have no windows, but two or three doors, always wide open and giving demi-daylight. The dwellings are built over the shops, with small balconies projecting over the street, some of them veneered with *azolejos*, or glazed tiles. The names of the streets are of the same ware in blue and white. The strangest sight in Horta is the capote of the women, worn alike in summer and in the rainy season: this cloak is of heavy, dark-blue stuff, falling in massive folds to the ankles, and surmounted by a stupendous hood, stiffened with whalebone and buckram, and of astounding shape and size. Some pretty faces may occasionally be discerned

THE PICO FERRY.

under this grotesque guise, although the women of Fayal are less pleasing than their sisters of Flores. At night the main street is dimly lighted, rather superfluously it seemed to me, as after dark very few steps are heard. Day or night, no place could be more quiet. The roar of the surf tumbling on the reef or against the sea-wall is about the only sound prevailing. Now and then the bray of an ass, or the bark of a dog, or the shrill voice of a peasant-girl — once or twice a day the harsh jangle of a tumble-down hack drawn slowly by mules — such are the sounds in Horta. Quiet reigns there, except at the landing-place near the fort: there the bawling of boatmen and sailors is often resonant.

On the third morning, after another early stroll about the market and the port, I ordered a donkey for the Caldeira, or crater of Fayal. The saddle, like those of Scio, is intended for riding sidewise, without stirrups, and is broad and well cushioned, with a bow at each corner by which the rider steadies himself. By the driver's advice, I sat on the "starboard" side of the little beast. We proceeded by way of the Flamengoz, a straggling village on the outskirts of Horta, once settled by Flemings, and the most attractive part of Fayal. Much of it lies along the course of a torrent deeply worn in a lava bed. At one picturesque spot a brown stone bridge spans the torrent with several arches; under them a small thread of water now percolated, in which merry-voiced girls were washing their clothes. Beyond the bridge, on a hill, stands a white church, from whose steps a superb prospect is gained. Pico rises in the background, garlanded with delicate clouds, yet towering as if close at hand; between the two islands lies the port, the roofs of Horta, and then the nearer hills which form the gorge through which runs the river, overhung with foliage in tropical variety and luxuriance. Here we left the good macadamized road, and struck into narrow bridle-paths. The cultivated fields were everywhere enclosed by walls or hedges of the Hortensia, profusely covered with massy clusters of white and purple flowers. Gradually we left all signs of civilization, and struck into a solitude, the donkey carefully picking a precarious foothold over lava soil scooped out, furrowed, ribbed and broken by the winter rains in the most inconceivable manner.

After several hours we reached the mouth of the crater, seven miles from Horta, and 3335 feet above the sea. Making the donkey fast to a bush, we descended into the crater, a feat more easily mentioned than accomplished, for it is 1700 feet to the bottom, and the sides are so precipitous and broken as to make the descent hazardous without a guide. A young American was killed some years ago going down into this abyss. The floor of the crater is overgrown with dry yet sponge-like moss, giving to the feet the sensation of a heavy Turkey carpet. Near the centre is a pool, tawny and turbid, of unknown depth, and close to it rises a smaller crater, resembling in size and appearance the liana-draped, age-hoary teocallis in the jungles of Yucatan. A few frogs, not in awe of the sublime loneliness of the spot once the scene of belching fires and subterranean thunders, gave an occasional croak by the edge of little brooks wimpling down from the clefts in the rocks. Before we began the ascent, the clouds came creeping over the edges of the precipices, assuming the form of water-falls dropping into space in eternal silence. This magnificent volcanic valley is nearly six miles in circumference and over a mile in its largest diameter, but so symmetrical is its form that it is with difficulty one can realize its depth and extent.

Before we left Fayal, I had time also to ascend Pico Peak, which is the central point and most interesting feature of the Azores. I crossed the strait in one of the feluccas which ply daily between the islands. The spirited action of the saucy little craft filled one with exuberant joy, her immense lateen-sails swelling and straining in the breeze as she drove careening over the waves with a bone in her mouth, and now and again a dash of spray over the bow; the groups of chatting, gayly dressed, black-eyed peasants clustered on the deck were also charmingly picturesque; sea and sky were a deep azure; and before us, a stupendous outline clean cut against the sky, towered the Peak, solitary and sublime.

Immediately on landing, I sent men in different directions to procure a mule for the ascent. But four-legged animals are scarce at Pico; and it was several hours before one could be found, and then only for the following day. This was bad. The time generally allowed for the ascent is two days, while the time at my disposal was short, and the weather looked threatening. Without clear weather, it is effort thrown away to climb the Peak. I decided to accomplish the trip in one day, and then walked up two miles to the village of Vellas, with Jorge, my guide, in whose house I passed the night. The village lies on one of the lower slopes of the mountain. It has no water, and the women bring all the water from wells at the sea-side two miles away, sometimes making the trip several times daily. They carry the jars on their heads, which gives them the stateliness of caryatides.

The women of Pico are the handsomest of the Azores, finely formed, and with features of almost classic beauty. Their wealth of massive black tresses are done up in a simple beautiful braid, crowned by a straw hat or a scarlet cloth. Blithe and buxom, they seem to bear the burdens of life right merrily. Where ignorance is bliss, there is indeed no greater folly than to be wise.

Jorge's house was the best in the village; it consisted of three small rooms and a porch, over a half-story containing a hand-mill and a stable. The garden was stocked with yams, potatoes, grape-vines, and fig and orange trees, fenced in with brown walls of loose lava, which looks massive and heavy, but is light and spongy, and is so irregularly shaped that walls made of it cling together without mortar. The villagers collected at Jorge's in the evening to gossip by the light of a feeble glim. They were ranged on the floor around the apartment, like sachems in a wigwam. The pipe of peace went around in the form of a meagre cigarette; each took a moderate whiff. Tobacco is too precious an article in the islands to be indulged in too prodigally by most of the people. After a while I was able to roll up in a blanket on the floor; but sleep was a scarce commodity that night. A baby with the colic, who at first excited my sympathy, finally aroused in me less amiable feelings. But the English language has a pliability and richness suitable to all occasions. Toward morning I caught a few winks, but was soon awaked by the girls tripping merrily by after the daily rations of water. Then came the mule. It was nearly four o'clock. Hastily despatching a cold breakfast, I mounted. The saddle was a crazy piece of antiquity; but it held together as long as I needed it. The muleteer and Jorge, the guide, followed on foot; and as we went on we were accompanied part of the way by villagers going out to work in the fields. The morning was glorious. Bay, oleander, and arbutus hedged the road; the whistle of blackbirds was heard far and near; sometimes we flushed a partridge or started a rabbit. The truncated outline of the cone was wreathed by light, rosy clouds, and its summit burned like a living coal in the glow of the rising sun, while the lower part was still hidden in shadow and mist. It seemed a huge altar on which the Titans of old were sacrificing their morning oblations to the Lord of the Universe.

After climbing four thousand feet, I was obliged to leave the mule behind in charge of a neat-herd, and scramble up the unbroken slope of the cone on foot. It was a very hard climb of over three thousand feet, without a break, as if one were to creep up a dome of that size. At one o'clock, after great exertion, we scaled the rocky wall of the first crater, and looked into it as one might look down into an ancient fortress from its battlements. The sides are perpendicular, averaging seventy feet in height, except in one place, where a breach has been made. It is apparently about three hundred yards in diameter, and offers the most complete spectacle of desolation I ever beheld. Masses of scoriæ and blackened lava lie strewn around its floor, like fragments of shattered towers; nowhere is there the slightest sign of life; not a bird, not a blade of grass, is to be seen. On one side is the little peak, soaring like the grim keep of a castle. It is three hundred feet high, and stands on a platform of lava, which is again supported by long buttresses, rugged and twisted, like the writhing limbs of tremendous dragons suddenly stiffened into stone.

The heat was intense in the crater, and my thirst was such as no wine could quench. Fortunately, we found a bowl-like hollow in the interior of a cleft of a lava bowlder, in which was mysteriously concealed a small pool of water, icy cold, enclosed like the bulb of air in a spirit-level. The aperture was just large enough to admit head and shoulders. Outside of the rock was the heat of the tropics, and within the coolness of winter.

Having lunched, we grappled with the little peak, an undertaking attended with some hazard, owing to its height, its excessive steepness, and the character of its formation. It is composed of loose blocks of lava, which are easily detached, and roll bounding to the bottom, threatening the footing or the head of the climber. When half-way up, Jorge, who was in advance, dislodged a large stone. "Look out!" he cried. I dodged my head just in time, but, instinctively raising my arm, received a blow which disabled my hand for several days. On reaching the top, we found a slightly depressed crater, perhaps twenty-five feet in diameter, out of which issued a thin, hot vapor. The stones were sufficiently warm to make a change of position agreeable. Sitting on the edge of this pinnacle, I felt much as one might if seated at the top of a lofty chimney. The long slope below seemed so perpendicular that it suggested the illusion that I might descend over seven thousand feet before touching bottom, if I chose to take the leap. I felt no sensation of giddiness, but a certain awesome solemnity, such as one might realize if he were on the apex of creation. One can only experience this effect on mountains which stand entirely isolated, like Pico, between sky and sea, and terminate, like it, in a minute point. Three thousand feet below, the scattered white clouds lay dreamily, like a fleet becalmed; and, below or beyond them, Fayal and most of the group of nine islands were seen inlaid on the amethystine floor of the vast ocean. The meeting of the sea and sky line was discerned with difficulty. The blue overhead was an intense and almost opaque cobalt. We seemed on that point to be ensphered midway between two semiglobes whose edges were joined at the horizon.

The descent naturally occupied less time, and at dusk we re-entered Vellas. The villagers were chatting in their doors; a guitar tinkled in the still air. But the tramp of the mule clattering down the steep streets, a sound unusual at Vellas, produced a sensation. A lad, half wild with excitement, dashed ahead, shouting, "The American is coming!" Much laughter and merriment ensued; once more they all gathered at Jorge's house, and, tired as I was, I could get no sleep for some hours.

Returning to Horta at sunrise on the following morning, I found an invitation awaiting me to breakfast at the house of Count Santa Anna. Performing a hasty toilet, I was in season for a charming stroll about the grounds. An elegant breakfast followed, graced by the ladies and gentlemen of his household. The count is a bachelor, but his sister's family resides with him. The *Jehu* had by this time returned from San Jorge, and, when breakfast was over, I hastened on board; we made all sail, and glided past Monte de Guia out to sea, bound to St. Michael. The distance is one hundred and fifty-six miles, east-south-east, and it took us just three days and four nights to do it in, owing to calms and head-winds.

On a fine morning in August we came up with the city Ponta Delgada. The appearance of the place—lying on a gentle slope, flanked by luxuriant orange plantations and volcanic peaks sharply serrated—is very pleasing from the sea. Other towns of the same size are also visible here and there, and the general aspect of the island is more prosperous and inviting than the shores of the other islands of the group. In effect, there is anchorage along nearly the whole southern side of St. Michael, although with southerly gales vessels are forced to make an offing. A breakwater was begun twelve years ago, on the outer lip of a sunken crater, in ten fathoms of water; it is expected to afford shelter for one hundred sail, and is now gradually approaching completion, in spite of the terrible shocks of the winter surges, which have several times opened large breaches.

The city is faced with a sea-wall, and the landing is within a handsome jetty, forming a square, snug boat-harbor. This, with the archways, church-tower, and entrance-gate, combines to impress one who lands there for the first time with an idea of local wealth and prosperity not entirely belied by further inspection of the place. Ponta Delgada is regularly laid out and neatly kept, the streets are underdrained and well paved, and the roads into the country are macadamized, and afford excellent driveways. The churches are numerous, and generally well built. The value of the arch and tower is understood at St. Michael. The cathedral is an imposing edifice; the belfry simple, but grand in its proportions, and hung with a chime of sweet-toned bells. Less can be said for the interior, although it is not without merit. I observed on the walls a Papal dispensation granting forty days' indulgence to those who should, in however small degree, contribute to the repairs on the roof. A quaint effect is added to the exterior by human-faced, lion-bodied gargoyles springing from the rear angles under the eaves. With the Church of San Francisco is connected a nunnery, whose windows are guarded by massive iron gratings; it resembles a jail for the confinement of the worst criminals rather than an asylum where pure young virgins flee from a wicked world to meditate on the Paraclete and Paradise. The convents in the Azores had become so corrupt that Dom Pedro I. abolished them some thirty years ago, as before stated; but this one is allowed to exist by limitation. Priests are numerous in the streets, which are otherwise cheerful and attractive.

There is considerable traffic between town and country, and much passing of peasants driving loaded asses and mules; and the rattle of crazy hacks, furiously driven and drawn by refractory mules, is not uncommon. Once a day an antique omnibus runs to Alagoa, a town nine miles off down the coast. Some really handsome equipages, with attendants in livery, are occasionally seen. St. Michael boasts a baron, a viscount, and a marquis, all of its own raising. The mansions and gardens of these gentry are sumptuous, well laid out and stocked with exotics, noticeable among them the Norfolk pine. But the orange plantations are the glory of St. Michael, and they spread over the whole island. Every plantation is surrounded by high walls of lava stone, within which are again planted rows of the insenso-tree, which forms a dense growth to a considerable height; and, protected by this double enclosure from the furious winter winds—for the Azores are in the line of the severest Atlantic gales—the orange-tree spreads its glossy foliage and bears its golden fruit; and an ample crop it is: 360,000 boxes, twenty to the ton, are annually exported. By the middle of October the long procession of mules and donkeys begins to wend down the mountains to the city, laden with the fruit which is to gladden many firesides in foreign lands. At the same time the schooners and barks begin to arrive from abroad to waft spicy odors to the wharves of England and America. This continues until April.

MARKET-DAY IN FAYAL.

Besides the activity of the orange season, Fridays and Sundays, being the market-days, are always blithesome occasions, full of bustle and life.

The people collect then in holiday attire to buy, sell, or exchange their wares, and one has a good opportunity of observing all classes in St. Michael. The people of that island more nearly resemble the parent stock than the natives of the other islands. The men are handsome, and the children are often exceedingly beautiful; but of the women less can be said. Pleasing in maidenhood, early child-bearing and hard labor in the fields soon rob them of their charms. The heavy capote is very common there, and the streets look as if every other woman were a nun, giving a sombre effect to street scenes, which, indeed, lack a certain something to give them character. On analyzing the question, I came to the conclusion that the addition of more variety and brilliance of color in the dress of the people is what is wanting to complete the effect one would expect in a place like Ponta Delgada. The population of St. Michael is about 115,000, of which Ponta Delgada contains 25,000. The females are 8000 in excess, owing partly to the lawful emigration of males to Portugal and Brazil.

Twenty-five miles from the capital are the thermal springs called the Furnas, whose waters, strongly impregnated with sulphur, have been a sanitary resort for many years. They are reached by an excellent carriage-road, winding through the most romantic scenery. These springs are apparently a sort of safety-valve for the volcanoes of the Azores. Although Pico is now half comatose, it has been active within a hundred years, while it is scarcely thirty years since St. George was the scene of a terrific catastrophe, the whole summit of that island appearing to be more or less overrun by subterranean fires and melted lava, bursting forth from many sources, and nearly depopulating it. Nor is it uncommon for islands to spring up in those waters, especially in the vicinity of St. Michael, and, after a short stay above the surface of the ocean, to disappear as suddenly as they rose.

After a stay of some days, we again embarked on the *John*, which, during the interval, had been lying off and on in charge of the mate, and started for home by way of Pico and St. George. Toward morning we took a breeze from son'-west, and the bark boomed along at a spanking rate. A heavy squall brought us down to close-reefed topsails, and under this canvas we flew till noon, when "Land ho-o-o-o!" was the cry; and there, sure enough, was the loom of land through the mist on the weather bow. But what land? Pico was the island for which we were bound, but some said this was Terceira; others, St. George. Yet how we could have deviated so as to make either of these in a run of only a hundred miles it was impossible to say. An hour brought us near enough to ascertain that it was St. George, and that we were over twenty miles out of our course. Had the gale continued or the fog not lifted, the consequences might have been serious. It turned out that a chisel had been thoughtlessly left in the binnacle, thus affecting the needle. St. George looked very grand and grim with the thunderous evening clouds enshrouding his brow, lit here and there by fiery gleams of sunset. For two days we drifted with the currents back and forth in a calm, between Pico, St. George, and Terceira. Angra, the chief town of Terceira, is the residence of the Governor of the Azores. Here also is a college, with law and theo-

HOSPITAL OF VILLAFRANCA DO CAMPO, FAYAL.

logical schools attached. The island produces oranges abundantly, and is noteworthy as the seat of intellect and the residence of the *crème de la crème* of Azorean society. A great naval battle for the possession of Terceira was fought off Port Angra, in the sixteenth century, between the Spaniards and the Franco-Portuguese fleet.

St. George, without presenting any striking isolated peak, is very high land throughout its extent of thirty miles, falling everywhere sheer down to the water from a plateau, except at the southern end, where it slopes very slightly, and its precipitous sides are deeply grooved. The villages are small and the population is thin, yet more than enough to till the arable soil. Wheat, cattle, and cheese are the products of this island. Beef and fowls are cheap, and canaries are plenty, as on all the islands of the group, of a russet-green hue, but warbling a full rich song: they serve a double purpose in the Azores—to sing and to furnish tidbits—and very delicate they are, whether in a cage or on a platter.

On the 21st, we approached St. George, and were boarded by a boat, which had eluded the revenue officers and come in quest of tobacco. Large quantities of the weed are smuggled into the islands, often by whale-ships, and at an enormous profit. In the evening signal-lights were seen both on Pico and St. George, indicating that fugitives were there waiting, as by previous arrangement, to steal off to the vessel; but she again drifted too far out with the current in the calm. Pico Peak showed magnificently at sundown, in one of the most superb sunsets I have seen at sea. On the 22d, we stood close in to Pico, giving the agent of the International Transatlantic Submarine Railroad an opportunity to identify the vessel and mature his plans. We also saw a revenue-boat keeping careful guard along the shore. About nine in the evening a brilliant flame, the concerted signal, appeared, flashing at intervals on St. George. We stood in, and at about ten a light suddenly shone out close to the ship, and a boat was soon vaguely discerned.

As they came up, "Is this an American ship?" was the hail.

"Yes."

"What's her name?"

"The *Surprise*."

"Is she going to Boston?"

"Yes."

"Does she take passengers?"

"Yes."

Then they pulled along-side and boarded us, bringing four passengers. Soon after midnight another boat came up with four more passengers, and informed us that several were waiting for us on the other side of St. George, where no guards are kept, owing to its inaccessible character, so that the embarkation can take place there in the daytime; although there they have to slip down steep ledges, and sometimes swim several yards through the surf to the boats, as the sea is often too high to allow a boat to land. An English brig had taken off eighty from that side a few days before our arrival.

At daylight we squared away for the eastern side of St. George, running under its lee with a very stiff breeze, coming down the gorges in terrific squalls—and what high land that is! From the central ridge the land slopes gently two miles, and then, along its whole length of thirty miles, falls almost perpendicularly from 900 to 1500 feet, usually nearer the latter than the former figure; a tremendous spectacle, as mile after mile was passed, and still no break in that Titanic wall, corrugated with black gorges and gulches. It made the scene still more impressive to observe how every available patch of earth is everywhere terraced and cultivated by man, who here seems fitted both with wings and claws to till the soil on bits of slope, at an angle of sixty-five degrees, to the very edge of precipices that drop hundreds of feet to the ever-beating surge below.

JETTY OF PONTA DELGADA, ST. MICHAEL.

About noon the treacherous wind lulled, and the bark began setting in toward the land. By great effort and by skilfully seizing a flaw, they contrived to work her out into the wind again and into control. Then smoke was seen on Ponto Ferrado. We sent off a boat, which met another coming off with a single passenger. The boatmen said others were waiting to come on board, and therefore returned; but as they were scattered about the neighborhood secretly bidding their friends farewell, it might take some time to collect them, so we braced the yards and stood over toward Graciosa, or the Beautiful Isle—rightly named, if one may judge from its appearance as seen from the sea. When we again stood in for St. George, a sail loomed up suddenly close to us, white in the light of the moon. Four more passengers now arrived, and the boat was then hauled on deck with its crew, including the agent of the I. T. S. R. R. We lay off and on all night, the squalls blowing with the fury of *pamperos*. A signal-light was seen several times; but at sunrise such a swell was rolling in, that landing was out of the question, and we stood on beyond the northern end of the island. After a few hours we again headed for the rendezvous, passing near to "Padre," a colossal statue 223 feet in height, off Rosales Point, hewn by nature out of the rock, and vividly resembling a venerable priest, kneeling, in his vestments. A boat was sent ashore, but not returning when expected, its loss in the surf was surmised, and another boat was sent in quest of it. After a long interval, both boats returned with only three passengers. A smoke being then discerned on another spot, a boat was again sent off, returning this time with a young fellow who had been burning brushwood for us all night.

But in the mean time those on board were fully occupied. In his anxiety to procure passengers, the captain had allowed his ship to come too near the land, which is so lofty that when it is blowing a gale of wind off shore, it is often a dead calm close in; and it is even more hazardous to be becalmed off St. George than off the other islands, because on that side, in addition to the currents, there is, even in the mildest weather, a heavy northerly swell tumbling in. About five it was evident that the ship was drifting landward; and it became necessary to put forth every effort, as we were nearing the cliffs fast. The three boats were got out, and all hands, including the male steerage passengers, were put to rowing, without, however, making any impression in checking the dead-drift of the bark shoreward. Black overhead loomed the tremendous cliffs, many hundred feet above us, frowning under a heavy canopy of cloud that gradually veiled the upper crags. Night was at hand, the barometer was low, and all signs were ominous of a change of weather. The writer was at the wheel, with orders to watch for the first breath of air, to bring the vessel up to it. There seemed a little trying to come from the north-east, but not enough to stop the ship in her drift toward the rocks, where the long ocean-swell broke with a sullen and ceaseless thunder. At last there came a smart shower, and then a gentle, almost imperceptible, flaw. "Keep her up!" roared the captain, half beside himself with anxiety. The air came again; the sails began to fill, and, gathering way, the bark again responded to the helm. Gradually she drew off shore, the boats were called in, and slowly we gained two miles, and began to feel more easy, although not realizing until later from what a shipwreck we had escaped. We were all at supper, when the cabin-boy came down and said, "It looks awful black to windward!" The cabin was cleared in half a wink; then the ship rung with the tramp of feet, the frantic shouts of the officers, the creaking of blocks, and the furious flapping of sails. The squall was very fierce. Not having sea-room for running off before it, as is usual with square-rigged vessels in such an emergency, the vessel was brought up in the wind's eye just in time to save going on her beam-ends or carrying away her spars. Either contingency would have resulted in the ship's drifting directly on the rocks, and going to pieces in the wild sea which accompanied the squall. But, though staggering under the blow, everything held; and having rolling topsails (a priceless invention), the *Jehu* was soon under close-reefed top-sails and courses, and with this canvas managed to claw off ten miles of lee-shore and make an offing.

A ST. MICHAEL WAGON.

It blew a gale of wind all night, backing more into the north at daylight, when we concluded to run for a lee under Fayal, thirty miles away. The wind shifting several points, we made instead for the strait between Pico and St. George, and hove to under Pico, the base of whose stupendous cone was wreathed with luminous clouds, running up the weather slope like surf dashing up the sides of a light-house. During the afternoon I saw at one time seven rainbows in a row, each brilliant and defined with perfect distinctness. The wind shifting to sou'-west, and blowing very fresh, we lay to around Pico until the 27th, when, although the weather was still very dubious, we again ran for the north side of St. George to land the agent of the I. T. S. R. R., who would land nowhere else, lest he be nabbed by the *guarda-costa*, and made to pay dear for running Portuguese off the islands. A boat with the second mate and the best half of the crew was sent ashore to land the agent, while we stood out to sea again, taking in sail after sail as we again passed Padre, and having a hard day's work of it, short-handed as we were. Mr. Looby, the mate, a very valuable officer, on whom, owing to his efficiency, the safety of the ship depended much more than on the captain, had not slept four out of the last forty-six hours.

Toward night we stood in and picked up the boat. Her crew were in high dudgeon, on account of the perilous expedition upon which they had been sent; but the captain had the good sense to hold his peace, treated the men to a stiff glass of grog, and the affair blew over. We lay off and on all night off St. George, and the next day ran out past Pico, returning between the two islands at sundown. It was now calm, the moon near the full; and soon the expected beacon-flame was seen blazing at intervals at Calheta on St. George. We ran in and showed our light in the rigging, and about eleven a large launch appeared bringing thirteen passengers, including several women and children. This completed the number we could get from St. George, full twenty less than promised. But the season was advanced, and the supply was running low, over one thousand having already left the islands during the summer, of whom the *John* had taken one hundred and twenty on her previous trip.

After dodging in this unsatisfactory way around Pico for several days longer, and finding at last that some unknown cause prevented the escape of those we were expecting from that island, we put the helm up and bore away for Flores. A glorious breeze on the quarter took us in thirteen hours to Santa Cruz, where we again landed and remained three days, which were passed with much pleasure rambling about the island, enjoying its unique scenery and its hospitable cheer, for which I am much indebted to the unaffected kindness of Dr. M'Kay, the English consul, and his amiable family; to Senhor Pedro Almeida, German consular agent; Senhor Constantine Almeida, collector of the revenues, and other gentlemen. The bark meantime lay off and on, taking on board water and provisions, and thirty-five more passengers, who had many of them been in America and were all able to obtain passports. Those who were already on board were kept out of sight until after *pratique* was obtained; after that it was easy enough, and quite *en règle*, for the guard left in the ship to wink hard when he saw strange faces from time to time creeping out of the steerage.

It was after nightfall of the 5th of September when everything was ready, and we bade farewell to our kind friends, who accompanied us to the beach. The islesmen carried us on their shoulders to the boat and shoved off. We rode over the rollers at the entrance of the little port, and pushed out on the wide ocean to seek the *John*, which had drifted with the current in the calm nine miles to the southward. Heartily the eight boatmen bent to the huge oars, accompanying the movement with a rude song. The night was perfectly still, but cloudy. Seaward a thin mist veiled the mysterious deep; on our right the steep crags of Flores loomed high and dim; the long swell of the ever-panting bosom of the ocean was like glass; and yet from the hollow caves came the eternal boom of the surf-billows that have beaten that wild coast ever since it first arose to view. At length the ship's light became faintly visible, and then the vague outline of spars and sails duskily limned against the sky, and forms moving eerily before the lights; and then was heard the sighing of the sails languidly swinging to and fro with the idle roll of the phantom-like bark; then the rush of feet on deck; the shrill orders of the mate; the shadow of the great fabric above us; the flash of a broad light in our dazzled eyes; the grappling with the ship; the hurried scramble up her black sides into the snug security and comfort of a good, trim clipper and a cosy cabin; and a rousing cup of tea, and a brace of as tender and savorily roasted ducks as ever tempted an anchorite to forego a while his crust and acorns.

For eight days we had mild, fair winds, and the guitar and the love-song rung through the ship early and late. By the starlight the steerage passengers gathered in the gangway and listened to the vocal songs of island improvisatores. One, with a guitar, sung a couplet ending in a female rhyme, and another responded, repeating the last line and adding a couplet of his own, the subject constantly varying, with allusions to whatever most interested singers and listeners. The versification was smooth, and the refrain, although monotonous, was not unmusical. Evidently we here had poetry in its bucolic form, as exemplified by Theocritus and Virgil; the Azorean bards gave us genuine eclogues even if rude. This blended form of poetry and music, still common in the East, is undoubtedly the earliest mode in which the twin arts found expression. One night we had a sort of rustic ball in the steerage; merry was the music of violin and guitar, and lively was the dancing by the feeble light of a smoky lantern, which gave a Rembrandtesque effect to this unique and romantic scene.

An affray between the second mate and the cook broke the calm in which we were basking, and seemed a fit prelude to the boisterous weather which attended us during the last fortnight of the passage. Captain Brown was playing cribbage with Mrs. Brown on the quarter-deck one afternoon; most of the steerage passengers were lying here and there sunning themselves, or embroidering and chatting together. The watch were engaged splicing ropes or patching old sails; and all was so peaceful that the musical plash of the water could be heard against the ship's side as she slipped along at a lazy six knots an hour. Suddenly angry voices, sharp and loud, disturbed the quiet, and in an instant Manuel, the second mate, had the cook on his back in the gangway and was ferociously thumping his head on the deck. All was then in an uproar. The combatants were from different islands; and while the women set up a wailing and shrieking, swaying their bodies back and forth in wild frenzy, the men, both crew and steerage passengers, began to take sides. In the mean time Captain Brown went on with his game, willing to let them fight it out among themselves until further developments. But the twitching of his face showed that he was keeping half an eye to windward. The crisis arrived when the man at the wheel struck eight bells, and the man who was to relieve him, instead of going aft, lingered to look on, and perhaps take a hand in the fight. "What are you doing there? why don't you go to your wheel?" roared the captain to him. "I will when I'm ready, sir," answered the half-mutinous Portuguese. Up leaped the captain, standing six feet two in his stockings, and heavily built at that; and as if the fire of youth were once more galloping through his veins for a moment, with three strides he reached the man, and hissing in his ear with almost Satanic passion, "You'll come when ye are ready, will ye! You go to that wheel, or by the living God I'll dash your brains out!" and clutching him by the nape of the neck, as one might hold a wet rag or a limp puppy, he fairly lifted him along on his toes to the wheel and planted him there. This action seemed to bring most of the rioters to their senses; they were made instantly conscious that they were going much further than they ever intended. The second mate and the cook were separated, and the former returned to the forecastle to continue the splicing of a pennant. But the cook, burning for vengeance, seized a cleaver, and, creeping stealthily up behind Manuel, was just about to split his skull, when the others interposed and caught the uplifted arm. A sullen peace was patched up after this affray, and the heavy weather which succeeded tended to distract the attention from a quarrel, which, as is not unusual, had originated about a woman—"There was a woman in the case."

Amidst a succession of variable gales, accompanied by enormous seas, we now worked our way laboriously toward Boston, adding a very narrow escape from destruction by fire to the other incidents of the voyage. On the twenty-third day we made Thatcher's Island in a fog, ran down to the Graves under a stiff breeze, and, rounding Boston Light, cast anchor off the quarantine—the first time our anchor had touched bottom since we had sailed from India wharf on the 23d of July.

CHAPTER III.

THE CHANNEL ISLANDS.

THE severest gale that had blown for several winters had lashed the shores of Great Britain. The whole country was covered with unwonted snows, and frozen by cold very unusual there. Many wrecks had occurred, and the Channel had, as usual, been swept by the tempest. A large steamer had foundered in its waters, and the costly breakwaters of Alderney and Jersey had been greatly damaged. Hardly had the waves yet subsided when the royal mail packet *Southampton* steamed down the Solent, past the Isle of Wight, at midnight, for the Channel Islands. But on getting out into the open sea we found the wind piping up again, and a high sea directly in our teeth. Accordingly, we put back, and lay till morning in Yarmouth Roads. The wind moderating at daylight, we weighed anchor and made a second attempt. All day it blew fresh, with quite "a lump of a sea" on; but toward night Alderney hove in sight, then the three light-houses, warning the mariner to give a wide berth to the Caskets, one of the most dangerous and most celebrated reefs

in the Atlantic. On these rocks Prince William was lost, the only son of Henry I., after which event it is said the king never smiled again. In later times, the wreck of a Russian line-of-battle ship, and of the English man-of-war *Victory*, with eleven hundred men on board, have, among other wrecks, given a melancholy celebrity to the Caskets. As we neared and passed this reef the waves became greatly larger and more broken, although the wind was less. This was explained as caused by the tides and counter-currents, which, owing to the very irregular character of the adjoining coast of Normandy and the numerous sunken ledges surround-

ST. PETER'S PORT, GUERNSEY.

ing the channel, combine with the extraordinary rise and fall of the tide to render navigation in this archipelago generally rough, and in the winter season hazardous.

Picking her way carefully between the various pitfalls which line the entrance to St. Peter's Port, the steamer moored along-side the pier after nightfall. As I wound my way up the steep winding streets to my lodgings, it seemed as if I had fallen upon some old fortified rock town of the Middle Ages, and the impression was not altogether contradicted by inspection of the place by daylight. St. Peter's Port has a population of 16,000, females being in an excess of nearly a third, as is also the case in Jersey. It is built on a slope of considerable steepness, rising two hundred feet above the sea, and consists of the old and the new town. The former faces the port, and is fronted by a pleasant esplanade, ornamented with trees and protected by a sea-wall. The port itself, originally built by Edward I., is entirely artificial, and has been enlarged in later years with great labor and expense. On a rock at the end of one of the piers stands Castle Cornet, a massive pile without much beauty, but dating back, it is said, to the Romans, and presenting various interesting additions since then. It suffered greatly, three hundred years ago, by the explosion of its powder-magazine, which was struck by lightning. The main pier or breakwater lies at right angles to the waves of south-east gales, which are very savage in those waters. Nothing can be wilder than to see an immense breaker swooping down on the massive wall, and then dashing to a great height into the air, a gray ghostly mist that is immediately torn away by the gale and swept across the harbor. Coming once from Jersey in a tremendous south-easter, the steamer I was on was taken by the undertow swelling up into a huge mound of green water as it fell off from the breakwater; she was lifted high in air, whirled beyond control of the steersman, and came within an ace of crushing in her side against the lee breakwater at the entrance. They concluded not to venture out again that day, but lay snug until the next morning, when the weather moderated.

On the esplanade is a really very fine colossal bronze statue of Prince Albert, and close at hand is a bronze plate stating that the queen and her consort landed on that spot in 1846. Immediately adjoining stands the parish church, as it is called, one of the oldest buildings in the islands, and in some respects the one most worthy of attention for architectural beauty. The style is Flamboyant Gothic, and it is enriched by beautiful stained windows. Wandering about the steep narrow lanes radiating from this choice and venerable relic of antiquity, one is astonished to find such stern massiveness in the buildings, such winding irregularity in the narrow streets, and a steepness that necessitates the most curious succession of long stairways, with cross-lanes meeting at the landings leading up to other narrower steps, all in the most quaint and unexpected manner.

The new town may be said to begin with St. Paul's Chapel, and extends back of the old town north and south, generally more level, and always pleasing. While in the old town the houses are almost entirely of sombre granite, in the new they are as universally stuccoed, and tinted of a soft cream or brown tint. I

MONUMENT TO PRINCE ALBERT, GUERNSEY.

think it would be difficult within the same space to find elsewhere so many charming streets and houses as in St. Peter's Port, giving an air of unostentatious competence. On almost every one is painted either the family name or some pleasing title in English or French, as "Merida Villa," or "Bon Repos," while in front are little garden-plots, neatly kept, or rows of ivied elms; ivy also clings lovingly to the surrounding walls. Everywhere

MARKET-PLACE AT ST. PETER'S PORT, GUERNSEY.

one comes across these cheerful, home-like streets, leading to pleasant inland views, with a central spire surmounting some time-worn chapel of past ages, where still the villagers meet with undiminished devotion.

Not an unimportant addition to the pleasure a stranger takes in rambling about St. Peter's Port is the physical beauty of those he meets. We find here the pure Norman race, the same as that which conquered Britain, but, unlike that, scarcely mixed with Saxon or any other foreign blood. The men have a fresh, ruddy complexion, an honest, frank, good-humored but manly expression. The women have a skin remarkably fair, delicate, and clear, and features regular, expressive, and often beautiful. If but their eyes were as brilliant and eloquent as those of their sisters of Greece or America, they would present a nearly perfect type of female beauty. And the children are, of course, charming; and even when they run out of the peasant houses in the remote districts and beg the passer-by for "doubles," there is a witchery about them seldom found in beggars elsewhere. But to speak of beggars in Guernsey is almost absurd, for extreme poverty is nearly unknown, while almost every tiller of the land cultivates a patrimony inherited from his ancestors for many centuries, and it is difficult to find evidences of squalor in the island. Even the houses of the peasantry are neatly kept, and a clean lace or cambric curtain veils the lower windows of the humblest cots, while flowers and vines are trained on the window-seat during the winter season.

The language is the old Norman French, pure and simple, although the dialect of Guernsey differs slightly from that of Jersey. English is now spoken by the better families, and often understood by those who do not use it among themselves. Services in many of the churches, and all proceedings in the courts and Legislature, are in French. Strange as it may seem to many, the islands are in their government very nearly independent of Great Britain, to which they owe a sort of feudal allegiance. In the transaction of their own affairs they are practically independent; and, stranger still, Jersey has a government and laws of its own, while Guernsey, with the dependencies of Sark and Alderney, is ruled by still another code and Legislature. The Legislature consists in each case of a Senate-house, composed of the bailiff, or chief-justice, and the jurats, and the Assembly, including a larger number, called the States, but of less influence. The laws still smack of the rough emergencies of the Middle Ages, and are sometimes very arbitrary. Any one who chooses to set up a claim as creditor has a right, on his bare assertion, to seize either the person or the property of the alleged debtor, whether a native or a stranger, and the debtor has no redress; on the other hand, the sheriff cannot enter a house unless the door be opened voluntarily, and, if he desire to

CHILDREN BEGGING FOR "DOUBLES."

arrest a man or woman, must sometimes resort to artifice to decoy the victim into his clutches, as, for example, to send an ally into the house on some errand, who can open the door when the sheriff knocks.

Notwithstanding this semi-independence, and the fact that French is the popular and official language, the queen boasts no subjects more loyal than these Normans of the Isles. To question their loyalty is to inflict insult almost amounting to injury. Some of England's most distinguished soldiers and sailors have come from these islands, where their names are cherished with patriotic pride. More than this: it is the common opinion here that, instead of being a fief of England, England herself owes her allegiance to the lords of the Norman Isles. For why: these islands are a part of Normandy, and were such when William of Normandy reduced

DOLMEN AND MARTELLO TOWER, GUERNSEY.

Britain to subjection to Norman rule. During all the changes that have happened in the succeeding centuries, they alone have survived of the Norman territory, and have preserved a remnant of that race intact and unmixed which laid England at its feet and has kept her subject ever since. This is not so absurd, after all. It is quite as reasonable for these little islands to be lords paramount of England as for the comparatively small England to hold sway, as once she did, over the whole of North America, Hindostan, Australia, etc.; and the apostolic succession of the Church is scarcely as clear as the descent of these Channel Islanders from the fellow-countrymen of William the Conqueror and Richard Cœur de Lion. It may be well to add here that one law exists in Guernsey advantageous to foreigners residing within its limits: they are not subject to the payment of taxes unless holding real estate in the island.

The ecclesiastical jurisdiction of the group was for several centuries under the control of the Bishop of Coutances; but after the doctrines of the Reformation were universally accepted by the people, they were transferred to the diocese of the Bishop of Winchester, who is represented in each island by a dean. The islanders are, with few exceptions, good Protestants; churches and chapels abound, and are generally well attended. Puseyism and ritualism have, so far, made little progress here; the Low-Church still continues popular, while the Non-conformists of all the leading sects are in a flourishing condition. Superstition is gradually losing its hold, and much genuine and intelligent piety doubtless exists in some of these islands. But in the hamlets most remote from town, and among the older people, curious superstitions still obtain belief. On Christmas-night there are some even in St. Peter's Port who will on no account go to a well to draw water. Others will not venture into a stable at midnight lest they should surprise the cattle, asses, and sheep on their knees worshipping the infant Saviour. A photographer is sometimes regarded as dealing in the black-art, and some refuse so far to compromise their character as to allow themselves to be photographed. In Guernsey, at St. George, is a well called "Holy Well," still visited by damsels, for on the surface of its waters maidens are said to be able to see the face of their future husbands. In Jersey, near St. Clement's, is the Witches' Rock, where, it is said, the witches hold their Sabbath: the belief in witchcraft is not entirely extinct here. The marks on that rock are confidently asserted to be the footprints made by his Satanic majesty during the visits which, it is to be feared, he makes quite too frequently in Jersey as well as elsewhere.

One of the first things the stranger hears of, on coming to these islands, is the exclusiveness of the upper class, their hauteur and pride, and the contempt in which a tradesman is held. It is stated that a gentleman will be on very good terms with a tradesman in his shop, but will not condescend to recognize him in the street, while at balls the line is drawn with painful distinctness. On the other hand, it is said that the distinction between the "sixties" and the "forties," as the two classes are termed, is wearing away. For an exclusiveness so much more pronounced than usual even in an English colony there was doubtless some ground originally, arising from local causes, which is now forgotten.

St. Sampson's is the only other town of any size in Guernsey after St. Peter's Port. It is named after some mythical Irish saint who came here in the sixth century. The place is about two miles from the capital, the road being by the sea, skirted with houses on one side and a sea-wall on the other, with here and there an old martello tower or a bit of an ivied castle to relieve the view. The port of St. Sampson's is a good one of its size. I counted as many as sixteen vessels there, loading with granite for England. The granite trade is the most important business of Guernsey.

HAUTEVILLE, VICTOR HUGO'S LATE RESIDENCE IN GUERNSEY.

The church of St. Sampson's was consecrated in 1111. It is the oldest building in the island, but offers no architectural attractions. More interesting are the Vale Castle adjoining and the Druidic remains. Long before Rollo the Norman visited and conquered these islands, long before St. Sampson and Julius Cæsar, the Celt had braved these perilous waters in his rude bark, and had scaled these almost inaccessible shores. Here, in those ages lost in the vague mists of unrecorded antiquity, the Druid practised his mysterious and bloody rites, and left numerous dolmens and cromlechs to tell the tale of a race that would otherwise have passed away from these isles into the utter silence of oblivion. Many of these remarkable vestiges have unfortunately been destroyed; of those which remain, one of the most interesting is at L'Ancresse Common, near St. Sampson's. It is covered by seven blocks, of which the largest, estimated to weigh thirty tons, is 17 feet long by 10 wide and $4\frac{1}{2}$ feet thick, while the whole dolmen is 45 feet long by 13 in width. Under the floor were found one hundred and fifty urns, human bones, amulets, and the like.

St. Sampson's and the adjacent portion of the little island are also interesting, as many of the scenes of Victor Hugo's impossible "Toilers of the Sea" are laid there. There is no foundation for the story, so far as I can learn, but it is very well told, and gives incidentally vivid and often truthful descriptions of the scenery and people, and should be read by every one contemplating a visit to the islands. Passing through the old part of St. Peter's Port, by the markets (well stocked with most excellent fish, beef of a very superior quality, and fine vegetables), and proceeding in the rear of Fort George, one comes to Hauteville, for many years the residence of Victor Hugo. He is now in Paris, but his mansion remains furnished as he left it, in a manner highly characteristic of the distinguished author. Keeping on in a southerly direction, one comes to the south side of the island, to the artist or scientific student searching for studies in geology or crustaceology, by far the most interesting part of Guernsey. As Guernsey is triangular in form, and only nine and a half miles on its longest side, much the pleasantest way to see its beauties is on foot. The southern coast is indented with several small but exceedingly beautiful bays, presenting a great variety of granitic forms, often almost volcanic in grotesqueness of shape, the cliffs rising sometimes over three hundred feet, often perpendicularly, from the silvery beaches of soft white

GUARD-HOUSE DESCRIBED IN "TOILERS OF THE SEA."

sand at their base. Wild caverns are hollowed into the sides of the cliffs, and rivulets, under the sylvan cover of many varieties of vines and shrubs, descend from the plateau above to these bays. Le Moulin Huet Bay, Icart Point, Petit Bot Bay, the Gouffre, Gull Rock, Pleinmont, are in turn the favorites of the enthusiast who visits them; but the stern, precipitous, thunder-scarred Titanic cliffs of Pleinmont seemed to me the grandest place for a sea-view in Guernsey, and one of the finest to be found anywhere. Near the brow of these precipices Victor Hugo lays the scene of some of the most striking passages in his book. The small guard-house, which he represents to have been haunted, and makes the rendezvous of smugglers, stands there still, entirely alone on the cliff.

In plain sight from Guernsey in good weather, twenty miles from land to land, in an east-south-east direction, lies the island of Jersey, twelve

THE CORBIÈRE AND LIGHT-HOUSE, JERSEY.

miles long and seven wide, in area nearly twice the size of Guernsey. St. Helier's, the chief town, contains over 30,000 inhabitants, and is situated on the bay of St. Aubin, a most beautiful sheet of water, skirted by a level sand beach, flanked by high slopes and cliffs, and ornamented on the opposite side by the charming little town of St. Aubin. The approach to St. Helier's from Guernsey is around the south-western angle of the island, bristling with reefs, showing their teeth to the mariner in a most threatening manner. Of these the most formidable is the Corbière, or "Sailors' Dread," the haunt of innumerable *corbières*, or sea-crows. A light-house has recently been erected on the highest point, but it is a most formidable foe, as the writer can testify from personal observation, having passed it twice, in a heavy gale of wind from the south-east, much nearer than was agreeable. It must be owned that few spots present a finer opportunity for studying the effect of a raging sea on a rugged shore. The undertow meeting the waves formed by the wind, and again affected by the diverse currents and tides, which here rise forty feet, produces off the Corbière, as off the Caskets, waves of extraordinary height, grandeur, and fury.

The entrance to the port is very dangerous, owing to the reefs that skirt the channel and extend miles to the eastward. The harbor is almost entirely artificial. On the left, on entering the mole, is a high rock surmounted by the remains of a hermitage many centuries old. St. Helier, Hilary, or Hilarius, was one of those shadowy Irish saints whose apocryphal adventures serve to adorn the saints' calendar with a species of pious "Arabian Nights" tales. From what is said of the good people of St. Helier's, one might infer that they had made the mistake of spelling his name Hilarious, and suited their lives to the name. To eschew the world, the flesh, and the devil is not enough the custom in this insular Paris. Just northward of the Hermitage, on a rock of some height, stands Elizabeth Castle, a rather picturesque pile, of which a portion once formed an abbey. The town is not very pleasing near the port, the streets being narrow and dark, but it rambles up on higher ground, and gradually assumes a more cheerful and inviting aspect. The shop windows often make a display of wares quite metropolitan. The markets are well worth a visit, and the market-women sometimes dress in a costume slightly peculiar, the only noticeable local costume in the islands. Generally the people of these islands dress and wear their hair with excellent taste, combining the English common-sense ideas of comfort with a certain French gracefulness that one too often fails to see in England.

Odd as it may sound, there are two Lilliputian railroads in Jersey, starting from St. Helier's — one running five miles to Gorey, called the Eastern Railway, limited; the other also extending about five miles, to St. Aubin. The latter cost a large amount, and swamped two or three local banks, producing much business prostration, and still further reducing the value of local currency. They seem to have been borrowing lessons from the United States in this island: paper money is issued in the most reckless manner, and much enterprise, in the form of hollow bubbles of speculation, has enriched a few and impoverished many; but the law, mindful of the claims of the sufferers and what it owes to the defense of society, has made an example of some of the leading offenders, from which we, in turn, can take a lesson from the island of Jersey. Considerable shipping is owned at St. Helier's, employed in foreign commerce or in the cod-fisheries.

After St. Helier's, or rather before it in interest among the objects to attract the visitor to Jersey, is Mount Orgueil Castle, at the village of

MOUNT ORGUEIL CASTLE, JERSEY.

Gorey, on the eastern coast. It is now dismantled, and occupied only by a warder, but this makes it all the more attractive. Perched on a rock washed by the waves, the highest parapet of the venerable pile is 270 feet above the sea. Built of stone the same as the rocks on which it is founded, it looks in many parts almost like a portion of the cliff. Setting aside the legends about Julius Cæsar, who is made responsible for the parentage of half the castles in Europe, there is no doubt that Mount Orgueil was occupied, if not built, by Rollo, the grandsire of William the Conqueror, whose escutcheon is still quite distinct over the main entrance to the keep. The crypt under the chapel, with a marble statue of the Virgin and Child, is in good preservation; also the apartments occupied by Charles II. while seeking an asylum in this island, which remained faithful to the house of Stuart. These apartments have unfortunately been modernized recently for barracks, although untenanted at present. The guard-room where military courts were held is gone, but the adjoining cell where criminals were executed remains, with vestiges of a secret staircase which communicated with the keep and the sally-port. The dungeon is a ghastly place, but the most interesting spot in the castle is the dark, dismal cell, some six feet by four, with but a small loop-hole over the sea, where Prynne, the Puritan, was confined for three years. He had ample time to compose poetry or philosophies in these close quarters, although the scene was not altogether congenial to tranquil meditation. That rheumatism, megrims, and misanthropy did not quite corrode his bones or his intellect is evident from the fact that he tried to write verse, as shown by the following doggerel lines, besides certain moral essays:

> "Mount Orgueil Castle is a lofty pile,
> Within the eastern part of Jersey Isle,
> Seated upon a rock full large and high,
> Close by the sea-shore, next to Normandie,
> Near to a sandy bay, where boats do ride
> Within a peere, safe from both wind and tide," etc.

From the battlements rusty chains still hang, by which criminals in those rough ages were suspended alive.

The view from the top commands the coast of Normandy and Brittany, including the Cathedral of Coutances on clear days, and, besides a prospect of the landscape of Jersey, gives one an idea of the dangers which beset the mariner in these waters. Scylla and Charybdis were very trifling affairs compared with the chevaux-de-frise of rocks under and above water which encircle these islands. If the sailor escapes the Caskets, the labyrinthine snares of the Little Russel are ready to trip him;

THE PINNACLE, JERSEY.

or, if sailing for Jersey or St. Malo, the St. Roquier or the Hanways lie in wait for him, or the Paternosters, so terrible that they are thus called.

perhaps, because there is nothing left to him who encounters their savage blows but to say his prayers. Escaping these, he still has the Corbière or

ST. BRELADE'S CHURCH, JERSEY.

La Conchière to avoid, and is not yet past dangers, for by no means the least savage yet lie near his path—the Chausseys, and the terrible Minquières, fronting the coast of France many miles, like a picket-guard; and the most awful and solitary of all, the Douvres, like an advanced post in the ocean, solemn and implacable. The coast of Jersey is also everywhere dangerous of approach, and rises in some places over three hundred feet on the northern side. Many very bold, striking cliffs are to be seen there, many rocks of remarkable form and size. The Jersey granite is considerably warmer in color than that of Guernsey, which renders its cliffs slightly less stern, and more in harmony with the vivid green of the surges that lash their feet and fill their vast caverns with the dread thunders of the storm. Boulet Bay, Grève de Leeq, Grève au Lançon, Cape Grosnez, the Pinnacle, or La Pule, at L'Etac, are a few of the many points deserving the investigation and the enthusiasm of the tourist, the naturalist, and the artist. St. Brelade's Church is the oldest building in Jersey, and is still well preserved, and quite picturesque.

The interior of the island is altogether belied by its coast scenery, for it is highly rustic and idyllic, intersected everywhere by winding lanes almost concealed by hedges, and banks abounding in ferns, mosses, and thick-embowering vines and shrubs. So very winding and intricate, in fact, are the rural lanes of Jersey that a cause is assigned for it: the island was in early ages infested by pirates, who carried off the people as well as their goods to that degree that, in order to mislead the freebooters and make it easier to cut them off before they could reach the sea, the paths were twisted into a species of labyrinth. These lanes are, however, gradually being replaced by more direct roads, and many of the old avenues of trees are falling before the axe of improvement or necessity.

Twenty miles in a north-easterly direction from Guernsey lies Alderney, called by the Normans Aurigny, in most respects the least interesting of the group, although the abruptness with which its elevated table-land plunges into the ocean presents some very striking scenes. But the table-land itself is generally flat and bare, and the town of St. Anne's offers few points of interest. The island is but three miles and a half long. It claims our attention, however, on two accounts. On its north-western side is Braye Harbor, celebrated for the breakwater or mole which the English Government has been building for many years at an enormous expense as a naval station and harbor of refuge, to offset the corresponding port of Cherbourg in Normandy, and enable the English to command the Chan-

VRAICKING.

nel. This breakwater has, very strangely, been constructed in a most blundering manner, at least in its form, so that it presents itself to the sea in such a way that it often suffers serious damage, and will eventually have to be altered. Alderney is also known for the breed of cows which bears its name. These are so called probably because the first ones ex-

CREUX HARBOR, SARK.

ported were from that island, although now very few that are sold as Alderney cows are directly from there. Those of that breed actually exported from these islands are generally from Jersey, where the cattle are much the same as those of Alderney, small, with tapering heads, and of a delicate fawn-color. The Guernsey cow is esteemed by some even more highly than the Alderney; it is rather larger, and more of a red, brindled, in color. The cows are milked three times daily, and the milk is churned without skimming. One pound of butter a day is by no means an uncommon yield for a good cow. The cow cabbage is made to reach a size so large that the leaves are used to wrap the butter in for market, while the stalks are varnished and armed with ferrules, and extensively used at St. Helier's for canes. The cows are very carefully coddled. The grass they feed on is highly enriched by the vraic, a species of sea-weed gathered from the reefs at low tide. There are two vraic harvests appointed by the Government—one in the spring, the other in August, although it is gathered at other times in small quantities. All hands turn out in the season with boats and carts, frequently at night, and it is a very lively, picturesque occupation, though often attended with risk and loss of life from the overloading of boats or sudden rising of the tide. The cows are always tethered when feeding; they eat less in this way, really giving more milk than if glutted with food; and while they are cropping the grass on one side of a field, it has time to spring up on the other side. When they have done eating, they are at once removed from the sun into the shade. The breed is preserved from intermixture with other breeds by strong and arbitrary laws very carefully enforced. No cattle are allowed to enter the islands except for slaughter within a certain number of days, with the exception of oxen for draught.

Opposite the eastern coast of Guernsey are the islands Herm and Jethou, about three miles distant from St. Peter's Port. The former is a mile and a half long, high, and in some places very bold, and possesses withal a sand beach abounding to a very unusual degree with shells of great variety and beauty. It is chiefly valuable, however, at present as a resort for sportsmen. Two or three houses are on the island, including a hotel, much resorted to in summer. Jethou is close at hand, but is much

ENTRANCE TO THE CREUX LANDING-PLACE, SARK.

smaller, and tenanted chiefly by rabbits. Beyond these islands, a little more to the southward, and only seven miles from Guernsey, is Sark, one of the smallest, most curious, most interesting, most elusive, most desolate, most beautiful, most dangerous, most sublime, of the Atlantic islands. The old legend-makers, who have sung such weird tales of phantom isl-

THE AUTELETS, SARK.

ands, now appearing close at hand, then vanishing like enchantment, must have drawn their inspiration from watching Sark from Guernsey. On some days it is so distinct, and looks so near, that cliffs and houses and even men can be distinguished with the naked eye, and the soft play of light and shade and color on the rocks. The next day one shall look in the same direction, and he will discern with difficulty the faint hazy outline of what seems an island forty miles away. The approach to the island is almost always hazardous, and except in the best weather no boat can land or leave, owing to the maelstrom-like velocity and turbulence of the tides, which rush raging in all directions around the shore, and fill the hollow caves with melancholy dirges, as for the many wrecked on that merciless coast. The late Seigneur of Sark was lost off Point Nez, and the present Seigneur and his family have had an escape bordering on the miraculous. Sometimes, even in summer, weeks will pass without the possibility of communicating with the island. In winter one must depend entirely on Sark boats of seven or eight tons burden, strong and weatherly. In summer a small steamer plies in good weather between Guernsey and Sark; but it cannot enter the port, which is doubtless the smallest in Europe. It is formed by a breakwater thrown across a miniature bay called the Creux. A little beach extends around the base of the vertical cliffs, and the interior of the island is only reached by an artificial opening actually pierced through the surrounding wall of granite.

Sark is about three miles and a half long, and is divided into Great and Little Sark, the latter being a small peninsula at the southern end, united to the main portion by a curtain of rock some two hundred yards long, called the Coupé. It is three hundred feet above the sea, on one side literally vertical, on the other nearly so. The path at the top is not over five feet wide. It is said one person who lived on Little Sark never dared during a lifetime to cross over the Coupé. Another old fellow, who used to like to take his grog of an evening in Great Sark, would, on returning to Little Sark at night, walk several times over a log that lay near the Coupé. If the result was satisfactory to his equilibrium, he would then venture to reel across the Coupé. The cliffs surrounding the island furnish an inexhaustible supply of the grand, the wild, the picturesque. The rocks are clothed with highly colored vines and lichens; the magnifi-

CREUX DE DERRIBLE, SARK.

cent caves, seemingly the abode of sea-fairies, teem with varied and beautiful submarine vegetation and diverse forms of life, shell-fish, mollusca, algae, and the like. Our limits forbid more than allusion to such spots as the Autelets, the Creux du Derrible, or D'Ixcart Bay.

The interior of the island is devoted to agriculture and pasturage, and,

NATURAL BRIDGE, PONT-DU-MOULIN, SARK.

although not generally wooded, and destitute of streams, presents many choice bits of rural underwood. The avenue leading to the Seigneurie is exceedingly beautiful, and the building itself is a very pleasing object. The huts of the peasantry are often of the most massive construction, having walls six feet thick.

Those who suppose Monaco, or Andorra, or San Marino to be the smallest state in Europe must awake from their delusion. Sark has, by the last census, only 546 inhabitants, and is practically an independent state, owing only a feudal allegiance to Great Britain by way of Guernsey. Traces of the Druids exist, showing their early occupation of the island. In the Dark Ages it was the haunt of pirates, who from this almost inaccessible eyry swooped down on ships passing the Channel. After they were exterminated, the French held Sark some time; but in the reign of Elizabeth it was taken by a very ingenious stratagem, of which only a brief recital can be given here. It seems a galley anchored off the island under pretense of being a trader whose captain had died on the voyage. To consign a Christian man to the deep seemed a gratuitous sin, when Sark was so near at hand. Would the garrison allow his comrades to land the coffin and bury him in consecrated ground? They would go ashore unarmed, and would allow themselves to be searched on landing. This request was granted after due deliberation. The coffin was landed, and in solemn procession borne into the church. The door was then closed suddenly, and before the French could discover the object of this manœuvre, the coffin, which was filled with arms, was broken open, and, arming themselves, the sailors rushed out and cut down the French right and left. In their panic some threw themselves from the cliffs, the rest surrendered. Since that time Sark has continued under the English flag.

The Seigneur is feudal lord of the island, and shares the government with the other landholders, about forty in all. The worthy pastor, Mr. Cauchmeyer, a Swiss, has not been off the island for thirty-seven years.

I can heartily and truthfully recommend the invalid and pleasure-seeker to give these islands a trial—with a bit of advice on a point not always regarded by persons culpably foolhardy or totally ignorant of boat-sailing, especially in these very dangerous waters: never set out in a boat here, or undertake to go to Sark or any of the islands, if the boatmen are reluctant to try it, or if you are advised by the natives to wait for a change of weather.

SEIGNEUR'S HOUSE, SARK.

CHAPTER IV.

THE MAGDALEN ISLANDS.

MY attention was first called to the Magdalen Islands, in the Gulf of St. Lawrence, when I sailed in the *Anna Maria* fishing schooner. The skipper had often cruised in their neighborhood, and strongly advised me to visit them. Accordingly, I packed my kit and started in search of this *terra incognita*, in September—two months too late to see them if one consults his personal comfort, although really the best season if the tourist wishes to gain a clear notion of the savage character of the islands, and the waters which encircle them, and of the isolated life which the islanders lead. I went by way of Prince Edward Island, and found it no laughing-matter either to reach or leave these dunes of sand, even so early in the autumn, although they are but fifty-six miles due north from Eastern Point, Prince Edward Island (the distance from Souris, where the boat touches, to Havre Aubert, Amherst Island, being but eighty miles). Twice a month, until navigation closes, the steamer *Albert* runs from Pictou to the Magdalens, touching at Souris to take the mails when the weather allows her to enter the exposed port of Souris. But her movements are very uncertain, and the sleepless vigilance which is said to be the price of liberty is trifling compared with the watchfulness required on the part of the voyager who has made up his mind to reach the Magdalen Islands, and to reach them by the steamer *Albert* from Souris. No one could tell me the exact day or hour she was to be looked for, and a gale of wind about the time we might begin to expect her seemed to render it very uncertain whether she would touch at Souris at all; but the postmaster promised to give me prompt information when they came for the mail-bag. At nine in the evening, the wind having moderated, the whistle of the steamer was heard shrieking in the port. I ran to the hotel for my carpet-bag, but the postmaster had, of course, forgotten to send me word according to promise, and every one at the hotel had gone to an itinerant show. With the bag on my shoulder, I ran a mile, and was able to clamber over the side of the steamer just as she was shoving off from the breakwater. A slight detention of five minutes, owing to a loose screw in the engine, was all that enabled me to catch the boat. The *Albert* proved to be, without exception, the most clumsy and dangerous craft I ever stepped foot on, considering the perilous nature of the waters she navigates. The weather was fine and the wind fair, so we managed to average nearly six knots, which took us in sight of the islands at sunrise. It was a clear, cheerful day after the storm. Nearly a hundred sail of our Gloucester fishermen dotted the horizon, and the crests of Amherst, Alright in the extreme distance, and Entry directly ahead and near at hand, were exceedingly beautiful, warmed by the morning sun, which mellowed their various vivid tints into pearly grays.

It may be said here that the name now given to the whole group originally belonged to the long narrow island which comprises the more

SAND DUNES AND WRECKS BETWEEN AMHERST AND GRINDSTONE ISLANDS.

or less lofty divisions termed respectively Amherst, Grindstone, Alright. Wolf, Coffin, and Grosse Isle—islands which are all more or less connected by a double row of sand dunes enclosing lake-like lagoons, but divided in some places by sea-openings fordable at low water, and at Basque Harbor, Havre aux Maisons, and Grand Entry Harbor deep enough to admit of the entrance of small vessels. Around the Magdalen Islands, never more than a few miles distant, are Deadman's Island, the Bird Rocks, Biron Island, Shag Rock, and Entry Island, which are now all comprised under the same name. The Magdalen Islands *par excellence* trend thirty-eight miles in a north-easterly direction, from Amherst to Coffin Island. A long spit, called Sandy Hook, and partially under water, extends due east from Amherst toward Entry, from which it is separated by a narrow and dangerous channel. Pleasant Bay is the bight formed by Sandy Hook round by Basque Harbor to Grindstone Island, and is a commodious and safe road-stead in all but easterly winds, when vessels must cut and run for the other side of the island, or make a dash for Havre Aubert if taken too suddenly. In the terrific gale of August, 1873, our fishing fleet was

lying for refuge in Pleasant Bay, when the wind shifted so rapidly and violently into the eastward that thirty-three schooners were driven on shore in an hour, piled together on the top of each other. The skeletons of some of these hapless vessels still bleach on the beach at Amherst.

Rounding the grand, gayly colored sea-cliffs of Entry Island, the *Albert* steamed up to an anchorage at Amherst, at the bottom of Pleasant Bay, and a boat carried the mails and one solitary passenger ashore through the surf. The curious little town of Amherst lies there, composed of perhaps fifty houses straggling up the flanks of the Demoiselle, a conical hill, which on the sea side falls vertically nearly two hundred and eighty feet. The business portion of the metropolis of the Magdalens clusters farther down, where store-houses and fish stages for the drying of cod are huddled together on a sandbar scarce a hundred paces across, which connects Mount Gridley with the Demoiselle Hill. On the north side of this bar is Pleasant Bay; on the south side is Havre Aubert, twisted by our fishermen into Harbor le Bear. It is a small but perfectly safe port, the best in the Magdalens, it is said; but the entrance channel is very narrow and shifting, and accessible only to vessels drawing not over twelve feet of water. On the flats in the centre of the harbor lies an old hulk rotting in the storms which howl around that devoted coast so much of the year—a characteristic object, looking as if planted there purposely to indicate the character of those desolate isles.

The passenger aforesaid found better lodging than he had reason to expect, at Mrs. Shea's little boarding-house. The variety in the larder was limited; but the eggs were fresh, the milk rich, and the tea good, and the total cost of board and lodging not over seventy-five cents per diem. Amherst town may be said to be the seat of the Government. Mr. Fox, the revenue collector and superintendent of wrecks, resides there, and also Mr. Painchand, the United States consular agent, who is very polite to our countrymen, and Mr. Fontana, the most important individual in the islands, the agent of Admiral Coffin, the proprietor, who holds them subject to the jurisdiction of the Dominion. In reward for his public services, Captain Isaac Coffin, uncle of the present owner, received a grant of these islands from the British crown in 1798. They were first discovered by Jacques Cartier, and were colonized by French, chiefly Acadians, who sought refuge here when expelled from Acadie. They have received accessions from Canada, St. Pierre, Jersey, and England, and now number about five thousand, nearly all of French descent, and speaking and retaining the language, customs, and religion of the parent country. They occupy the land generally by leasehold, under various conditions, and the rents are devoted by the proprietor to the laying-out of roads and other public improvements. But great dissatisfaction has grown out of the existing tenure of lands. It is alleged that the prosperity of the islands is hindered by the present arrangement, and strong efforts are now made to bring about the transfer of the islands to the Dominion. The admiral asks eighteen thousand pounds, which would not seem excessive, considering that the area of the Magdalens is seventy-eight thousand acres, of which fully one-third is arable, and another third not wholly useless, while the fisheries add greatly to their value.

AMHERST, LOOKING TOWARD DEMOISELLE HILL

The lions of Havre Aubert were soon visited, including the English chapel on Mount Gridley, the new Roman Catholic church on the Demoi-

LANDING ON ENTRY ISLAND.

selle Hill, and the jail and post-office, which are within the same enclosure, and under the charge of one superintendent, whose official duties are not exhausting. There is a mail but twice a month, and for five months there is no mail at all, for the shore ice forms around the islands while the Strait of Northumberland is closed, and navigation ceases in the Gulf from December to April inclusive.

It was important to visit Entry Island, and to seize the first good weather, as the passage of nine miles in a small boat may prove very difficult in case of a sudden change of weather, always liable to happen after the 1st of September; and, in fact, at all seasons the sea rises in the Gulf of St. Lawrence with great rapidity, always rugged and tumultuous, with vast combers that break, owing to the tides and currents and the shoalness of the water and the undertow, all aiding to render navigation there excessively hazardous, combined with the frequent fogs.

Some men had come from Entry Island to attend the sale of wrecked goods at Havre Aubert, and I was able to return with them. We sailed in the broad light of the full moon, skirting Sandy Hook. A number of the islanders with their dogs came down to help us beach the boat and land the cargo on a long low sand spit on the northern side of Entry; and the scene by moonlight was very picturesque, and seemed more as if on the shore of some tropical isle surrounded by summer seas and balmy breezes than in the almost hyperborean regions of the St. Lawrence.

Mr. James Cassidy, the keeper of the light-house, cordially invited me to lodge with him. A long mile over a rolling moorland, with shadowy hills on our left and the moonlit sea and red star of the light-house before us, led through the frosty air to a warm fire in Mrs. Cassidy's comfortable kitchen, where a cup of tea and some of the capital island mutton added very materially to our well-being. "Look well to the commissariat," is ever the motto of your experienced traveller.

Entry Island is pentagonal in form, only two miles long in its greatest length, and for its size offers a greater variety of scenery and attractions probably than any other island of the Atlantic. The western half of the island forms a gentle slope, broken into pleasant *intervales*, divided into charming meadows and pasture-lands, overgrown with potatoes or waving grain and fragrant grasses, and ending abruptly in cliffs fifty to a hundred feet high. Bits of dwarf woodland scattered here and there give a very picturesque effect to this pastoral landscape, which is also heightened by the numbers of cattle, horses, and sheep everywhere visible, and the farm-houses of the ten families who here pass away their uneventful but not unhappy lives. They are all of Irish and English descent, and such a thing as want is probably unknown on Entry Island. It contains

OLD MAN AND OLD WOMAN.

about thirty-two hundred acres, an average of over three hundred acres to a family. They export some stock and provisions, including considerable butter. Mrs. Dixon told me she owned fifty-five cows; the milk is excellent, and to be had for the asking. The people appear to be thrifty, and yet it does not seem that they make the most of their opportunities. But who would blame them for this? They have enough, and are content. The women do not have to buy four hats a year, or study the fashions from Paris; the men do not need to pore over the daily financial reports, or discuss the public-school question in a place where all are Protestants, where there are no schools, and only a minister twice or thrice a year to marry and christen. At the same time, I saw books and papers in every house I visited, including the old family Bible, and the people are as intelligent as they are hospitable. They use, in common with all the Magdalen Islanders, a peculiar square cast-iron stove set on high legs between two rooms, fitting in an opening in the partition wall, thus heating both apartments equally, and economizing both labor and fuel. Here during the long winter days, when shut out entirely from the rest of the world, they sit and spin yarns and woollen at the same time. The old-fashioned spinning-wheel is used in all the islands, and most of the people are clad in homespun.

The eastern half of Entry is of quite another formation — bold and mountainous. Although the highest elevations are but lofty hills, yet they are really so high, considering the small area from which they rise, as to give in miniature the effect of a very rugged and mountainous land. The highest summit is six hundred and eighty feet above the sea by the latest survey, and it looks higher, it is so steep. The prospect from the top on that calm September day was one of rare beauty. The tints of sea and sky were soft, yet rich as those of southern latitudes. At our feet were spread the rich uplands and lowlands of Entry Island encircled by a line of silver foam. Beyond lay the group of islets clustering around Pleasant Bay, the red and gray precipices of Amherst, Alright, and Grindstone, bathed in hues so tender and beautiful I could hardly believe it was not some fair scene in the Ægean pictured before me like an exquisite dream. In the extreme distance, fifty miles away to the southward, could be discerned the faint outlines of Cape North and St. Paul's Island. As this hill, the highest elevation in the Magdalens, and commanding a view of the Gulf of St. Lawrence nearly one hundred miles in diameter, has remained without a name up to this time, the writer has ventured to name it St. Lawrence Hill. To the eastward of St. Lawrence Hill is Pig Hill, about fifty feet lower, but equally well defined. From these two peaks radiate a number of miniature gorges and dells thickly overgrown with savage woodlands of dwarf spruce, intermingled with birch, pine, and sassafras, and terminating on all sides but the land side in astonishing cliffs, generally vertical, and in some cases actually overhanging the sea. These magnificent precipices are three hundred and fifty feet high at the east end, gradually rising to over four hundred feet on the southern side. The loftiest of these cliffs, for lack of any other name, is here called the Watch Tower. Scarped and sculptured in a thousand fantastic shapes, and brilliantly hued with the lively and variegated tints of the new red sandstone, intermingled with gray gypsum and warm ochres, the cliffs of Entry Island scarcely yield in beauty and grandeur to the famous rocks of the Channel Islands, which, indeed, never reach an altitude of four hundred feet. Devil's Island is a perpendicular isolated mass connected with the main island by a zigzag curtain some thirty yards across, over three hun-

DRAGGING THE HULL OF A SCHOONER TO THE BEACH.

dred feet high, and tapering up to an absolute edge scarce an inch thick. The sheep wiggle across this edge, which may be likened to the bridge of Al-Sirat, to browse off the acre of grass on the summit, where they keep company with a colony of freebooting foxes, which, gradually driven from one post to another, have taken a last refuge in this almost inaccessible stronghold of despair, and raid on the hen-roosts o' stormy nights. Near the Devil's Island is a pool which has been sounded farther down than the sea-level without finding bottom.

I returned from Entry to Havre Aubert when a gale premonitory of the equinoctial was setting in, and was obliged to wait for clearing weather before starting for Grindstone Island. At length the elements seemed propitious, and we set out. The equipage, driven by Jean Nedean, who can be recommended as a competent guide across the fords and quicksands of the Magdalens, consisted of a cart hung on what were intended for springs, but they did not fulfil the intent of the maker. The jolting I received that day was fitted to search out every weak spot in one's anatomy, and would sorely have tested the quality of false teeth. One could readily realize in Jean Nedeau's cart what may be the sensation of having the spine piercing upward into the skull. The sturdy roan pony that dragged us along at a three-mile-an-hour pace was of a decidedly domestic turn, and was strongly averse to leaving home.

THROUGH THE SURF.

Our road led around the southern side of Amherst Island, which is eleven miles long, east and west, very hilly in the interior, being five hundred and fifty feet high, and generally cultivated. Near the fishing hamlet called the Basin we saw a very beautiful view. In the middle distance rose the Demoiselle Hill like an acropolis; in the background lay the purple heights of Entry Island like the main-land; and in the foreground the blue waters of the Basin, girt with green meadows, where the peasants were harvesting the hay. No scene on this side of the Atlantic has ever reminded me so vividly of historic bits in Asia Minor. Passing the hamlets of Pont-du-Moulin and Anse au Cabane, the road skirted the perpendicular red sea-cliffs on the left, while the wind sung a wild music in the spruce forests on our right. Here we saw a schooner on the stocks on a cliff, from which it would be slid on to the ice in the winter. Many small vessels are built on these islands, and it is not uncommon to construct them in the midst of the forest, over half a mile from the seaside. In the winter, when the men cannot farm or fish, the ship-builder buys a few gallons of gin, and then invites his neighbors to the launch. The cradle on which the hull is laid is placed on runners, and drawn over the snow by many willing hands tugging at the cables. When they reach the cliff's edge, the vessel is lowered to the ice, forty or fifty feet below, on sloping ways, by the aid of crabs and a few oxen. When the ice breaks up, she becomes a thing of life, and goes forth to battle with the storms.

At ten o'clock we came down to the lagoon called Basque Harbor, and began the toilsome journey along the dunes which protect it on the north-western side. After proceeding a couple of miles, shielded from the sea by a range of low sand hills, we came to a break where the tide rushed through like a mill-race: here we waited for the tide an hour, with ample time to study one of the wildest and most desolate scenes on the face of the earth. Sharp-speared salt grass scantily covered the tops of the sand hummocks, and relieved the uniform white, which only seemed more repelling when the surf lashed it with the foam of a storm that was gathering in the south-east, threatening and terrible in its gloom. Wrecks, or bits of wreck, were everywhere visible, partly covered by the shifting sands. Seaward, Deadman's Island was distinctly seen—a large rock resembling a corpse laid out. When the tide had fallen somewhat, we ventured to cross, feeling our way along a shoal near the centre of the lagoon. The water was up to the hubs of the wheels, and any deflection from the landmarks which guided us might have proved hazardous. After wading two-thirds of a mile, we once more stood on dry but not on firm land, for that epithet will hardly apply to bars more or less affected by every storm, and in places completely covered by the sea in a gale of wind. After this, we proceeded along the open beach, with the surf breaking among the spokes of the wheels. Curlew, plover, and wild-geese seemed to abound. In one spot two wrecks lay close together; one of them had been there

PORT AND VILLAGE OF ETANG DU NORD, GRINDSTONE ISLAND.

ten years, and was still in tolerably good condition. She sailed out of Miramichi, a noble vessel of twelve hundred tons, just off the stocks. It was her first voyage. She had proceeded less than two hundred miles when she brought up on the Magdalen Islands. The owner got his insurance, but the circumstances were against him. The far-sighted and resolute audacity that will build a vessel to cast it away is almost sublime. while one hardly knows what to think of the sailor who will deliberately destroy a ship on her first voyage.

Fording one or two more small inlets, we at length reached the end of the dune, twelve miles long, and entered the curious fishing-village of Étang du Nord, on Grindstone Island. In summer many of the people leave their houses inland and come down to this place. The men go a-fishing when the weather is at all practicable, while the women and children dry the fish and have a warm meal ready when the men return. A large fleet of strong fishing-boats of large size crowds the little port, just outside of which lies the curious rock called Gull Island. The shore of the haven is lined with rude houses on stages in the water for the storing of the fresh fish, and the huts of the fishermen are ranged behind these. A quaint place is Étang du Nord, with its French people and manners; and as I took a capital fast-day dinner in the snug house of M. Bourque, I could almost imagine myself back in the fishing-towns of Brittany. From here in the dusk we jolted through the woods, down hilly paths, to the house of M. Nelson Arseneau, at Havre aux Maisons, where I was hospitably entertained for several days: "Vous êtes chez vous, monsieur," as mine host said to me, with unaffected cordiality.

Part of the little settlement of Havre aux Maisons, or House Harbor, is situated on Alright Island, which is reached by a ferry. Both islands have some remarkable headlands over three hundred feet high, notably Cap au Meule, Cape Grindstone, and Cape Alright; while each contains much fine farming land, with comfortable farms and pretty valleys, affording pasture to numerous flocks and herds. Abundance of grain is raised on these islands, but the general complaint is that there are no mills to grind it. Brooks there are which, by the aid of a dam, could furnish the power; but I could not but think it very strange that, with such a capital situation and such abundance of wind, they do not use windmills, which are quite inexpensive. Cranberries grow on the islands, and the cultivation of that beautiful berry might easily become profitable.

Havre aux Maisons is a port of much importance as the seat of the seal fisheries, in addition to what is done there in the disposal of shore mackerel and ship-building. In the last century the walrus frequented the Magdalens in vast numbers, but they were at last frightened away by the prodigious slaughter. But the seal has always been common around there, and sometimes the catch is important. In the winter of 1875 over 20,000 were taken, valued at $60,000 to the hunters, and yielding several thousand barrels of oil in addition to the skins. The oil is tried out in vats. The blubber is thrown in at the top, which is left open; when the spring sun arrives, the warmth melts the blubber, and the oil runs into the tubs below. The seals are caught on the floating ice, which sometimes extends many miles, but is liable to be blown away from the shore ice with a change of wind. Immense is the excitement throughout the whole settlement when news runs from one end to the other like wildfire that the seals have arrived. Every soul turns out, including the women, who stand on the beach with refreshments. Every party of hunters carries a small skiff, with which to return in case the ice moves off. Dragging the dead seals over the ice is a very exhausting labor; some now use horses and sledges for this purpose; but at best it is a fearfully labori-

CAP AU MEULE AND WRECK, GRINDSTONE ISLAND.

ous and dangerous work, and many have lost their lives, carried away on the ice.

It may not be generally known that our fishermen have for years frequented the Magdalen Islands for mackerel. It is not uncommon to see a fleet of two hundred schooners in those waters, taking home annually 30,000 barrels of mackerel, worth over $350,000 at a low estimate. But the fishermen of those islands also pursue the shore fisheries with profit in boats. Nine thousand barrels of mackerel and ten thousand quintals of cod, worth in the aggregate $100,000, are set down to their credit, exclusive of what were caught by the Yankee fishermen, during the not very profitable season of 1875. The herring fisheries are also of great value and importance at the Magdalen Islands.

North-east from Grindstone Island stretches the broad and navigable lagoon formed by Wolf and Alright islands on either side, with their long

PART OF CAPE ALRIGHT.

sand dunes that unite them with Grosse Isle and Coffin Island. Grand Entry Harbor is a fine port of refuge between the two latter islands, which are the most common resort of the seals. Detached from these to the north are the Bird Rocks, and Biron Island, which is inhabited by a few families who cultivate its rich soil and raise stock; but it is inaccessible, except when the weather is serene and with the wind off shore. Owing to the lateness of the season warning me to seize the first opportunity to leave, and the fierceness of the equinoctial gales, which lashed the Gulf surges into rage unwonted even in that turbulent sea, I was unable to visit the remaining islands. Passage was kindly offered me in the small schooner *Sea Foam* to Souris; but, on account of the heavy surf on the bar, we could not avail ourselves of the favorable wind after the gale, but were forced to wait a day. The ship-channel of Havre aux Maisons is very tortuous, in some places scarcely a ship's width, and lies so near the end of the spit that it can be touched by an oar in passing, while the current of the incoming or outgoing tide rushes through with such violence that in a moderate breeze it is extremely difficult for a vessel to get by the spit without being headed off by the tide and slewed on a bank. Three times we got aground, and each time waited for the tide to lift us off. The same thing happened to the schooners in company with us. Finally, by the aid of a kedge, at slack tide, we were able to slip through the channel and put out into the open water of Pleasant Bay. But our fair breeze had failed us, and the weather looked dubious and threatening, with light and baffling winds all night, which took us to the southward of Entry Island, when the wind settled in the south-west, with lightning, a heavy sea, and a very wicked-looking sky in the offing. A storm was brewing, and after a hasty consultation the helm was put up, and we bore away again for Pleasant Bay, where we dropped the mud-hook under the lee of the Demoiselle Hill, and were soon joined by a fleet of schooners. It blew fresh all day, shifting into the west, with a fine clear sky. In the afternoon we got up the anchor and moved farther up the bay, opposite Basque Harbor, to make a lee in case the wind should shift to the northeast in the night. There we lay until the following afternoon. The time was pleasantly whiled away exchanging visits with the neighboring schooners. Some very sensible, good fellows, with now and then a comical genius, were discovered in the diminutive cabins of these little craft, and the conversation, the merriment, and the yarns never flagged. On board our schooner we numbered six, consisting of the owners, the passenger, the skipper, the officers and crew, combined in the burly person of one man named Jim, and Joe, the cook, who professed to be from Gloucester, and was one of the most singular characters ever seen on board a schooner. Cleanliness in his person or apparel was not one of his prominent traits. I know he has washed his hands at least once in his life, because I heard the owner of the schooner send him on deck to do so just as he was about to knead some dough. As a cook, he was voted to be the greatest failure of the season, although he limited himself to cooking only salt-horse, codfish, and potatoes with their jackets on.

THE SERENE JOSEPH.

But the imperturbability of his disposition, combined with an impudence that almost exceeds belief, afforded us a compensating fund of entertainment, aided by the undying feud that existed between this hopeful disciple of Soyer and the skipper.

"Blast your eyes!" roared the skipper, at dinner, "why don't you put the beef to soak before you boil it, you young pirate?"

"It was soaked," said the serene Joseph.

"And who was it but myself who put it in to soak at the last minute?" replied the skipper.

"Well, if you put it in to soak, what was the need of my doing it, eh?" answered the respectful youth.

"D——n your impudence!" yelled the skipper, now fairly shaking with rage, and hurling a hatchet at the brazen-faced youth, who dodged it, and it struck the side of a bunk, just over his head.

The whole morning Joe lay in a sunny spot on deck, out of the wind, in a brown-study. In the evening he handed around a greasy note-book, in which he had put down the result of his meditations in the form of a satirical poem on the captain, which was not altogether destitute of literary merit.

It was very interesting, while we lay there, to watch the gannets diving for mackerel. Rising to a great height, they suddenly turned head downward, and, folding their wings close to the body, dropped into the water with the speed and violence of a shot, splashing the spray well into the air. When a flock of them were diving in this way over a school of fish, the effect was that of balls falling into the sea during a naval battle.

On the following day by noon the wind got into the north-west, and it was decided to make another attempt to get across. We ran through the channel between Entry and Amherst, passing near to the *Tigress* steamer, which was wrecked on the former island in the late gale two days previously. The sunset that evening was one of the most superb it has been my fortune to see. The waves were of the most exquisite emerald hue, tossing up their spray like diamonds, while sixty-five of our schooners fishing close together under the lee of the purple hills of Amherst Island, their main-sails touched with a rosy flame, and flocks of sea-birds darting hither and thither like bearers of light, or shooting-stars, their white wings illumined by the glory of the setting sun, combined to compose a marine view of unsurpassed magnificence. But after the sun went down, the weather looked less satisfactory; however, it was decided to keep on.

All night the wind was fresh but steady: all hands took turns at steering and watching, and a sharp lookout was kept for East Point Light, on Prince Edward Island. This was made more difficult because a number of fishermen were tacking about or lying at an anchor, and their lights sometimes looked surprisingly like the gleam of a light on shore. After taking another look, the skipper went below again to catch forty winks. Jim was at the wheel, and the writer, leaning against the foremast, and dodging the spray which shot over the bow, was on the lookout. But Jim also wanted to go below, ostensibly to get his sou'-wester; and I went to the wheel. However, when he found himself in the warm, snug cuddy, he stretched himself along-side of the other four, and there they all lay on the floor, snoring as if we were a thousand miles from land. It was, however, not a bad night to have the deck to one's self, to hold the old schooner heading sou'-west and by south by the feeble glim in the binnacle, to keep a sharp lookout for the light under the leech of the main-sail, an eye to windward for squalls, and also find an odd second now and then for reflections suggested by the scene. It was a murky, restless night about two in the morning; the wind growing fresher, and coming in flaws moaning through the rigging, and driving dark clouds across the stars that twinkled here and there. Everything betokened a change of weather and a storm before long. The schooner, close hauled on the starboard tack, held bravely on her course, careening over gracefully as a stiff puff would strike her; then a turn of the wheel shivered the headsails, and she was all right again. But at last I became convinced that a light on the lee bow could be no other than the one we were looking for, and I called up the skipper. Immediately on seeing it, he ordered the helm to be put up, and, slackening the main-sheet, we bore away to give the reef off the point a wide berth. In the August gale of 1873, two of our schooners running before it, and with no other possible course that they could take and live, ran over the reef, and, owing to the depth of water then on it, might have escaped if they had not lost headway when their foresails jibed. An enormous breaker overtook and swooped over them at that critical instant. In a twinkling they were seen to capsize and go down, and not a vestige of them was ever seen again. Beating under the land against a strong breeze, accompanied by a fleet of schooners running for a lee, we reached Souris at noon, just escaping a hurricane, which came on soon after and destroyed many vessels.

CHAPTER V.

MADEIRA.

"MADEIRA is an island lying off the coast of Africa, in the latitude of Charleston, S. C., a resort for invalids. It is said to be exceedingly rich in natural beauty, and its wine is famous."

That was all I knew about the island—quite as much, if not more than is known probably to most Americans; but a trip made the previous summer to the Azores had whetted my appetite, and happening, about the time I was thinking of another cruise, to come across Captain Hardy, of the bark *Ethan Allen*, his glowing description of Madeira easily induced me to take passage with him, engaging the same state-room as on a former voyage. We had been twenty days out of Boston, running, generally, with a fair wind and less incident than usual, when "Land ho!" was the cry, and there, indeed, was the loom of land faintly discernible under a mass of cumulus cloud on the weather bow. For several hours it was doubtful whether what we saw was Madeira or its neighbor, Porto Santo; but, after a while, three isolated hummocks, pale-blue, under the lee bow, gradually assuming the peculiar outline of Porto Santo, indicated that Madeira was the land on our right, enveloped, as usual, in a curtain of vapor, and sixty miles distant. Porto Santo, twenty-two miles north-east of its neighbor, is small and barren, chiefly valuable for its limestone quarry, a geological phenomenon in the group. Until recently it was also a penal settlement to which convicts from Funchal were transported.

The lightness of the breeze made our approach very slow, and it was only on the following morning that we drew near Madeira, and, very fortunately, obtained an uninterrupted view of its magnificent outline, falling at either end abruptly to the sea, with lofty precipices and vast detached rocks of ragged and fantastic shapes and rich volcanic tints, along the whole coast-line; while from the sea the land arose rapidly to the centre, where a cluster of peaks, closely grouped, deeply grooved and turreted, suggesting the bastions and pinnacles of a gigantic fortress, were cut clearly against the sky with the sharpness of sculpture. Passing San Lorenzo

Point with a leading wind, we were immediately headed off by one of the numerous air currents which prevail on the southern side and neutralize the north-east trades, and fetched a tack across to the Desertas, three rocky islets belonging to the Madeira group. Very narrow, like a winding wall, they rise to the height of two thousand feet, and are next to inaccessible; while the violent squalls, which spring unawares from the cliffs, oblige the mariner to exercise unusual vigilance in their vicinity.

Off the end of Chao, the northernmost, is a needle-rock, one hundred

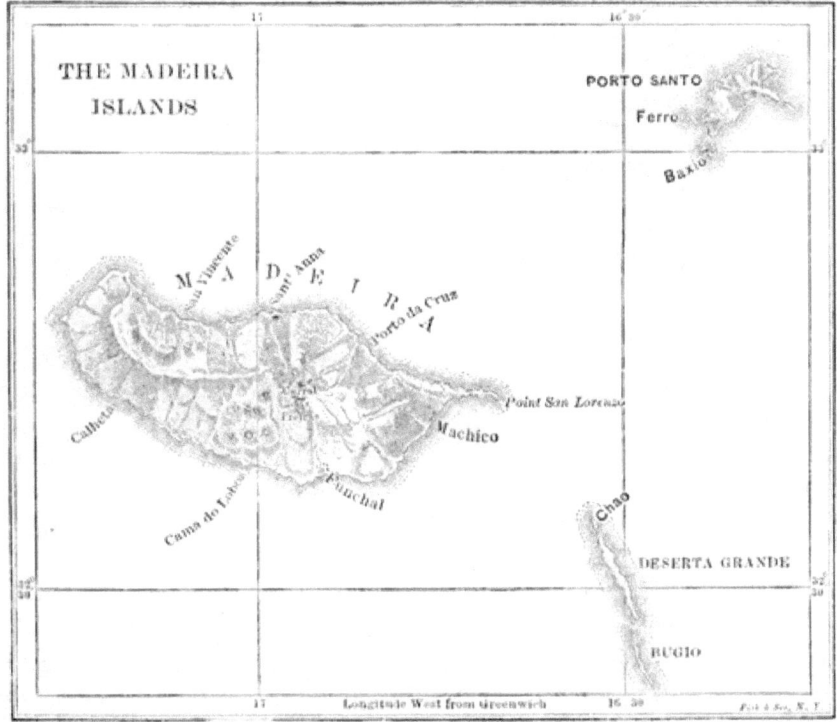

and sixty feet high, resembling a ship by the wind, as seen from the stern: it is naturally called Sail Rock. A handful of fishermen share the Desertas with the cats, which have colonized and overrun them, and gather orchilla and catch shearwaters by swinging over the precipices. The birds are pickled, while the plumage is reserved for the beautiful feather-work of Madeira. When a supply of these is collected, an immense beacon-fire is kindled on the highest peak to summon boats from Funchal, thirty miles

FUNCHAL HARBOR AND BRAZEN HEAD.

distant. It is more than surmised that smuggling is also successfully carried on at the Desertas.

The port of Funchal is only a slight curve between two headlands, with a sea exposure reaching to the south pole. Yet ships lie here all the year round. During the winter months vessels sometimes have to slip and run for an offing; but the rest of the year the hazard is slight. A brig took out and repaired her main-mast while we were there as fearlessly as if moored in a dock in a snug harbor. There is no landing-place except the beach, and boats of the most diminutive size venture out into the bay. Nothing so much impressed me with a sense of the mildness of the climate of Madeira as the security of this exposed roadstead. The boats are pointed at both ends, the keel-piece being carried several feet above the gunwale. The stern-post is rounded at the heel, and a rope is passed through it; a triple keel keeps the boat in an upright position on shore. When the beach is reached the boat is turned stern foremost, and men bared to the hips rush into the surf, and by the aid of the rope lift the boat up the steeply shelving shore. Ships are loaded and discharged entirely by large lighters, which are drawn on the beach by immense capstans, called crabs. An army of yelling, bare-legged boatmen is required to land or launch a loaded lighter. The beach of Funchal—crowded with rows of picturesquely shaped, gayly painted boats; enlivened by the roar of the surf, and the constant landing of boats, and the Babel-like vociferations of boatmen and the drivers of ox-teams; and flanked at one end by the governor's residence and a noble avenue of plane-trees, and at the other by a shaded Praça and an old red fort peaked with pepperbox turrets, the warm cliffs of Brazen Head rising behind it, and the soft violet outlines of the Desertas in the offing—presents one of the most interesting scenes on the island. Loo Rock and the castle (which seems an integral part of it), dovetailing with the jagged pinnacles of the rock, form one of the most effective features of this scene, standing isolated and picturesque against the sky.

The port of Funchal is often enlivened by steamers and ships touching there from the coast of Africa. Their decks are crowded with crates and cages full of tropical fruits, and parrots and monkeys, the screeching and chattering of the latter being distinctly heard at some distance. This gives rise to many amusing incidents. Boys go off from the beach to

LOO ROCK.

these steamers in tiny boats, and, clamoring loudly for pennies, dive to a great depth in the clear turquoise-colored water and fetch up coins. Now and then a shark's fin stealthily and ominously appears on the surface; but accidents very rarely happen.

Soon after I arrived the first time at Madeira, a Greek polacre brig came in from Sierra Leone, bound for Marseilles with a cargo of peanuts. She had been becalmed in the doldrums, and had been ninety-five days making some fifteen hundred miles. No sooner had she anchored than a negro sailor escaped from her and came on board our vessel. As he seemed determined to stay, Captain Hardy finally concluded to send him back to the brig, and, as I spoke Greek, asked me to go with the boat and explain the matter to the captain of the brig.

I found the vessel apparently in the last degree of neglect, the counterpart of scores of similar craft I had seen in the Levant. Neither paint nor tar seemed to have touched the hull or rigging since she had been built. Everything was slack and in unmentionable confusion. The peanuts fairly bubbled on deck over the open hatches; and monkeys and parrots snapped or winked at one from their cages or hiding-places under piles of old spars. A curious scene was the deck of that brig, rendered more singular by the handsome and tidy appearance of the captain, who stood by the companion-way and received me with the courtesy of a prince. He spoke French and Greek alternately, and with almost equal facility, and ordered the cabin-boy to bring up some Madeira wine, which, I regret to say, was of a poor quality. I then gave my message regarding the black sailor, who was now sitting on the rail dangling his feet over the water.

The Greek listened with simulated nonchalance; but when I had done, his fury exploded. Seizing a calker's mallet, and hurling terrific imprecations, he flew at the negro with a ferocity that led me to expect to see his brains dashed out on the instant. Raising the mallet, the Greek brought it down with great violence to within an inch of the negro's skull, and let it stop there. He then flung down the mallet, and came back as serene as if nothing had happened. But the negro, who had neither flinched nor winked, still remained in his place. After talking with me a few minutes, the Greek captain was seized by another paroxysm of frantic rage, and, snatching up the mallet again, rushed at the negro with even more violence than before; but again the mallet stopped within an inch of the victim's head. Here was a blending of frenzy and self-control that was most extraordinary and unaccountable. Coming aft again, with a sardonic smile on his classic but rather piratical features, the Greek called for another glass of wine, and chatted in the most unconcerned manner, until a third fit of fury came upon him. This time he was undoubtedly in earnest; for he did not take up the mallet, but making a dash at the negro, seized him with a death-like grip, and, in spite of his efforts at resistance, hurled him over the ship's side into the boat, where he struck on the thwarts, severely hurting himself, and nearly breaking his back. Calling away the boat's crew, I now returned aboard the bark. The poor negro deserted again the next day.

Funchal, seen from the sea, lies on a slope of extraordinary abruptness, rent into three divisions by two gorges whose sides are ragged and nearly vertical. At the head of these ravines, immediately behind the city, peaks 4000 to 5000 feet high appear through rifts in the canopy of

THE SLEDGE-HACK.

clouds. A gray old castle, perched on a spur projecting from the mountains, whose teeth have been drawn—for its quaint outlandish brass pieces have flashed the grim menace of war for the last time—assists the eye to realize the suddenness of these precipitous ranges, and greatly adds to the effective prospect of the town. On landing, the stranger very soon learns the actual steepness of the place, and finds that your true Madeirian walks on three legs, or, in other words, assists nature with a staff, which, by often saving one from a severe fall, becomes literally the staff of life. The streets are paved with round pebbles, whose natural slipperiness is increased by friction, and also by the grease-bags of the sledges, insomuch that they are often worn flat, smooth as glass, and scarcely less treacherous. I found myself sometimes clinging to the walls on a steep incline with the tenacious grasp of ivy. The sledges alluded to are the nearest approach to a wheeled vehicle used on the island. They are drawn by oxen guided by leathern thongs passed through the tips of the horns. The drays are a mere slab twelve to eighteen inches wide, strengthened by a rim on the upper edge, and are of the same form, whether used by farmers or draymen. The hacks resemble our old-fashioned covered sleighs, except that the runners are of wood alone, and a cross-bar rests on the floor inside for the support of the feet when climbing or descending the steep declivities. The driver carries a grease-bag, which he lays at intervals in front of the runners. One of the most characteristic cries of Funchal is the yelling of the ox-drivers, " Ca, para mi, boi! ca, ca, ca, ca! o-o-o-ah !" (Come here to me, O oxen! here to me! whoa!)

The hammock, carried on men's shoulders, is another conveyance peculiar to Funchal. While this is of especial advantage to the invalid, men who can reel off their ten miles before dinner without inconvenience do not disdain to avail themselves of the luxuriant motion it affords. Strange to say, the apparently severe labor of hammock-bearer is preferred by the natives to any other form of open-air work. Horses imported from abroad, and generally trustworthy, are also used to some extent, shod expressly for the roads of Madeira with spiked shoes, which, in travelling over some parts of the island, have to be renewed as often as once in every three days. But the character of the roads, even in Funchal, is so trying to the nerves that many prefer the other modes of conveyance.

But the coasting-sledge of Funchal must claim pre-eminence over all known forms of locomotion except sailing. I know of no other place in the world where business men slide down hill to their counting-rooms. In summer many gentlemen reside in villas, which are a continuation of Funchal, reaching as high up as the Church of Nostra Senhora do Monte, 2000 feet above the sea. I rode up one morning to breakfast at the villa of the Austrian consul, Signor Bianchi, situated on a level with the Mount Church. The ride was up a very precipitous incline; but the horses were on their mettle, and went up the unbroken ascent at full trot, the muleteers running close behind: they rested but once, and neither horses nor men showed shortness of wind. Behind us, at the end of steep streets, stretched the ocean, whose dim horizon-line grew rapidly more distant and faint as we rose. On either hand the road was shut in by high walls, overhung with a profusion of purple and scarlet flowers, which loaded the moist morning air with perfume. The terraces above were darkened by the lace-work of wavering light and shade cast by trellises supporting vines weighted with clusters of Muscatel grapes, "wanton to be plucked." Having partaken the genial hospitality of our host and hostess, we walked across the head of a ravine to a sledge "stand" by the Mount Church, and seated ourselves in a vehicle of basket-work, fixed on wooden runners, with a cushioned seat for three, and a brace for the feet. The attendants, seizing a leathern guiding thong, leaped on the rear end of the runners with one foot, gave the sledge a start, and we were off. With the foot that was free the men controlled their flying sledge as a boy guides a sled, only with more skill. We dashed down the narrow way at a speed almost frightful, but gloriously exciting, going around abrupt turns with a slide to leeward which only the astonishing dexterity of the guides prevented from becoming a hazardous capsize.

THE MOUNTAIN SLED.

Soon the increasing number of people in the street obliged us to slacken our pace; but toward the end we overtook another sledge, and, ordering our engineer to put on steam, away we went again at prodigious rate, gradually overhauling the chase, until we suddenly turned into a dark lane. The sled stopped, and, presto! the excitement was over; but not the memory thereof. We made something over two miles in eight minutes and a half. The distance has been done in five minutes, when, earlier in the day, there was a clear road. Another time I made the descent at ten o'clock at night, when all was darkness ahead, intensified, if possible, by the lantern we carried at our feet. This sliding into mystery, swiftly slipping through impalpable gloom, down apparently fathomless abysses, is wonderfully stimulating to the imagination.

Funchal improves on acquaintance. As one grows familiar with its narrow and somewhat intricate streets, he rapidly discovers objects of interest which relieve the sameness of the heavy stone buildings. I never was in a town of 20,000 inhabitants so well built, so cleanly and prosperous, and so well situated, in which architecture as an æsthetic art had been so entirely ignored as in Funchal. The Sé, or cathedral, is a building of some size, and its spire is surmounted by a gilt globe symbolizing the former world-wide dominion of Portugal. It is said to have been designed by Mattheus Fernandez, one of the great architects who constructed the famous church and cloisters of Batalha. The Sé is pleasing in its general plan, while the poverty of the founders probably prevented much elaboration. But the ceiling of the nave and transept, beautifully carved out of juniper, and tinted and gilded, deserves careful attention. The Church of Santa Clara is an interesting old building. It contains the grave of Zarco, the Portuguese discoverer of Madeira.

On the way to the Mount Church is an old dwelling, whose two front windows, mullioned in stone, are suggestive of Moorish art. But if art has done little for Funchal, nature has done much to atone for this. Many of the solid but unpretentious houses conceal rare attractions within their gates, revealed like magic to him who steps within, unprepared for the sight, and finds terraced gardens overlooking the ocean and the mountains, and stocked with the profuse vegetation of two zones. The palm and the pine, the cypress and the magnolia, the pomegranate and the banana, the walnut and the guava, the apple and the coffee-tree, the rose apple and the chestnut, intertwine their various shades of perennial verdure in a fraternal embrace that seems to unite different climes as in Eden; while the oleander, the fuchsia, the geranium, the hortensia, the bougainvillia, the heliotrope, the acacia, the jessamine, and numerous other flowers of brilliant hues and spicy odors, growing wild in vast quantities, clamber over trellis and wall, and blend their fragrance from one season to another; for on this enchanted isle neither the frosts of winter nip their buds, nor the rage of the dog-star fades their scarlet and blue.

The market-place of Funchal is also an object of attraction, although the many varieties of fruits and vegetables displayed in its stalls do not generally reach the excellence of their native climes, excepting the grape, the fig, and the strawberry; the latter lasts all summer, and is superior in flavor to our best. The peach is not comparable to a good Jersey peach; apples and pears are hard and tasteless; but the flavorless character of the fruits of Madeira must be owing chiefly to the little attention paid to improving them, for agriculture is conducted in a primitive manner, while the mildness of the temperature and fertility of the arable soil would seem to offer the conditions essential to successful husbandry; but it may be that this very mildness is the cause of this defect in the vegetable productions of Madeira. A sharper air in winter, a fiercer heat in summer, may be necessary to complete excellence. The oak, for example, flourishes here, and its foliage is perennial; but the wood is soft and comparatively valueless.

Venomous insects and serpents, which are one of the scourges of the tropics, are happily almost unknown in Madeira, with the exception of

CHURCH OF NOSTRA SENHORA DO MONTE.

a small species of tarantula, which is not common. Its bite, although very painful, is not often fatal. I once had an adventure with one which afforded me a little exciting sport. I was occupying at the time a small building containing two apartments, standing alone in the vineyard behind Holway's Hotel—a very cosy little box, where I passed many a pleasant evening. From the balcony I could overlook the lights of

Funchal or of the ships at anchor, and listen to the music of the bells stealing up from the town, or the regular beat of the surf on the shore. Often the upward rush of scores of rockets, blending their red, blue, and green stars with the stars which spangle the serene skies, added to the interest of the prospect from my window. Nowhere is there a greater delight taken in fireworks than in Madeira. Every saint's day is celebrated by the explosion of hundreds and thousands of rockets, and the birthdays of the wealthier citizens afford fresh opportunities for the explosion of these aërial baubles. Every church in the island has also its *novana*, or nine days' *fête*, and during the whole nine days rockets are sent up at intervals by the score.

Well, on the evening in question I was quietly reading, absorbed in Byron's tragedy of "Werner," when I became conscious, without knowing exactly why, that there was something in the middle of the floor which had not been there a moment before. On looking around, I saw a tarantula deliberately marching across the room and coming toward me. He evidently wanted my chair, and I concluded to let him have it. As more light on the subject was desirable, I then went into my bedroom and brought out another candle. When I returned, he was sitting exactly in the centre of the chair I had just vacated. The cushion was scarlet and he was black, a sort of velvety black, like a large button of that color. But I could not stop to admire the harmony of colors, for he was closely watching my motions; and as the tarantula is aggressive, and can jump several feet, he is not to be trifled with. I went after a heavy walking-club in the corner of the room, and meantime he hopped on the flap of the table-cloth which was close to the chair. This was a false move on his part. Gently raising the end of the cloth below him with the stick, I gradually coaxed him on to the top of the table, which was exactly where I wanted him. Quietly I removed everything off the table, in order to have a clear field of operations. He watched me intently with his bright, intensely black bead-like eyes, quickly turning around to face me every time I moved. It was a fair game on each side, but he did not improve his opportunities. When all was ready, I took up a volume of Ruskin's "Modern Painters"—a work which has proved itself of great weight, and has demolished more than one reputation—and, taking deliberate aim, brought it down with great force on the devoted tarantula. When I took up the book the creature was not there. It was now of the last importance to find out if he had jumped on me. The dark color of my clothes, and the fact that I could not very well see my own back, made it difficult to settle this satisfactorily for some moments.

Further search, however, showed the tarantula under the sofa in the corner of the room. I hurled the club at him, end on, with a fury which indented the wall, but he briskly avoided the danger; and another hunt revealed him under a chair, this time thoroughly frightened, it would seem, for he allowed me to lift the chair and carry it away. Still confident in the destructive powers of Ruskin, I brought the volume down once more on the tarantula, and this time his back was broken. I still have faith in Ruskin, at least under certain circumstances. Leaving the tarantula on the field where he had fallen, I then went to bed, thankful to feel that I was rid of a very unpleasant bedfellow. I have known several cases where a tarantula has crept between the sheets unbidden.

The next morning I arose and went to look at him; he was still there. I returned to bed and took another nap and a cup of chocolate. But when I looked for the tarantula a second time I found that the cockroaches had completely devoured him, excepting the two hard, black, glistening eyes, which lay on the floor like bits of polished jet.

But Funchal is not the whole of Madeira: it is, in fact, but the vestibule to scenes of greater interest and beauty, and it was therefore with much satisfaction that I completed a bargain for a boat-cruise along part of the southern coast. I had a crew of four stout fellows, and an able boat provided with sail and awning. We started about sunrise, and skirted cliffs standing many hundred feet perpendicularly above the sea, richly colored with volcanic tints, sometimes showing spots of pure vermilion inlaid with burnt sienna and Indian red. Reeds and grass grew on the ledges, partially draping the nakedness of the precipices as a cincture of leaves dangles around the tattooed waist of a Feejee warrior. Little boys and girls were barely discernible here and there, skipping like goats from ledge to ledge at dizzy heights, gathering grass on these unpromising spots. Passing under the remarkable promontory called Brazen Head, we came to Atalaya Rock, which resembles a vast oak riven by a thunderbolt. We continually met boats bound to Funchal with vegetables and firewood, until, toward noon, we reached Santa Cruz, where our boat was hauled on the beach, and I proceeded on a quiet ramble, finishing up with dinner at the charming hotel.

Santa Cruz is at the opening of one of the profound torrent gorges which are a distinguishing feature in every Madeira landscape, and affords some fine bits of scenery. A sail of an hour from here took us to Machico, where the boat was beached, and after some search I obtained a room in a private house for the night.

Anna Dorset was sought in marriage, in the days of Edward III., by

Robert Machin, a gentleman, and they both lived in Devon by the sea. But he was of lower station than the lady— at one time, and, unfortunately, still too often, the accursed cause of much heartache and the separation of souls whom God, if not the priest, has joined. Her friends made haste to patch up a marriage between Anna and a nobleman, whose birth, if not his wits, was equal to hers. But Machin—and who that has loved can blame him?—was not of the stuff that can tamely submit to such petty tyranny. He persuaded one of his friends to enter the service of the lady's husband, and in that capacity become her attendant. By this means it was planned that she should elope to France. A galley was procured, and one night the lady fled from her lord's castle, and embarked with her lover at Bristol, forsaking her native land, never to return. The night was wild and dark with threatening tempests, but they had no alternative but to put to sea. Scarcely, however, had they cleared the coast, when a north-easter struck the vessel and forced them to bear away before it. Thirteen days they scudded, and at last made land—a strange, cloud-hidden, unknown, and uninhabited land, offering only tremendous precipices and surf-beaten rocks on its northern coast; but, on rounding a savage cape, they came to the southern side, and there, at the bottom of a snug little bay, stretched a beach, on which they landed, and found themselves in a grassy vale, well watered, musical with the melody of birds and streams, and shaded by majestic trees, seemingly sheltered from the boisterous world by lofty mountains. Here Anna and her lover rested three days—perhaps, in each other's society, forgetting the land they had left behind and the stormy scenes which had intervened, and hoping that in this paradise they had at last gained an asylum where they might pass their remaining days in peace. But another storm drove the galley to sea, and, overcome by this new calamity, added to her already terrible suffering of body and soul, the lady expired. Five days passed, and Robert Machin, too faithful in his love, also succumbed to the anguish of these accumulated afflictions, and was buried at her side. Their surviving comrades erected a cross over the grave of the lovers, and then embarked in a rudely constructed craft and were blown to the coast of Africa, whither the galley had already been driven, and her crew reduced to slavery by the Moors. A companion in their captivity was the Spaniard Juan de Morales, who was eventually ransomed and sailed for Spain; but he was captured on the way by the Portuguese navigator João Gonsalez Zarco, who learned from him the story of Machin and Madeira. Associating Teixera, an experienced pilot, with himself, and also taking Morales, Zarco sailed in quest of this island. The remains of Machin and Anna were found as described, and a small chapel was erected over them, which exists to this day.

Such is the one legend of Madeira, a tragedy replete with pathos, the substantial truth of which has been confirmed by recent investigations. Machico and its valley, named after its ill-fated discoverer, seemed to me well fitted to be the scene of a story so tender and affecting. The town, once a rival to Funchal, is now only a humble farming and fishing village. A few barefooted, poverty-stricken peasants cultivate the terraced sides of the valley; a few fishing-boats lie on the beach; an old fort, half-hidden by overhanging plane-trees, points the cobwebbed muzzles of dismounted guns, at fleets which pass at a distance and aim at it nothing fiercer than the lens of the perspective glass. The only garrison of this

HAMMOCK-RIDING IN MADEIRA.

grizzly veteran of sieges and bombardments that have never been fought were a whiskered Portuguese and a portly dame, apparently the guardians, possibly the parents, of a maiden whom I saw embroidering in one of the embrasures, singing to herself and tapping an old cannon with her foot —one of the very few really beautiful girls (let it be breathed in a whisper) whom I was privileged to see on the island. Several quintas are scattered about the valley, and on a spur projecting from the mountain-sides, a mile or two from the shore, are the gray ruins of a nunnery, which the abolition of convents throughout the Portuguese dominions has left roofless and desolate. It is superbly situated, and commands at sunset a prospect of surpassing beauty and grandeur.

The long beat of the surf on the shore lulled me to early dreams after a prime cup of tea and a dish of broiled mullets just out of the sea.

The shouting of the fishermen starting on their daily trip to the fishing-ground aroused me at three next morning; and, after a breakfast the counterpart of the meal of the previous evening, we shoved off and sailed away with the morning-star for our beacon, the dawning splendor of pearl and gold broadening in the east. We reached Fora Island about eight o'clock. This is a bold cliff at the extreme end of San Lorenzo Cape, over three hundred feet high, and surmounted by a light-house erected but six years since, which is the only guide for the mariner to be found either in the Madeiras or the Azores—a circumstance very disgraceful to Portugal. The keeper of the light-house and his assistant welcomed us with the cordiality of men whose social advantages are Crusoenian. As a dingy, greasy copy of Camoëns's "Lusiad" was the only sign of print to be seen on the premises, the mental resources of these stylites appeared not less meagre, although good so far as they went. The Connecticut clock in the entrance-hall also indicated that these recluses took "no note of time," for it was one hour and three-quarters slow. Justice requires me to admit that the lantern itself is mounted in a building admirably adapted to the purpose, and is one of the finest Fresnel lights on any coast, revolving twice a minute, and visible thirty miles at sea: it is also kept in excellent order.

Setting my easel on the terrace at the summit of the Rock, I devoted several hours to putting on canvas a sketch of the Point and the mountain ranges in the background. We then lunched, and launched away for Funchal before the fresh north-east trade-wind which carried us rapidly as far as Brazen Head, when a counter-current of air and a calm forced us to lower our sail and try a "white-ash breeze." We reached Funchal at sundown, after an excursion full of novel pleasure and incident, of which the foregoing is but a mere outline.

On the following Monday I made an early start on a wiry gray horse, and attended by a *burrequiero*, or muleteer, for the ascent of Pico Ruivo, the highest point in Madeira. As the road to the summit from the southern side, by way of the Torrinhas Pass, was at the time impracticable, which is saying much in Madeira, it was necessary to cross over to Sant' Anna on the northern side, and ascend from there—a very pleasing alternative, as it proved, for it carried me through some of the finest scenery of the island. Dashing directly upward, we soon gained the Mount Church, and passed into the clouds. Nor was it long before we reached a cooler atmosphere and a resting-house at an elevation of 4500 feet. Not very far beyond we came up with the lofty summit of Poizo on our right, and the gorge of the Ribeiro Frio, or Cold River, a winding cañon, narrow and thousands of feet in depth, clothed with verdure, beautiful with exquisite gradations of light and shade, and festooned with lazy mist trailing from crag to crag. Immediately opposite to where we began the descent rose the central range of the island, the sharply pinnacled group of Ruivo, Arriero, Sidrão, Torres, and Canario; while to the left the ravine of the Ribeira Metade, next to the Curral the grandest gorge of Madeira, lost itself in the heart of the mountains. The rapidity of the descent almost took away my breath; but I soon became seasoned to anything no steeper than this, for the whole road to Sant' Anna was very much like going over the teeth of a saw lengthwise. Mounting by zigzag roads up the sides of a perpendicular cliff, we would reach the ridge only to descend at once on the other side by a road perhaps more precipitous, where a misstep of the horse would plunge the rider into an abyss.

Often we passed the peasants at work in the fields, which in Madeira

VILLAGE OF CAMA DO LOBOS.

are mere narrow shelves on the mountain-sides, which are terraced as high up as 3000 feet, involving an amount of labor and climbing almost beyond belief. So scant are the level spaces that even the threshing-floors are often mere terraced platforms overhanging the precipices. The lungs of the peasantry must, I am sure, be abnormally developed, for men and women alike travel all day up and down these steep ascents, bearing heavy loads on the head, at much more than the average pace of a good walker on a level road in other countries, and with no other aid than a stout staff; and merrily they do it, too, without signs of fatigue, and singing as they go. They are a musical race, challenging each other to improvise as they meet on the road, or chanting while the oxen are treading the wheat; but it is a very lugubrious music, resembling snatches of a funeral dirge very dolefully rendered. It is pleasing to the stranger chiefly because it indicates a cheerful, contented spirit, the practical philosophy of a simple-hearted people who live out the celebrated maxim about the folly of exchanging ignorance for wisdom. To practise philosophy is the lot of those who are too ignorant to understand its meaning; to analyze and preach, but not to practise it, is the privilege of the few whom the world has seen fit to regard as sages.

A THRESHING-FLOOR.

The dwellings of the peasantry on the north side of Madeira are generally thatched cabins rudely constructed, having but one room, divided by partitions of matting. The people themselves are thrifty, but by no means comparable with the Azoreans in personal beauty. They have, especially in the western half of the island, a large infusion of African blood, for slavery once existed there. Their language is a patois of the Portuguese, subdivided into almost as many shades as there are valley parishes — a circumstance sufficiently strange, considering that Madeira has an area of only 240 square miles. They speak with a shrill rising inflection and a plaintive, pleading tone, which gives a ludicrously pathetic character to the merest gossip or idle banter.

Cultivation is largely dependent on irrigation, for while Madeira is not destitute of streams running at all seasons, the water, at its sources, falls from great heights to the bottom of the ravines which radiate from the central mountain group, and, as the arable land is almost entirely along the sides of these ravines, the water would seem unavailable; but the problem has been solved by the display of considerable daring and engineering skill. The streams are tapped far up near their sources, and diverted into *levadas*, or channels, averaging fifteen inches in width, meandering along the vertical sides of stupendous precipices, and by easy gradations coursing by all the gardens and terraces of the island. Sixteen hours in every forty days are allowed each landholder for the use of the current dashing past his grounds, and he must be ready to avail himself of it whenever notified that his turn has come; so that it is a very common circumstance to see a man in his garden at midnight groping, glowworm-like, among the beds with hoe and lantern. One of these currents is drawn from the cataract of Rabaçal, where one may see accomplished one of the most daring engineering feats of the age. The water-fall is on the north side, and has a sheer descent of 1000 feet at the head of a narrow gorge; for a large part of the year it is rather a meagre stream slipping down the side of the cliff. The curtain which here divides the northern and southern slopes is but 1400 feet thick; and a native of the island, an officer of engineers, conceived the idea of catching the water in its descent, and by a tunnel conducting it to the south side, where it was most needed. To accomplish the undertaking, it was necessary for the workmen to lower themselves from the edge of the precipice, and thus, suspended in the air by ropes 400 feet from the abyss below, and constantly drenched by the cataract, these unrecorded heroes labored at their fearful task. When blasting, they would swing out and lay hold of a bush or a crag, and thus await the explosion. A number were killed before the work was completed. At last a trench was excavated in the hard rock of the cliff, by which means part of the water-fall was intercepted and conducted to the tunnel bored

A GRIST-MILL.

through the mountain, and thus reduced to service. It is the old story over again of Pegasus curbed and harnessed to the plough.

The parish of Sant' Anna is a large, straggling village spreading over a plateau somewhat less broken than the ridges over which I had been riding. As I entered its limits, the road became wider and less precipitous, often overarched with interweaving shade-trees, presenting many delicious nooks, with here and there a picturesque grist-mill overgrown with ivy and moss enlivening the still air with its chattering. The thatched huts were also very pleasing, embowered in the foliage of chestnut and bay trees clasped by the creeping arms of grape-vines, and enclosed by hedges of fuchsia and geranium growing in rank profusion. About 3 P.M., I alighted at the hospitable gate of Senhor Acciaoly, mine host of the Sant' Anna Hotel, as well as the respected mayor of the parish. Affable in his address, he has in his day entertained many strangers from abroad who have sought the island for health, science, or pleasure. On the pages of the hotel-book are the autographs of Commodore Hull, Sir Charles Lyell, and other celebrities. The hotel is on the brow of a precipice 1100 feet above the sea. From its windows may be seen Ruivo to the south, and in the foreground to the eastward the pointed peak of Courtado, which has a sheer descent of 2000 feet to the surf that dashes below. I found myself rapidly becoming accustomed to look at the most tremendous precipices with the familiarity, but, I trust, not the indifference, of those native to the soil.

It rained hard during the night, and the next morning the mountains were concealed in compact masses of cloud, to the last degree unpromising of clear weather on the heights. To undertake the ascent of Ruivo on that day seemed a hopeless task. But, about nine, the clouds began to roll up a little, and, contrary to the advice of all, most especially of my grumbling muleteer, who did not care to make the trip—and I did not blame him—I decided that, at any rate, no harm could come from trying, while we might, by a bare possibility, succeed in obtaining the view desired. I had not come so far to give up without at least making an attempt to scale the mountain citadel of Madeira. A guide from Sant' Anna accompanied us. Part of the way we had a steep cattle-path, but the rain had made it very slippery, and the panting horse had to be urged hard up the rapid, crooked inclines, in order to hold his footing, and, after a while, not even a bridle-path was to be seen, but he had to pick his way carefully from crag to crag. The fog, in the mean time, was so thick that nothing was visible beyond the ground we trod on. It was often accompanied by heavy showers, and the guide strongly urged our return, but, determined, at least, to stand on the summit of Ruivo, I kept on. An isolated row of basaltic columns, joined in a gigantic wall, served to shelter us from the driving rain as we rested at noon, and somewhat disconsolately discussed our cold chicken and wine. Occasionally, tantalizing glimpses of ragged cliffs and gorges appeared in the gray mist only to disappear in a twinkling. An hour later I was obliged to leave the horse with the *burrequiero*, and, with the guide, climb the remainder of the way on foot. Passing through a cleft in the ridge, we gradually ascended the precipitous sides of Ruivo, threading a tortuous path among enormous heath-trees of a hoar antiquity, dating, perhaps, beyond the dawn of history. Weird beyond description did these antediluvians appear in the ghostly folds of the dripping mist, their limbs and trunks violently distorted and convoluted in multitudinous grotesque shapes, as if here the Dryads and Mænads had heard the cry, "Great Pan is dead!" and had been suddenly fixed while writhing in the despairing agonies of dissolution.

At length the last rock was surmounted, and the guide impressively said—at least it sounded impressive to me—"Pico Ruivo!" We stood 6200 feet above the ocean. But clouds were overhead and beneath us and around us. Nothing but opaque masses of cloud, frantically driven past us by an angry wind, frore as if directly from the frozen north. Closely wrapped in my overcoat, I waited anxiously for some break in the clouds that would at least partially repay me for the trouble of the ascent. Half an hour went by, and I was about to descend, when, far below, the clouds seemed to grow thin, and the shoulder of a peak was seen coyly appearing. After this, glimpses of the landscape became quite frequent; then, of a sudden, as if a curtain had been withdrawn at a signal, the clouds parted above, revealing the clear sky intensely blue, and, at the same instant, Ruivo and its group of Titanic companions uncovered their heads and came forth in all their majesty, heightened, if possible, by the mantles of cloud which gathered, fold on fold, in the gorges, deepening by contrast the glory of the sunlight which illumined the thunder-scarred faces of the upper cliffs, then suddenly seized by the gusts that swept through the passes, surging upward in curling, roseate columns like the steam arising from a vast caldron in the bowels of the earth. Around Ruivo towered Sidrão, Torres, Torrinhas, Arriero, Canario, and Pico Grande, at an elevation of from 5500 to over 6000 feet, all within a radius of three miles, and cloven to their bases by ravines of stupendous depth. Around the angle of the vertical wall of Torres, the gorge of the Grande Curral das Freiras was partially visible; to the south-east rose the Lamocciros

Pass and Penha d'Aguia; in the north, the Arco of São Jorge; and around all, only five miles distant, north or south, rolled the ocean, appearing dark sapphire through rifts in the tumultuous array of clouds which seemed let loose in aërial battle over its apparently boundless surface; for the horizon-line often blended with the sky, and soared far up toward the zenith. Along the verge of ocean, clouds reposed in ranks, gleaming pure as beaten gold, and resembling icebergs at the pole. Never have I gazed upon a scene equalling in sublimity that awful and overpowering spectacle from the summit of Ruivo—a scene to mould the character and stamp its memory on the soul forever.

How long I should have remained riveted to that spot entranced I cannot tell, if the clouds had not closed over it as suddenly as they had opened, and in an instant all again became gray and dim, as if what I had just gazed upon were but the wild vision of a brain steeped in the subtle fumes of opium.

On the following morning I was again in the saddle for Funchal, returning by way of the Lamoceiros Pass. From the smiling plateau of Sant' Anna we dived into a narrow but beautiful valley, where culture and nature held united sway, and then scaled the steep side of Courtado. At the summit, I checked the horse to gaze over the superb scenes we had just traversed; then, turning his head, I passed, without warning, through a cut in the razor-like summit of the ridge, and came with startling suddenness upon the edge of a precipice falling 2000 feet, with the ocean directly below, but so far down that the roar of the surf reached the upper air like the echo of voices long missed but still ringing faintly in the memory. The effect was precisely as if one were to open a door to step from one room to another at the top of his house, and be arrested on the sill by finding himself stepping into space, and the half of his house prostrate at his feet. Before us rose the rock of Penha d'Aguia, or Eagle's Eyry, a cube of volcanic stone high as Gibraltar, on all sides nearly perpendicular, and projecting into the sea, where three cañons (the Ribeira Secco, the Ribeira Metade, and the Ribeira Frio) converge and unite their torrent streams. On one side of the Penha is the village of Faial; on the other, Porto do Cruz—each on a small bay, almost inaccessible, however, as a harbor, owing to the vast rollers which tumble in at all seasons of the year. From Courtado Peak to Faial the zigzag road was paved with small triangular stones along the face of the cliff, but it was very narrow and frightfully steep; in fact, the steepest road in the world attempted on horseback, and entirely unprotected by a parapet. Gradually picking our way down to Faial and across the stony bed of the three torrents around the basis of the Penha d'Aguia, we came to the romantic village of Porto do Cruz, after climbing a bit of road so steep and broken, it was only by severe and constant application of the whip that the horse was kept on his feet, while the rider leaned well forward to retain his seat, and momentarily expected a dangerous fall.

From this village to the Lamoceiros Pass was a steady, rapid, zigzag ascent of 2300 feet, but the road was wider and in better order. A waterfall, flashing down the mountain-side near the road, added greatly to one of the most magnificent prospects in Madeira. After gaining the Pass, we turned to the south side of the island, across the head of the valley of Machico, descending into the green recesses of a glen upon whose lush grasses the Lotus-eaters might repose content, and dream years away, lulled by the carol of streams wandering under the rustling foliage of aspen, laurel, and chestnut trees. We lunched by a brook-side, and, climbing again, reached the elevated table-land of the Santa Serra, overgrown with broom, and entirely different from the scenery we had been traversing. After a while we came again to deep ravines, and ascending and descending, and deviously wending,* the usual mode of travel

PEASANTS' HUT AND PEASANTS.

in Madeira, came to the village of Camacha, where the charming villas gaze on the ocean far below, through the branches of chestnut-groves. I afterward spent two months in Camacha, and can truthfully recommend it as one of the most delightful summer residences in the world, and the nearest approach to an ideal paradise I have ever seen. Farther on, Funchal, gleaming like pearl in the slant rays of the setting sun, burst on our view, thousands of feet below. At this point I found a sledge station, and dashed down to the city, over three miles, in fifteen minutes.

Another excursion, oftener made than any other, because more accessible, is the trip to the Grande Curral. The last time I visited it I was *en route* to San Vincente, and as parts of the road to be traversed are un-

---

* Ἄναντα κάταντα πάραντά τε δόχμιά.—Iliad, xxiii.

travelled by horses, I took a hammock. The hammock was stretched on a pole, and shaded at the head by a canopy. The ends of the pole rested obliquely on the shoulders of two stout bearers, who started off at a swinging pace between a walk and a trot, which was kept up most of the distance to the Curral, not less than ten miles, with a rest once in three miles at a *venda*, when a *pour boire* was expected and sometimes obtained. The men showed little sign of fatigue, although, like all Madeira roads, this was always up and down steep grades. Soon after leaving the limits of Funchal we came in sight of the village of Cama do Lobos and Cabo Giram, a vertical cliff 2185 feet high, bathing its feet in the sea waves. It is the loftiest sea cliff in the world. Leaving this on our left, we entered the Estreito district, which is virtually the wine-growing district of Madeira, the slopes being densely covered with vines trained on trellises which often overarch the road. The little wine raised on the north side and at Porto Santo is of inferior quality, and is changed into brandy, which is mixed with the best Madeira. The vine was first introduced into the island from Cyprus in 1425, and the red volcanic soil gave it a flavor which brought it into rapid repute. The Shakspearian student will remember Poins's allusion to it when he says to Falstaff, "Jack, how agrees the devil and thee about thy soul, that thou soldest him on Good-Friday last for a cup of madeira!" Until 1852 this noble wine continued to sparkle on the board of those whose cellars contained the rarest wines. In that year the yield was about 20,000 pipes; then, without warning, a blight—a fungus on the plant and fruit, called the *oïdeum Tuckeri*—made its appearance, and in 1853 the yield fell to 100 pipes! This has continued until within twelve years. The suffering resulting from the sudden collapse of the wealth-bearing resources of the island was beyond computation. After a while the cultivation of the sugar-cane restored a portion of Madeira's lost prosperity. Still later, a way was found of counteracting the spread of the blight, and partially resuming the production of wine. This is done by blowing the powder of sulphur flowers over both vine and grapes, a very laborious process, as may be easily imagined. Madeira wine, *par excellence*, is made from the mixture of grapes dark and white, and from a light claret color gradually pales into a topaz hue of surpassing richness. Four other sorts are also produced—Malmsey, Bual, Sercial, and Tinta, all excellent. The first is too well known to require further mention; the last, from the Burgundy grape, is a mild, red wine.

From the Estreito district our hammock-bearers gayly swung us from height to height, under the shade of ancient chestnut forests. At noon we reached the edge of the woodland, and a few rods of steep climbing brought us suddenly to the brink of a basin of appalling depth. We stood on the edge of the Grande Curral das Freiras, and gazed upon one of the most sublime landscapes on the face of the globe. The form of the valley at once suggests a crater, but geologists assure us that such is not its character. The bottom of the gorge is 2500 feet above the sea-level, while the average height of its vertical sides is over 2000 feet. At the north-eastern end are grouped Ruivo, Torres, Sidrão, Canario, and Tor-

PENHA D'AGUIA.

rinhas, rising nearly 4000 feet above the torrent which courses along the bottom of the cañon and slips away to the sea through a cleft too narrow to permit of a road. The ragged ridges and needle-like pinnacles towered rosy-red against a sky of an azure far deeper than is seen in our climate. In the centre of the Curral, on a small green plateau, stands the white Church of Nostra Senhora de Livramente, surrounded by the thatched roofs of a hamlet, appearing at that depth like mites. Of less extent than the Yosemite, the Curral scarcely yields to that in actual grandeur.

There is the same abruptness of precipice, the same impressive sublimity in the grouping of peaks, to produce, within a narrow compass, an overpowering effect; the massing of light and shade is perhaps superior, presenting contrasts of terrific strength as cliffs project into space ruddy as living coals in the blaze of sunset, while the ravines recede into unfathomable depths of Tartarean mystery and gloom. The local coloring is also varied and rich, affording the artist not only *chiaro-oscuro* and form, but also color, the musical or emotional element in landscape.

From this spot we proceeded somewhat over a mile farther, until we could look into the gorge of the Serra d'Agoa, which, in the form of a right angle, runs from the Curral to the sea, and is but little inferior to it in sublimity. Winding along a narrow dike, which separates the two gorges, we came to a place where the dividing rock was not over twenty feet wide. On either side was a chasm not less than 2000 feet deep. Among so many astonishing views it is difficult to select the finest; but after surveying about every striking prospect in Madeira, I am inclined to think, excepting the view from Ruivo, that this one is the most impressive; and as few travellers ever go beyond the first halt on the edge of the Curral, I most heartily advise them to push on a little farther, to the dike, and to the rock called "Boccha dos Inamorados," in spite of the remonstrances of the hammock-bearers. Skirting the perpendicular, streamy sides of Pico Grande, we descended into the romantic recesses of the Serra d'Agoa, densely wooded with primeval forests of the grotesque and dusky *til*, which is found only on this island and the Canaries. The forms and grouping of the castellated peaks, as seen from the *venda*, where we halted for *agoa diente*, is extraordinarily beautiful. From here we again scaled the ridge which separates the northern and southern sides, and, almost falling down the steep slopes of the Pico das Freiras, plunged into the valley of San Vincente, the finest of the cultivated gorges of the island. It is of considerable length, and the sun had already robed the regular bastions, 3000 feet high, of the eastern side of the valley, in golden light, and shrouded the walls of the Paul de Serra, 5000 feet high, on the opposite side, in purple gloom, as we passed from stream to stream, and, amidst the mingled music of peasant-girls and cascades, arrived at the inn. The building stood on the edge of a natural terrace, in the centre of a valley whose loveliness beggars all description. On three sides the closely grouped mountains enclosed this idyllic spot with a tremendous forest-clad wall crowned at one end by the pinnacle-like Pico das Freiras, soaring to a height of 6000 feet. Numerous streams tripped their musical journey down this magical valley, while on the fourth side the ocean was seen close at hand, through a gate-way in the mountain barrier, tumbling for evermore on the beach with the ceaseless surf of the trade-winds, and chanting a thunderous monotone, sublime and seemingly as eternal as time. My room overlooked the mountains and the sea. The floor was covered with beans spread out to dry, but the sheets of the bed were clean and scented with rose leaves laid between them, reminding me of Izaak Walton's Bleak Hall, where the linen was scented with lavender. But the landlord was half fool, half knave, and, like some men of that description in other countries who get office, was also *corregidor*. His wife endeavored, with well-meant politeness, to make up for what was lacking in the character of landlord and provisions. The latter consisted chiefly of chickens dressed up in various fashions, all equally tasteless. Like most of the poultry served up to tourists in Madeira outside of Funchal, the chickens aforesaid had hardly learned to peep before they found themselves in the soup-tureen. But the tea was good, as it generally is when prepared by the Portuguese.

The next morning we were off for Seixal. Proceeding down the valley of San Vincente, we reached the shore through a narrow passage between lava cliffs, and for a mile or two kept on a level with the sea; then the road assumed another character. The northern coast of Madeira is for the most part a perpendicular cliff, divided here and there by ravines, and occasionally presenting a narrow shelf at the base. Nothing like a sandy beach is anywhere to be seen. Until within ten years, Seixal could only be reached by perilous goat-paths over the mountains, or by boats in summer-time. But the road we passed over has been more recently hewn by pickaxe and gunpowder out of solid rock in the vertical face of the cliffs, at an average height of 150 feet above the sea, while the precipice towers many hundred feet above. The road we found wholly without a parapet, and rarely over five feet wide; in some places, between three and four feet only. Occasionally we came to a water-fall having a plunge of 1000 feet or more, and the road was then tunnelled under the cascade. I confess to an "awesome feeling" when we came to an angle in the road so abrupt that the hammock-bearers stood on opposite sides, while the hammock actually, and without exaggeration, hung in mid-air over the surf which thundered far below. After that I concluded to get out and walk. Several fatal accidents have occurred here. The road was interrupted by the Ribeira do Inferno, a highly romantic gorge, and then continued of the same character several miles farther to Seixal. After lunching on the porch of the village church, which commands a glorious prospect of land and sea, we returned to San Vincente for the night, and started next morning for Funchal by way of Ponta Delgada and Sant' Anna, along the sea. Much of the road on this day resembled the road to Seixal, never quite so narrow, however, and generally protected by a low parapet, so that it is passable by horses; but it is much higher, and at Boa Ventura springs suddenly to the height of near 1000 feet, and one must have a cool head when he looks over upon the ocean below.

Another most delightful trip is to Calheta, the Rabaçal (already alluded to), and Ponto Pargo, at the western end of the island. One can make the excursion entirely by land; but it is well, at least, to go one way by water, in order fully to realize the tremendous height of Cabo Giram, and to see some of the remarkable volcanic rocks of the southern coast. One should, however, be careful to choose the weather, and have reliable boatmen, as it is impossible to land anywhere if it should blow fresh from the southward. At Ribeira Brava I was obliged to lodge in a peasant's hut; but the view of the sunset from that spot toward Ponte de Sol is well worth the sacrifice. On my return, with a rashness which cannot be recommended, I started from Calheta with the wind blowing from southwest, and a high surf rolling on the beach; but we hoped the wind would moderate toward mid-day. It did exactly the opposite. There was nothing to be done but to run before it under a rag of canvas, the whole rugged coast everywhere presenting an unbroken line of raging breakers. The wind followed us around into Funchal Bay, and it was with some difficulty we effected a landing. But this was in March. Later in the season there is less liability to southerly winds.

Every day of my residence in Madeira increased my enthusiasm for the inexhaustible variety, beauty, and grandeur of its scenery and the deliciousness of its climate. Four times have I visited it, once remaining there six months, and rambling over it and painting its landscapes at leisure; and the more I reflect upon its scenery, the more do I feel that neither language nor pencil can exaggerate the natural attractions of this, the finest of the Atlantic isles. In climate Madeira may well be reckoned among the Isles of the Blest, for, in a word,

> "The climate's delicate; the air most sweet,
> Fertile the isle, * * * much surpassing
> The praise it bears."

CHAPTER VI.

TENERIFFE.

TO ascend this celebrated peak had long been my ambition, as well as, more recently, to discover if the climate and scenery of the Queen of the Canaries were equal, not to say superior, to those of Madeira. I was glad to find the two islands so different that comparison was unnecessary, while I was, on the whole, not disappointed by what I saw at Teneriffe. Although on a far grander scale, it resembles Pico Island in the Azores. But the peak of the Western Islands, although but 7615 feet high, has not only been seen one hundred and ten miles at sea by observation, but is often visible for half or two-thirds that distance; while Teneriffe, 5000 feet more lofty, is rarely seen at a distance, especially from the north, owing to

PLAZA DE LA CONSTITUCION, SANTA CRUZ.

peculiar atmospheric conditions, particularly after the trade-winds begin, in April. It was therefore almost useless for me to strain my eyes to discover it on the voyage, although the weather was fine, for the breezy ides of May were against me. But the light near Anaga Point was visible thirty miles out, and the fearfully ragged and desolate volcanic peaks and cliffs of the south-eastern coast were in plain sight close on the starboard beam as we rounded Anaga in the pearly gray of dawn. Ere long Santa Cruz appeared on the shore directly ahead, with the mountains rising behind in ever-ascending scale, and at last the extreme summit of the great cone

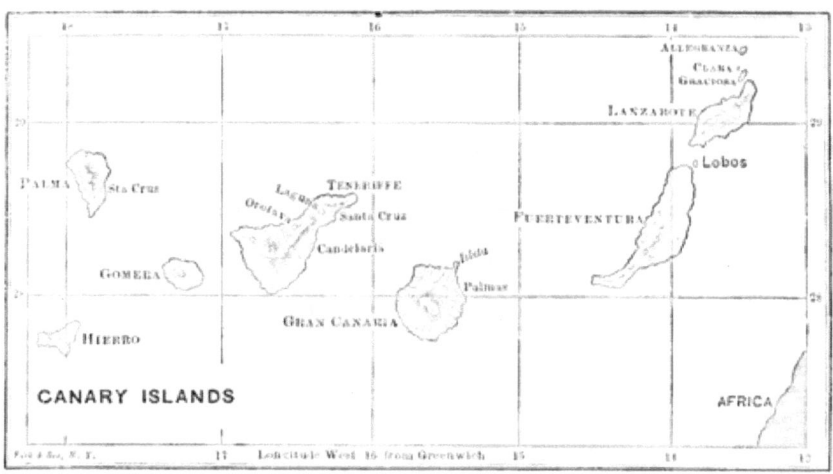

called the Piton towered before us, clearly cut against the azure of the sky. As the sun arose, the yellow pumice-stone and snow of the little peak assumed a rich roseate hue. The whiteness of the peak gave to it and to the island its name. *Thener ife* (the white mountain) it was called by the aborigines of Las Palmas, for so it looked to them sixty-eight miles distant. The Piton is also called the Pico de Teyde, a corruption of Cheyde, the Guanche word for hell—a title whose appropriateness is at once apparent to one who ascends the peak.

The harbor of Santa Cruz is only an open roadstead, whose sole protection is the regular character of the winds and climate, and the nature of the anchorage, which is so steep that a vessel cannot drag ashore, although she may be driven out to sea occasionally. But even when it is calm, the water of the port is always more or less agitated by the heavy swell rolling in from the trade-winds blowing outside. The landing-place is within an admirably constructed mole. It was here that Lord Nelson made his attack on Santa Cruz, July 14th, 1794, losing an arm in the fight, but winning knighthood for his gallantry and skill. The traveller, on landing, is beset by two contrary emotions, caused by the exorbitant demands of the boatmen and the carters, and the immense and rather unwonted relief at finding no custom-house—no officials in dirty livery to turn the contents of his trunk inside out; that, in a word, although under the Spanish yellow-and-scarlet flag, Santa Cruz is a free port.

In 1852 this island, with those adjoining, obtained permission from the Home Government to abolish all duties on goods entering the Canaries, provided that they made up any deficit that might result to the revenues of the crown from the adoption of this measure. The commerce of the islands since then has been tolerably prosperous, and the importers have thriven on free trade; but lest the advocates of free trade should cite this as a proof of the truth of their theories, it is only fair to add that the deficit in the national revenues has never been made up, and already amounts to millions, the possible collection of which is held over the people as a rod of terror, while the taxes have been so increased in proportion by the Home Government as to cause much grumbling among the landed proprietors and peasantry.

The English hotel, I found, had been recently closed for lack of patronage. It was therefore with dread that I turned to the Spanish *fonda* kept by Durvan, adjoining the captain-general's; but I was agreeably disappointed to find a comfortable and well-sustained hotel. Santa Cruz is not the only place of that name in the Spanish dominions. There are several in the Canaries alone, including two on the island of Teneriffe;

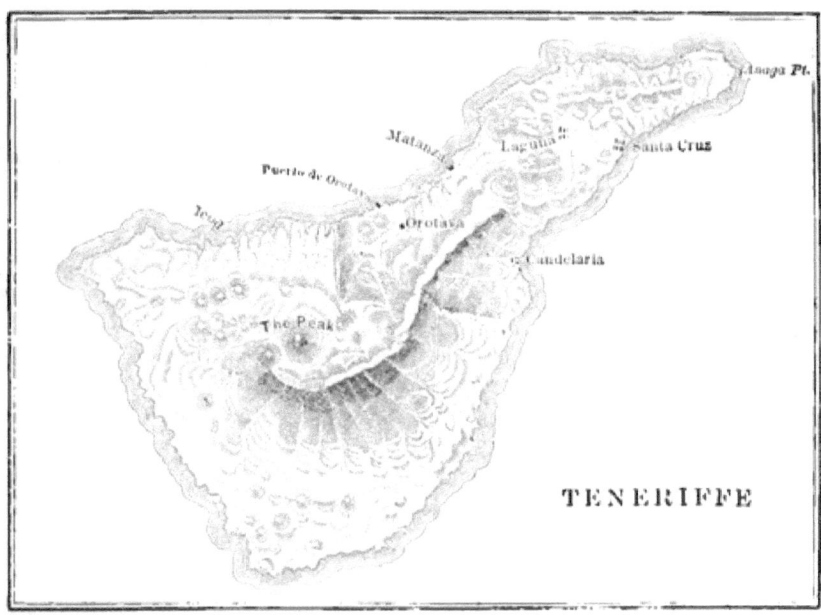

but this one is the most important town of the group, numbering some 15,000 inhabitants. Las Palmas, in Gran Canaria, contains a larger population, but it is of less relative consequence. Santa Cruz de Teneriffe is regularly laid out on a gradual slope, flanked by very savage, volcanic precipices and ravines, which are not so near, however, as to justify Humboldt's statement that it lies under a perpendicular wall of rock, unless his words be accepted in a figurative sense.

SPANISH SEÑORITA.

Lest the people should forget the name of their city, a massive marble cross stands at the head of the Plaza de la Constitucion, near the jetty. The houses are often of only one story, and rarely more than two, though a partial third story is not uncommon in the form of a tower surmounted by a terrace. The roofs are flat, and offer a pleasant promenade in the cool of the evening. The two-storied dwellings are in the form of a hollow square, in Eastern style. One would not suspect this from their appearance on the street. From the outer door, which is always open until late at night, one passes through a passage, corresponding in length with the width of the rooms, to the inner door, which gives into the *patio*, or court, open to the sky, and frequently planted with bananas, orange-trees, roses, and jessamines. Around the *patio* on the ground-floor are store-rooms and offices. The family occupy the next floor, the rooms opening upon verandas overlooking the court. A cluster of small bells is attached to the inner door. When a visitor arrives, he pushes it open; the bells sound the alarm, and a shrill voice answers above, "Quién?" (Who is it?) Should there be no bells, the visitor claps his hands.

As in Las Palmas, there are a number of the lower class who live in caves in the outskirts of the town. The Guanches, or aborigines, were troglodytes. At Gran Canaria remains of stone dwellings still exist; but the Guanches of Teneriffe seem to have been uniformly troglodytes, and the custom of turning the numerous air-vents, or caves, of this volcanic soil into dwellings has not yet been quite abandoned. Some of them have been improved by face-walls and other "modern improvements," but their essential character as cave-dwellings is unchanged. The windows of all the houses in Teneriffe deserve especial mention. A massive frame like a box fits into the aperture, but, unlike an ordinary casement, projects some inches from the wall. The blinds are heavily panelled with square bevels, and in the lower half of each is a smaller blind swinging out from below. This is called the *postigo*, and plays a most important part in the uneventful lives of the inhabitants, especially the female portion of the community. Is any unwonted sound heard in the street, up go the *postigos*. Early in the day, women with frowzy tresses and children just out of bed, scarcely awake and entirely unwashed, lean languidly on the sill and gaze at the passer-by behind the *postigo*. Later in the day the dark-eyed señorita, her toilet completed, shoots dangerous glances from behind this convenient ambush, and perhaps drops it suddenly just as one begins to realize the charms it coyly reveals. In the evening the lover converses with her, standing under the half-raised blind of the magic *postigo*, while she, seated on the window-seat, leans her round arm on the sill, and listens to the passionate words he utters in low tones, and perhaps with her fan coquets with another admirer across the street.

The Plaza de Príncipe, in the centre of the town, is very pretty, enclosing a fountain, and embowered with plane and pepper trees. It is the great resort on fine evenings, and few others ever occur. A band of music plays very tolerably, although the romantic guitar tinkling in the side streets is more in consonance with the hour and the clime. One is surprised to see so many handsome ladies in so small a place. They invariably wear that most graceful of all head-coverings, the mantilla, either black or white, and of lace or silk. The ladies of Teneriffe, having found a graceful costume for the head, are sensible enough to know when they are well off, and do not change it. Not until half-past eight does the band begin to play. It continues until eleven, when the "serenos" take up the cry in turn. This is the humorous sobriquet applied to

THE POSTIGO.

the night-watchmen or police, who every half-hour sing out, often very musically, "*Ave Maria purisima!*" then they give the hour, and end with "*Sereno*" (all serene). Hence the epithet; for so almost invariable is the weather, it very rarely occurs that it is necessary for the watchmen to alter the cry; and sometimes when it is actually storming they still, from habit, shout "*Sereno!*"

But to linger long in Santa Cruz when the valley of Orotava is yet unseen and unexplored is unpardonable. An excellent carriage-road connects the two places, and the distance is about twenty-five miles. The island itself is sixty miles long, and Orotava is on the northern coast. I therefore started one fine morning for the valley Humboldt considered the most sublime and beautiful landscape he had ever seen. We began to ascend immediately toward the ridge at whose summit, 3000 feet above the sea, lies that quaint and sleepy old town, Laguna, of all drowsy places one of the most peaceful and somnolent. It was once the capital of the island. Wealth was in its borders. Marquises and counts dwelt there in considerable splendor. The *adelantado*, or first viceroy, also reigned there, and his palace, built over four hundred years ago, still remains. But now the grass grows rank in the streets of Laguna; the house-leek is abundant, springing from the mossy tiles of the dilapidated roofs and the crevices of the forsaken *jalousies*. Stately gate-ways are walled up, and "the spider hath woven her web in the palaces of Afrasiab." Yet, owing to her exceptionally cool, moist climate, Laguna continues a resort in summer for those who desire to exchange the parched air of Santa Cruz for a more bracing atmosphere. Even in summer mists and rain are not uncommon there, with abundant breezes; while the charming meadow-lands and intervales surrounded by sharp peaks commanding wonderful prospects over land and sea, in the midst of which the little city is situated, afford a limitless variety of charming rambles. But, then, your true Canary Islander is not much of a rambler. A slight infusion of Anglo-Saxon blood is essential to develop the rambling propensity.

MILK-VENDERS.

The peasants of Laguna still retain one of the ancient costumes of the island. White drawers cover the whole leg; over these breeches of blue cloth come down nearly to the knee, bound with a scarlet cord, but so slashed or cut away over the hips that the garment really consists of little more than flaps in front and behind, resembling cuisses of steel armor. Formerly every village had its own costumes, some of them very picturesque; but, excepting in the more remote districts, like Chasna and Icod, they are gradually passing away. In some of the other islands many curious garbs are still in common use. In Teneriffe the country-women invariably wear a white cloth over the head and neck, or a shawl extending down the back, evidently to protect the spine from the sun; over this a straw or felt hat is also *de rigueur*. The men of the lower classes wear a blanket cloak, that swells out in stiff and unwieldy barrel-like rotundity, and is absurd enough when the mercury is at eighty. The purchase of one of these cloaks is a matter of great importance, as certain qualities enter into its composition without which it is simply useless to offer it for sale over any counter in Teneriffe. It must be white, white as snow, although immediately after purchasing it the wearer may perhaps fling it into the dirt, and it will never henceforward be other than a dingy brown. It must have a blue stripe, with a narrower one of the same color on each side near the lower edge; it must be of uniform thickness—a thin spot would ruin it—and the nap must run one way, and that downward, in order to make it water-proof. These and other conditions are required by the Medo-Persian inflexibility of public opinion among the peasantry of Teneriffe.

We passed many women carrying on their heads boxes containing the cochineal bug, which they had bought in Santa Cruz, and were taking to the north side to put on the plant. As is generally known, the cochineal deposits its young on the leaf of the cactus. The mothers are laid in thin cambric bags, which are then wrapped around the plant and left on until the bug is deposited on the leaf. After reaching maturity the bugs are scraped off, and dried in an oven or in the air. Much of the island is covered with cactus, and two crops of cochineal are gathered in many places; but the beauty of the landscape is marred by the unsightly fields of cactus bound with white rags. The cochineal, originally introduced from Mexico by an enterprising priest who suffered much persecution from the peasants for injuring, as they supposed, a plant whose prickly pear supplies them with a staple food, became a source of large profit at a time when the disease of the vines cut off the wine crop. But the discovery of aniline colors has greatly reduced the demand for cochineal, although they can never altogether supersede the little insect from which are obtained the most exquisite red dyes known in modern times. The

CAMELS AND COCHINEAL-CARRIERS.

deficiency that might result in the commerce of the islands is at present partially made up by an increasing production of onions and potatoes, which are largely exported to the West Indies. The climate allows three crops of potatoes annually. The cultivation of the vine is also in a measure reviving, and perhaps 3000 pipes of various sorts were made at the last vintage. The annual yield was formerly over 30,000 pipes. The best canary is, like most wines of warm climates, strong. It has a rich golden hue and a fine fruity flavor, although inferior to old port or madeira.

The fig grows in Teneriffe abundantly, producing several excellent varieties. During the season the trees are frequented by the capirote, which nestles in the dense shade, and feeding on the fruit, gains inspiration for the exquisite strains which the livelong day add the charm of melody to the loveliness that meets the eye at every turn. The notes of the capirote rival those of the mocking-bird and the nightingale in variety and richness, and it can be easily tamed and taught to imitate the notes of other birds; but this modest, pearl-tinted little songster is so sensitive that all attempts to acclimate it in other countries have failed.

After leaving Laguna we saw many palms, sometimes in clusters; but, except at Santa Cruz, they do not produce dates fit to eat. They give an Oriental aspect to the landscape, which is heightened by the camels that one encounters on the road. But camels are less employed in the island than formerly, and, like those of Lancerote, are scarcely tame. It is not uncommon for them to charge furiously upon men, not even respecting their masters. I have heard that people have been killed in the Canaries by camels. This certainly belies the reputation for meekness that they have earned in Eastern lands.

Our road beyond Laguna lay by the sea, or rather at a height of 2000 or 3000 feet above it, sometimes on the brow of a slope approaching a precipice, or again separated from the deep-blue ocean below by a valley studded with hamlets. At noon we stopped at the village of Matanzas to lunch and bait the horses. Matanza means "slaughter" in Spanish, and the name was given to the place in memory of the severest drubbing the Spaniards ever received, in proportion to the numbers engaged on each side. Jean de Betancourt, a Norman lord, having heard of the distant Canary Islands, and moved by the roving impulse inherited from his ancestors, set out to visit and perhaps conquer them. Finding no Frenchmen ready to accompany him, he went to Spain, where he was joined by a cousin, who induced some Spanish adventurers to embark on the galleys of Betancourt. The history of the subsequent conquest by Betancourt and his successors, and of the singular people they found and subdued in those islands, is full of romance and interest. Lancerote was the first island seized. Grand Canary was subjugated only after seventy-seven years

GROUP OF CHOZAS, OR HUTS, NEAR LAGUNA.

of heroic defense on the part of a people who were not destitute of some civilization, who displayed many magnanimous traits of character, and who yielded at last only when their king had been seized by treachery, and when their numbers were reduced to five hundred. Teneriffe was not even visited until after all the other islands of the group had come under the Spanish yoke. There are grounds for believing that the Fortunate Isles, with the exception of Teneriffe, were colonized by exiles of war, expelled from Barbary in Roman times. Aside from traditions to this effect, there are many dialectic analogies between their language and that of the Berbers, as well as resemblances in customs. But the natives of Teneriffe differed so much in language and customs from those of the other islands as to throw great doubt on their origin. The colonizing of Teneriffe by such exiles may, however, have been secondary to a previous occupation. In those primitive days communication between the islands was rare, and it is even asserted that boats were unknown there.

Some stones have recently been discovered in Hierro and Las Palmas bearing sculptured symbols similar to those found on the shores of Lake Superior. This has led M. Bertholet, the enthusiastic historiographer of the islands, to the conclusion that the first inhabitants of the Canaries and those of the great West were one in race. Although he has arrived at this result rather hastily, as it would seem, when one considers the universality of some of the ancient symbols, there is apparently some reason to urge further investigations of the subject.

TENERIFFE COSTUME.

Only to the tribes of Teneriffe does the term Guanche apply, although often given to those of the other islands. The island was divided among nine chiefs or kings, and there was a complete organization or feudal system, composed of a wealthy class, and of serfs who took charge of the flocks, which formed the riches of the island. The code of laws, though unwritten, was well defined and strictly administered. One of the upper class who so far lowered himself as to milk a goat was degraded to vassalage; but capital punishment was not allowed. Wars were common, chiefly regarding boundaries. The weapons were elaborately carved, and the arrow and spear heads were made of obsidian. The food of all classes was generally *gofio*, a palatable mixture composed of wheat, corn, or barley, roasted like coffee. It is afterward ground in hand-mills, and the flour, mixed with water or milk, is then thoroughly kneaded in a goat-skin. This dish is still almost universal among the peasantry of Teneriffe. The Guanches drank no cold water for half an hour after eating, to avoid injuring the teeth. After death the Guanche was embalmed and sewed up in a tanned goat-skin, and deposited in one of the numerous caves with which the island abounds. Four or five mummies, one of them a princess, another the remains of a *guarnateme*, or chief, of Teyde, in Gran Canaria, are preserved, with a few other Guanche relics, spears, hand-mills, leather pitchers, and the like, in a small private museum which I visited at Tacaronte. But the mummies have otherwise been wantonly destroyed wherever found by the peasantry, who regard them with superstitious dread. Some were discovered in a cave at Santa Lucia while I was at Teneriffe, and were immediately broken up. There are mummies still known by tradition to exist in caves on the edges of precipices, especially at Guimar, and inaccessible unless one chooses to be lowered a thousand feet by a rope. The bodies were thus let down and deposited on ledges in the cave mouth, where they probably remain to this day.

In 1464, the Spaniards, under Diego de Herrera, lord of Lancerote, made a landing at Teneriffe. They were peaceably received, and were permitted to remain and construct a fort. But the Spaniards having been guilty of a gross breach of faith, the honest Guanches were so irritated that they arose and swept fort and garrison out of existence. Naturally infuriated at the conduct of barbarians so simple as to be exasperated by mere perfidy, Alonzo de Lugo landed one thousand men, in 1493, and, as the natives were taken by surprise, was able to scour the land as far as Orotava. But the chief of that valley

GUANCHE MUMMIES AT TACARONTE.

sent forward three hundred men under his brother to waylay the Spaniards on their return, while he bestirred himself to rouse the rest of the island. At Matanzas, previously alluded to, the invaders were attacked, and, although armed with mail and arquebuses, they were put to route, losing not less than six hundred men in the battle, or rather slaughter. On reaching the coast, Alonzo de Lugo was again attacked, and lost one-fourth of his remaining force; he thought himself happy to be able to re-embark with only three hundred out of the thousand men with which he had landed a few days previously. Nothing daunted, however, Alonzo de Lugo reappeared at Teneriffe with a still larger force; and now the Guanches displayed a common sense rare in history. The leading chief of the island reasoned that, although he might be able to cope with the army just landed, it must be of little ultimate use; for an enemy who, after such a disastrous defeat, could so soon put a larger army into the field, must by sheer weight of numbers gradually wear out the limited population of Teneriffe. The wisest plan, therefore, seemed to be to submit while it was still in their power to impose certain conditions, of course accepting Christianity, without doing which they would all have been roasted. By the influence of this king all the island was brought to submit to the Spaniards. Alonzo de Lugo became *adelantado*, leaving a large posterity to transmit his name, and the Guanches, instead of being exterminated, were absorbed into the Spanish race. But the peasant of the western part of the island still shows the lineaments of a race that peopled these islands before the Goth had issued from the North, or the Saracen from the South, to form, in Iberia, the present race of Spain. Until quite recently, Guanches of purely aboriginal blood were still to be found at Chasna.

While we have been glancing briefly at the history of the conquest, the bony horses, three abreast, and well-nigh devoured by the flies, which, it must be confessed, are sufficiently numerous to amount to a plague in Teneriffe, have carried us past Sansal, where the peak should burst on the sight, revealing its proportions as from no other part of the island. But the peak was concealed in dense layers of the trade-wind cloud, and continued so for ten days after my arrival. This sublime prospect was therefore reserved for my return, as the final picture in a succession of magnificent scenes, which were revealed one by one, during my sojourn at Orotava. Could I have arranged everything with the purpose of producing the most effective impression, it could not have been better devised. Five hours brought us to the valley of Orotava, although another hour or two was required to complete the journey to the *fonda* at the *puerto*, which could be reached only on donkey or horse back.

Situated 300 feet above the sea, Mrs. Turnbull's comfortable little boarding-house was perhaps too inconveniently located for transient visitors; but for those who, either for pleasure or health, desire to spend delicious days of poetic indolence gazing on the noble prospect — the mountains and the valley, and the sea that lashes the volcanic beach from age to age—a more admirable situation could scarcely have been selected. As regards climate, the temperature at that height cannot be surpassed on this imperfect planet of ours. The trade-winds, which are hardly felt at the sea-level, there impart a reviving coolness to the air of midsummer. Fifty-eight degrees Fahrenheit is the lowest the mercury falls in winter. From sixty-eight to seventy-two degrees is the average height it reaches in summer. In the *puerto* below, the glass descends to sixty-four in the house in winter, and never rises above eighty. Add to this that the cli-

CITY OF SAN JUAN OROTAVA.

mate is dry—more so than that of the Bahamas or Madeira, both celebrated resorts for invalids—and the winds moderate. Santa Cruz is generally too warm, although the heat is not so much excessive as steady; while Laguna, to which residents of the island resort in summer for a more bracing air, is perhaps too damp and windy for invalids who come from abroad. But Orotava seems to combine all that is desirable from a sanitary point of view for those who are afflicted with pulmonary complaints, rheumatism, or neuralgia in its protean forms; also, perhaps, for those wasting away with that terrible malady, Bright's disease, if they can endure the voyage.

The valley of Orotava is more properly a slope than a valley. From the crater of the Cañadas a central ridge, called the Cumbre, runs to Laguna, where it is continued by a ridge of another formation running to Anaga Point. From this ridge, where it meets the Cañadas, a magnificent bastion, called Mount Tigayga, stretches for several miles, like a stupendous wall, on one side of the slope, throwing out into the valley buttresses of astonishing grandeur, often nearly vertical for thousands of feet. On the eastern side another mountain, nearly as sublime, bounds the slope. Between these two lateral mountains the celebrated valley of Orotava rises by a very gradual but unbroken ascent from the coast until it reaches the central ridge, some 7000 feet above the sea. The shore sometimes terminates in abrupt precipices of lava and basalt, or in a rocky beach of slag, whitened for evermore by the surges of the hoarse Atlantic. Three miles from the coast lies Orotava, an ancient-looking town of perhaps 6000 inhabitants. Here are houses quaint with dilapidation and a certain musty air of decayed splendor. It is still the residence of several Spanish families of title—counts, marquises, and dons of high and low degree. A church of some architectural merit, but incomplete, occupies a prominent position; and some of the gardens of the place are stocked with exotics.

DRAGON-TREE AS IT WAS.

I observed here a very pretty custom, common in other towns of the island, but seen in its perfection at Orotava. On the fête-days of the Church the streets through which the procession passes are strewn with carpets of flowers. This is done by gathering the petals of various brilliant flowers into separate baskets. A mould is laid on the pavement representing the pattern. In one compartment rose petals are dropped, in another marigold, in another violet, and so on. All the divisions having been filled with petals an inch deep, the mould is carefully removed, and a most beautiful painting appears, magnificent as the richest of stained-glass windows. Before private houses the ladies sometimes assist in this pious and poetic art, which, as may be easily understood, would be impossible in a land where flowers are scarce or where the winds are rude.

In the garden of the Marquis of Sansal stood what was considered on the highest authority to be the oldest known tree in the world, the famous dragon-tree of Orotava. Five thousand years was the least age that could be assigned to it. It was over eighty feet high, and of enormous circumference, but had been reduced to a mere shell, although still green at the top, and with a possibility of centuries yet before it. The marquis paid no heed to its decrepit condition, and the venerable patriarch was left without support. Eight years ago a hurricane swept the island, and in that wild night, while the thunders raged, while the winds screamed over houses unroofed, while ships foundered with all on board, the old dragon-tree that had survived the fall of empires, and the earthquake-shocks and fiery torrents of volcanoes, at last went down. What relic-hunters and fuel-seekers—with shame, be it said—have left of this patriarch now lies a mere heap of red bark, and nothing more. The dragon-tree, so called from its red sap, formerly used as a dye, is common in the Canary Islands, and many very fine specimens of it are to be seen there.

BOTANIC GARDENS, OROTAVA.

Below the town is the celebrated botanic garden of Teneriffe, which would be more properly termed a garden of acclimation. Great hopes of its usefulness were entertained at its inception; but a larger experience, and the extensive greenhouses put up more recently in northern climes, have to a degree neutralized its value, although it is still well tended by the intelligent superintendent, Mr. Wilpert. The Puerto de Orotava is a sleepy little place of about the same size as the villa, or upper town, but, on the whole, more cheerful, and with a certain amusing assumption of thrift, not to say bustle, about it during the onion and potato season, when the diminutive mole is piled with the odoriferous bulbs, and the lighters row out through the narrow passage among the rocks, and ride over the heavy swell, upon which the ships pitch and roll in a most uneasy manner, moored by the stern as well as the bow, and with the breakers often just under the quarter. The regularity of the winds makes accidents rare, but I should, notwithstanding, wish a ship well insured if I were to send her to Orotava for a cargo of onions. The number of crosses at the port, in shrines, on the house-walls, or over the gates, is remarkable.

Three miles to the westward of the port is the Val Taoro, a regular depression of the slope, but with a steeper incline. Here is the straggling village of Realejo, very striking and picturesque. The women of this place are more fair and plump than most of the countrywomen of Teneriffe, because, some say, of the wonderful air of the locality, and others because of their Norman descent. In the small church attached to the convent of San Francisco there is a carved cedar roof, exquisitely beautiful.

The flora of Teneriffe is said to be exceedingly rich; this, however, must be taken as implying variety in its botanic specimens rather than such a general luxuriance of verdure as is found in Madeira or Jamaica. The chestnut forests which once covered the valley have been largely cut down to make room for the culture of the cochineal; and the vestiges of volcanic action abounding on all sides in the form of streams of lava or slag, in dark-brown cliffs and mounds, and numerous walls and huge piles of lava stones, of which the fields have to be cleared before they can be cultivated, together with long stretches of unsightly cactus or poisonous euphorbia, sometimes give the landscape an air of desolation. But these features are soon forgotten in the grander objects which Orotava presents. To appreciate the valley of Orotava, one must give to it weeks and months of passive, reverent observation and reflection. It is not in the minute details, but in its general effect, that it should be regarded, like a painting executed broadly, and leaving the imaginative mind to supply the details. So viewed, the majestic slope of Orotava, encircled by the mountains and the sea, wearing on its bosom its cluster of beautiful towns, and robing itself in the vegetation of all climes, offers one of the most remarkable landscapes on the globe, if not indeed the most remarkable. Whether seen from Icod Alto, on the brow of Tigayga, or from the opposite side, or from the beach, or from the town, it everywhere overwhelms one more and more with its matchless magnificence and sublimity. The last time I saw it from the shore was at sunset. Not a cloud obscured the vast amphitheatre before me. The upper heights were bathed in purple. Be-

VIEW OF THE PEAK FROM OROTAVA.

yond Tigayga, far up in the blue, the white cone of the peak towered in regal solitude, a wreath of golden clouds above its head, and seemingly ablaze in the ruddy glow of the sun dropping below the ocean's verge. Purple shadows crept over the lower part of the slope until they gradually mantled the ridges of Tigayga and the Cañadas. But long after, like a star in the firmament, the extreme summit of the Piton gleamed alone in the heavens.

From Orotava I made a trip to Icod, distant twenty miles to the westward. The road was remarkable only for its rugged, not to say dangerous, character. We scaled the lower heights of Tigayga, and, passing the village of Guanche, reached Icod toward evening. The volcanic desolations through which we had picked our way moderated somewhat as we approached the little place, and it was almost with surprise I found myself in a well-built, picturesque town with considerable pretensions to beauty. The situation is certainly very fine. The view of the peak is the chief object of interest at Icod, and one who has never ascended it can obtain a better idea of the cone from Icod than from the valley of Orotava. There is in the garden adjoining the *fonda*, at Icod, the oldest and noblest dragon-tree now known to exist. It is in excellent condition, and can hardly be less than 3000 years old. Another object of interest is the cave of the Guanches, close to the town.

A formidable supply of pitch-pine fagots having been prepared, I followed the guide through a crevice so low that one must enter it on his knees. The cave is long, narrow, and winding, generally from ten to fifteen feet high, but sometimes so low that we were forced to crawl. It is also so regular in its width as to seem like an artificial subterranean passage. After walking a third of a mile in darkness, a gleam of light was seen at last, and we reached the other end of the cave. Here it widened to a moderate-sized hall, and remains of mummies were to be seen on the ground and in crevices in the wall. Although there were some dusky rays of light here, there was no exit; only a low aperture where the light came from, which I was able to reach by creeping face to the ground. I put my head out and found myself directly over a lofty precipice, at the foot of which the ocean dashed with unceasing roar. Burial-place more impressive could hardly be imagined.

Three miles beyond Icod is Guarachico, which once owned the finest harbor in the Canaries, and was a city of commercial importance. But two centuries ago the town was overwhelmed by volcanic eruptions and the port filled up with a torrent of lava. A little fishing village now stands where the former port *was*. Guanche was written on the face of most of the peasants I saw in that district. On Corpus Christi Day they were all out, and I had a good opportunity of observing them. It may be added that the *fonda* at Icod is very comfortable, and visitors are not badly entertained. The return by a lower road along the coast, through the villages of Santa Caterina, La Rambla, and San Juan de la Rambla, was very pleasing. The road, although very rough and stony, offers many striking views and objects of interest.

Before leaving Orotava I ascended the peak of Teyde. It was toward the last of May, but still somewhat earlier than it is usually attempted, and mine was, therefore, the first ascent of the season. The number who go up the peak during the year is always very limited, perhaps a dozen, and generally they are travellers from abroad, who come there expressly for that purpose. The difficulty of the undertaking and lack of enterprise deter most of the residents from trying it. The muleteer and guide were my only companions. We started at five in the morning. My mule, when I mounted him, acted in a manner that aroused grave suspicions as to his character, and his subsequent conduct during this and the following day confirmed my suspicions. The sumpter-mule generally comported himself with propriety. Not only the mules, but also the horses of Teneriffe, bear a very bad reputation. We passed through Realejo up the Val Taora, and for several thousand feet the ascent was moderate, although the road soon degenerated into a rough bridle-path. At a height of 3000 feet we entered the stratum of trade-wind cloud, which continued to conceal all objects from view except those in the immediate vicinity, and at the same time tempered the heat of the sun. This continued up to nearly 6000 feet above the sea, when we suddenly emerged and saw the vast sheet of cloud spread like a snowy table-land

A PEASANT WOMAN OF ICOD.

between the island and the offing. The entire absence of running streams, and the perfect stillness of the air—undisturbed by the music of woodland water-falls or any other appreciable sound, except now and then the voices of peasants descending the mountain under their loads of brushwood—became very noticeable soon after we left Realejo.

Five thousand feet up, we left behind all traces of vegetation except grass and ferns. The ferns kept us company until we reached the stratum of heather, as it may be called. After a while the heather became scarce, and the *retama* began to appear, until, at a height of 7000 feet, nothing green was to be seen but tufts of *retama*. The *retama* is a species of broom peculiar to the Canary Islands; that of Teneriffe is, again, a distinct kind, found nowhere else, and never there below 6000 feet above the sea. It reminds one alternately of the yew and the cedar, reaching a very good size sometimes, although diminishing in growth as one ascends the mountain. In summer it is covered with clusters of white flowers.

The approach to the Cañadas grew more and more rugged and sterile. Pumice-stone, volcanic rocks, and lava towers became more frequent, until we finally scaled the slope which seemed to keep us still within sight and sound and reach of life, and entered the vast crater called the Cañadas, on the eastern side, where its sides are most broken. The formation of the peak now for the first time became clear and intelligible to me. We found ourselves on the floor of a crater ten miles in diameter, thirty miles in circumference, circular, but slightly elliptical, in shape. This floor is covered with yellow pumice-stone, generally level, with here and there a moderate depression, and resembling in barrenness, atmospheric dryness, and concentration of heat a section of the Desert of Sahara. Around it rise the sides of the crater, sufficiently bold to convey the idea of a surrounding wall, sometimes springing aloft in splintered perpendicular peaks 2000 feet high; the loftiest of them is named Guajara. The soft purple hues of these crater walls and battlements, contrasted with the sea of glaring pumice-stone, was very beautiful. Near the centre of the Cañadas the great cone swells abruptly with a dome-like outline, suggesting in its proportions the peculiar curve of the cupola of St. Sophia, although certainly more steep as seen from some points. The great dome is supported on the east side by the Montaña Blanca, a huge mound covered with pumice-stone, rising like a buttress from the Cañadas. Vast cataracts of brown and black lava, solidified into permanent forms, corrugate the sides of the peak. The peak or dome rises over 4000 feet above the Cañadas, and terminates in another crater, called the Rambleta. Out of the Rambleta rises the little peak of Teyde, or the Piton, 600 feet higher, conical, and at an angle excessively steep, terminating in a point and a third diminutive crater, above which we discerned very distinctly, against the blue sky, thin columns of white vapor shooting up with an uncertain motion, like tongues of white flame from a smouldering fire.

Such was the scene before us as we entered the Cañadas, majestic, solitary, desolate, beyond the power of language to describe. It seemed best, before going farther, to fortify ourselves for the additional labors of the day with a substantial lunch; and in the absence of other shade we took shelter in the shadow of one of the great rocks which strew the Cañadas—a mystery to scientific experts, although nothing seemed plainer to

PEAK OF TENERIFFE, AS SEEN ON APPROACHING THE LARGE CRATER.

me than that they must have rolled down from the lava torrents on the slope of the peak.

A long and hot, but not tedious, ride over the Cañadas and the Montaña Blanca at length brought us to the foot of the peak, and to a serious consideration of the task yet to be accomplished. Rugged Plutonian ridges of black lava, warmed here and there by brown slag or gleaming in the sun like glass, where a mass, breaking off, had left a smooth surface, rose above us like some Titanic fortress. A very severe climb brought us to the Estancia de los Ingleses, over 10,000 feet above the sea. Here are some rocks so clustered as to afford a shelter, so that it is generally the spot where travellers halt for the night. It has been called after the English, because they furnish the largest number of visitors to the peak.

As daylight was yet abundant, I concluded to abridge the labors of the morrow by ascending a thousand feet higher and spending the night at Alta Vista, a plateau two or three acres in extent, occupied by Professor Piazzi Smyth when engaged in taking astronomical observations at Teneriffe, in 1856. He spent several weeks on Guajara, and then removed to Alta Vista, where he pursued his labors for a month. The numerous corps of attendants at his disposal enabled him to erect two little huts there; but few vestiges of these now remain to indicate that human beings ever occupied that lonely height. The *retama*, which had been growing more and more scarce, ceased, together with all other signs of vegetation, soon after we left the Estancia, and we were obliged to carry up bits of dry *retama* to our halting-place for the fire, which was indispensable. A fragment of one of Professor Smyth's walls afforded a partial shelter; on the other side a black mass of slag contributed its aid, but roof, of course, there was none. The fire was soon going, but the water the muleteers had brought was so muddy that we should have been poorly off for tea if there had not been a bank of snow within a dozen feet of the fire. With melted snow a delicious cup of tea was brewed very soon, but it was noticeable how rapidly it cooled at that height.

Below us lay the yellow floor of the Cañadas; beyond that, the stratum of trade-wind clouds; and below these, the sea fading into the sky. Around us circled masses of lava presenting an astonishing, singularly grotesque variety of form: here a ridge of Moorish battlements; there a gigantic goat, standing against the sky as if startled and on the alert; then it seemed to be a dragon or a griffin sculptured out of lava that met the eye. As the view was unobstructed toward the east, we saw the shadow of the peak thrown across the sea at sunset, and reaching up toward the zenith as the sun declined. The color of the shadow was of the most exquisite purple, delicate and elusive at the edges, but at the same time very impressive. Twilight was soon over, and the full moon suddenly appeared. A low wind from the eastward now began to blow, increasing until it became a gale, boisterous and gusty, the blasts coming sometimes from every quarter at once, as it seemed to us. This wind continued all night, intensely searching and violent. The muleteers tended the fire, and bent over it wrapped in their huge mantles. Two blankets, two coats and an overcoat, two pairs of pantaloons, and a carpet under and over me were insufficient to drive away the sensation of cold, and I slept not a wink all night. Soon after 3 A.M. we took some tea, and by the light of a lantern started for the summit. We entered immediately on the Malpays, which can only be described as a mass of lava blocks, from one to twenty feet long, but generally not above five feet square, of all shapes, heaped together like ice hummocks in the most inconceivable manner. Often there were cavities between them, into which one might easily fall several feet. The stones were piled one over the other to an unknown depth, and great caution was required in springing over them, especially with only the dim glimmer of a lantern to guide us. After climbing up a thousand feet over this volcanic débris, we came again in sight of the little peak, and, passing some vents, through which issued jets of vapor, emerged on the Rambleta, or second crater, which is covered with pumice-stone. We were soon across this, and grappled with the Piton, which is not less steep than the largest of the Pyramids, but probably contains twice the number of cubic feet. It is about 600 feet in height, chiefly of pumice-stone, with bits of rock projecting here and there, and serving as resting-places for the climber. When we were half-way up, the sun burst suddenly above the sea, apparently out of instead of beyond it. The variety and beauty of the tints in the lower sky at the time were very remarkable. The peculiar golden-yellow glow thrown by the sun on the trade-wind clouds directly under it, which lasted for two hours, was such as I have seen under no other circumstances, nor does it appear to have been observed by other travellers.

This part of the ascent was very fatiguing. Humboldt said that Teneriffe was, with the exception of Jurullo, in Mexico, the most difficult mountain he had ever ascended. He did not exaggerate the difficulties. Professor Smyth rather takes him to task for this statement, unreasonably, as I think, for the professor did not himself undertake it until he had seasoned his lungs to the rarefied air on Guajara for six weeks. He then spent some days at Alta Vista; and after a capital night's rest, without having wasted his energies on the previous day in climbing, went up to the Rambleta. There he ate a hearty breakfast before attempting the little peak, and then, after all this preparation and training, he undertakes to assure us that Humboldt, a veteran mountain climber, overestimated the difficulties of Teneriffe.

While we were still over one hundred feet from the summit, a gust of wind suddenly wafted the fumes of sulphur so strongly from the crater that for a moment I was almost overcome by it; but as we neared the top, the oppression grew less—a phenomenon I find it difficult to explain. The crater which fitly terminates the celebrated peak of Teneriffe is perhaps seventy yards in diameter, with a rim abrupt and sharp, but rather lower on the western side. It appears to be gradually filling up. Professor Smyth, twenty years ago, observed that it was more shallow than as described by Humboldt or Van Buck, and the floor seems now still more elevated; I say elevated, for that must be the process, since there is nothing from outside to account for the decreasing depth. The different tints of the stones in or on the edge of the crater are varied and beautiful; but the prevailing colors which strike the eye are the straw-yellow and pale-green of the sulphur, which lies in separate masses, or covers the rocks with moist sulphur crystals. Vapor constantly arose from the bottom of the crater, and the soil was warm, although a little snow still lingered in the crevices. The wind was keen and violent. The sky above was unclouded, and of a deep azure. This intense hue of the heavens has been the subject of philosophical speculation; but it was not as dark and opaque as I have repeatedly seen it at the top of Pico Ruivo, and other mountains of Madeira, which have only half the altitude of Teneriffe. Several thousand feet below us the impenetrable curtain of trade-wind cloud was spread like a frozen land at the pole, and like the sea dovetailing with the land, filling every bay and inlet, and dashing surf-like against the cliffs, yet calm and noiseless, altering its forms so slowly as to be imperceptible. The higher ridges towered above it like islands, while here and there slopes could be seen below it,

COSTUME OF PEASANT.

but veiled in a dark purple gloom that seemed to isolate them from the rest of the world forever. Beyond this cloud-land arose the edge of the ocean, joining the sky by an invisible line. The trade-wind caused a haze, which concealed several of the Fortunate Isles; but Grand Canary, Hierro, Gomera, and La Palma, with its astonishing outline, containing the deepest crater on the face of the globe, were quite distinct. The extent of ocean visible from the Peak of Teneriffe is nearly 300 miles in diameter in very clear weather, or about 900 miles in circumference. In winter, when other winds prevail, the whole group is distinctly seen; but few have ever cared to ascend the Peak when deep snows envelop it with almost arctic austerity.

On returning over the Malpays, we stopped to examine the ice-cave, where, alone on the mountain, snow and water can be found at all times of the year. It would seem to be a sort of vent, or air-bubble, in the lava, made when it was at its hottest. On reaching our bivouac, we breakfasted as well as the circumstances would allow, and then packed up the "traps" and prepared to go. But the unexpected conduct of the mules delayed us for nearly two hours, incredible as it may appear. Three times my mule kicked off his saddle, which, after the girths were torn to pieces, was with great difficulty made fast by a bit of rope. To mount the brute was about as difficult as to saddle him. The sumpter-mule also astonished us by suddenly laying back his ears, throwing up his heels with a snort that was quite satanic in its tone, and, without the slightest provocation, flinging the basket of crockery and provisions over his head. Plates, bottles, and cups were demolished in the general wreck. In order to mount, I had to approach my mule from his head, and seize my chance when he seemed exhausted with his diabolical efforts. He might have repeatedly flung me a thousand feet in the air as we descended the precipices of Tigayga, and effectually prevented the writing of this veracious record. As he did not thus take advantage of me when I was on his back, it is only fair to suppose he had a little conscience left, and he should have the benefit of the doubt, since I finally succeeded in reaching Orotava without further mishap than a face burned almost beyond recognition by the winds of the Peak and the scorching sun of the Cañadas.

10

CHAPTER VII.

NEWFOUNDLAND.

EARLY in August, I took passage in the little English brig-schooner *Clara*, for St. Johns, Newfoundland. It was a pleasant morning when we cast off from Long Wharf, and dropped down the harbor before a light breeze, which gradually fanned the deeply laden craft outside of Boston Light. The wind freshened, and everything promised fair until after nightfall, when the heavy curtain of gloom which overhung the land behind us, from whence issued ominous flashes, and the low growl of distant thunder indicated a severe storm travelling along the shore. It was evident after a while, from the increasing vividness of the lightning and the mist that was encircling us, that we were not to escape a touch of the storm. About midnight the wind struck us with the force of a heavy squall from the south-west. The storm was moving in a circle. We were now past Cape Cod; so the brig ran for an hour under easy sail before the gale, when, finding the wind likely to hold, Captain Byrnes hove to under close-reefed foretop-sail, and fore and main staysails. The sea was rising fast; but the *Clara* rode like a duck, dry and easy on the seething waters, and about sunrise the force of the gale blew itself out. An observation at noon showed us to have been driven, by wind and currents combined, to the south of the "Georges." All sail was now made, and I then had an opportunity to take a quiet survey of the ship's company.

All on board were natives of Newfoundland, excepting the captain, who was a native of Dublin; a Prussian before the mast—the best sailor on board; and the writer; and all, with two exceptions, were of Irish descent, and good "Romans." I shared the diminutive cabin with four seal-hunters and sailors, who had turned junk-dealers for the nonce, and had just disposed of a cargo of junk in Boston, and were returning with an assorted cargo, part of which—a deck-load of apples—contributed toward making the brig roll hard, and so overcrowded the deck that it was a ticklish operation passing fore and aft in bad weather to shorten sail, when blocks and sheets were snapping furiously, and she was laying her scuppers under. A young mechanic, with his wife and another young woman, completed the list of *first-class* passengers. The young wife was very pretty, but she had a temper rougher than a file, and a sea-voyage did not improve it. To say that the accommodations were of the most limited and primitive character, and that the fare was far inferior to

THE SPOUT OFF CAPE BROYLE.

what is furnished to seamen in the forecastle of American ships, is no exaggeration. Salt junk of the very worst description, and pilot-bread highly seasoned with the flavor of the kerosene oil and tar in the run, formed our diet, with a few potatoes, which soon gave out, and some tomatoes, intended for the owner, but served out to us in small rations as fast as they decayed. The unfailing good-humor of Captain Byrnes, whose broad face presided benignantly at the table which he and the owner had conspired to furnish so meagrely, and the Attic salt and Irish wit of the junk-dealers, were of some avail in covering the deficiencies of the *Clara's* lockers. Nothing could exceed the garrulousness of these worthy islanders; and only the flashes of genuine humor and wit which enlivened their talk made their everlasting chatter endurable. Early and late they maintained the wordy Donnybrook, the endless discussions on questions suggested by their own experience regarding salvage, invoices, the rights of ships as carriers, quirks of marine law, the treatment of wives, and the like—all stale and prosy enough, but rendered novel by the animation, earnestness, dogmatism, and occasional shrewdness displayed, and the strongly marked individuality of the speakers. The debates were always spiced by the sallies of Johnnie Feene, who, though usually on the wrong side of an argument, often, by a neat repartee, threw unexpected confusion into the ranks of the opposition. Amidst a number of pithy sentiments which passed at random from one side to the other, two or three struck me as meaning more than, perhaps, the speakers themselves realized at the time. Said one of the disputants, "Ay, but remember, sur, that Newfoundland is two cinturies behind the times;" a strange admission from an old sea-dog, and a Roman Catholic at that, who boasted elsewhere of the influence of Romanism on the island.

Another said, "Maybe ye're right, but thin there's a great difference between justice and law." So there is, my man, thought I; and bad luck to them that have wrought this divorce between right and intellectual might!

A third, in reply to the observation, "Shure, but ivery man defers to his own opinion," replied, "And of coorse; for ivery man's mind is a kingdom to him." Now, here was a man who could not be accused of ever having read "Percy's Reliques," or any extracts therefrom, giving utterance to this idea in words almost identical with the first line of the beautiful piece well known to all lovers of English poetry, "My mind to me a kingdom is." The fact is, that the same thoughts in similar language often occur to different minds without collusion, in different ages and countries; and what critics who have not studied their own or others' mental phases choose to stigmatize as plagiarism, is of much less frequent occurrence than they represent. Indeed, I am inclined to think that very often this charge is made simply that the critic may display his own acquaintance with the passage he cites, in proof of the charges so lightly adduced by his officious pen.

But if there was one topic more discussed by these junk philosophers than another, it was the supernatural. Bushnell would have found them in full accord as to the reality of the supernatural and its relation to nature; and Robert Dale Owen's "Foot-falls on the Boundary of Another World" contains nothing more startling than the weird, mysterious yarns which were nightly told from actual personal experience in the little crowded cabin of the *Clara;* told, too, in earnest tone to listeners who heard with bated breath, and, on occasion, corroborated the truth of the most impossible incidents. By attending with becoming gravity and an air of implicit faith, which, sooth to tell, almost turned sometimes into actual belief, I was permitted to hear the story of many a rare adventure or encounter with the powers of darkness.

As I listened one night by the smoky lantern, with the gravity of a thorough believer, the captain asked me in a whisper how I could keep

ENTRANCE TO THE HARBOR OF ST. JOHNS.

such a sober face, for he knew I did not believe a word that was said, and he did not believe more than half of it himself.

"Ah! but don't you see," I replied, "that if I were to laugh, or appear incredulous, it would shut them right up? And I like to hear a good yarn as well as any man."

One of the narrators had fought an hour with the body of a deceased friend; another had been stopped on the public road to Waterford Bridge by a "sperrit" in the shape of a black dog; another had been within an ace of recovering hidden "threasure" from a foundered frigate; while a fourth had assisted in drawing "an irron chist of threasure" to the water's edge, when the ghost of a man, who had been killed and buried with it to keep watch over it, suddenly appeared, and, giving him a blow in the face, spirited the chest away, nevermore to be seen by mortal eye.

Johnnie Feene, of course, had his quota of marvels to relate, all of them sufficiently entertaining. One of his stories recounted the experience of a friend who, four years previously, had left his family starving at Bay of Bulls village, and gone to St. Johns in search of employment. Failing of this, he started for home, and was met after nightfall by a black dog, who addressed him, and then assuming human shape, informed him that he was an enchanted person fixed by a spell in a subterranean cavern near the Bay of Bulls, and that his enchantment could only be abated by the entrance of some one sufficiently bold to brave the guardians of the cave and carry thence the riches it contained.

Overjoyed at the suggestion, the fisherman gladly volunteered to accompany the enchanted stranger, who accordingly introduced him to a subterranean hall, vast, and gorgeous with Oriental magnificence, where the wealth of the Indies lay apparently at his disposal, and he had it in his power not only to relieve the poverty of his condition, but also to become the most opulent of Queen "Victhoria's" subjects. But suddenly he was assailed by a troop of unwholesome ghouls, who so disturbed his resolution that he fled to the upper air, renouncing possession of the riches in his grasp, and leaving the enchanted man enchanted there forever.

Very naturally, I was led to conclude that a more behaunted, bewitched, and ghost-ridden country nowhere exists than this same Newfoundland, which seemed to be an outlying station of Pandemonium, as full of hidden treasures as the old haunts of Captain Kidd, as beset with enchantments as the brain of Don Quixote, as packed with ill-omened spirits as Alloway Kirk. The imagination of these prosaic, storm-beaten old fishermen of Labrador teems with the feverish fancies of a nervous child. The black dog figures in most of their legends, and is evidently the *bête noir* of the Newfoundlandic imagination.

But all this time we were sailing toward our destination slowly, but steadily. The dashing tide-rips indicated that we were on the "Georges," "the graveyard of Cape Ann," as those shoals are rightly regarded, and the fishing-schooners dotting the offing showed we were on the fishing-grounds. It is very strange that no light-ship has ever been stationed on these dangerous shoals; many a ship must have met her fate on Cultivator's Ledge, where the depth is but three feet at mean low tide. It is not too late for Government to put up a beacon there, and thus mitigate the perils of one of the sailor's worst foes. A south-wester took us toward Sable Island, but the currents seemed to combine with calms to set us nearer a direct line with that island than was comfortable. Somehow the brig failed to make the desired northing, and two successive observations did not allay the difficulty. It happened about this time that I took a trick at the wheel. We were running with the wind just abaft of the starboard quarter, and I noticed that the vessel, being too much by the head and carrying too weather a helm, from the pressure of her large main-sail, "griped"—that is, had a tendency to fly into the wind—which rather aided in giving us a drift to starboard. On informing the captain of this, he immediately took in the main-sail and gaff-topsail, and kept the vessel away two points. The next observation indicated a very decided improvement in the ship's course, and on the following day we had the satisfaction of seeing in the southern horizon the low globular clouds called wool-packs, which in clear weather hang over the island and show where it lies when too distant to be visible.

ASCENT TO A "FLAKE."

Sable Island is the bugbear of the mariners coasting in its vicinity. It is so low that it cannot be descried until close at hand; and is besides enveloped in dense fogs half the time, and so beset with swift tides and currents as to make it a very treacherous spot. Simply a sand-bank scarce elevated above the ocean level, its sands are constantly shifting and altering its shape; so easily, in fact, are its sands blown to and fro, that shipmasters who are wrecked there are recommended to make no effort to escape, as the sand will at once begin to gather around the grounded vessel and form a breakwater that will enable the crew to escape at their leisure. So soft and yielding is the beach that, some years ago, on a quiet moonlight night, a vessel went ashore there so easily that none of the crew were aware when it happened; the watch were asleep, including the man at the wheel; the captain was in his bunk. And there she lay until daylight; then the master went on deck, and behold! his vessel was hopelessly aground on Sable Island! He afterward received another ship, but contrived to leave her ribs also bleaching on the same unlucky spot, and it is almost needless to say was not again intrusted with a command. The island is inhabited only by a corps of Government wreckers, who communicate with the main-land once a month, and two or three hundred wild ponies, bred from a stock wrecked there in colonial times.

From Sable Island we beat up abreast of Canso, and made Scatari Light, at the extreme eastern end of Cape Breton, on the tenth evening. Louisburg, or what grass-covered mounds remain of that once famous fortress, lay hidden in the gloom to leeward, even its light being invisible. The light-keeper had probably gone off to a dance. It was a black night, and unpleasantly calm considering the proximity of the shore, and that the tide was swinging us helplessly toward the rocks, against which we could hear more and more distinctly the deep rote of the long ocean swell. But about nine we heard a wind rushing over the water, which soon filled our sails, and sent us plunging toward Cape Race, three hundred and fifty miles away; and a race indeed we had of it, running before a stiff breeze under press of sail, rolling gunwale under in the heavy following surges, the porpoises playing around the foaming bow with phosphorescent trail, and not rarely a huge whale starting up and spouting alongside. One fine morning a school of eight whales—good-sized fellows—passed close astern, remaining at the surface and tossing smoke-like jets of spray into the air for some time.

Those who voyage in steamboats, while they gain in comforts suitable to the invalid, lose, on the other hand, much of the zest and flavor of sea-life. Not for them is the adventurous sensation imparted to one who roughs it in a sailing-vessel, and enjoys the variety and excitement which come with the trimming of sails and the management of a ship in a blow. In addition to this, the constant grumble of a steamer's machinery prevents a full appreciation of the solemn grandeur of the ocean, deadening the wash of the waves and the sublime chant of the wind in the rigging. For the voyager on the sailing-vessel is reserved that most weird of ocean sounds, the muttering and shrieking of Mother Carey's chickens—those wandering gypsies of the sea—floating over the water through the gloom of a dark night, like the eldrich laughter of lost spirits. Only on a sailing-vessel can one realize in any degree what the navigators of other days have endured, and imagine, as he tosses on the buffeting surges, that he is bound with the intrepid Vasco to discover the Indies, with Columbus seeks to evoke land from an unknown void, with Magalhaens is encircling the globe, or with Raleigh or Sir Humphrey Gilbert is traversing the endless spaces of waves to discover El Dorado or quaff at the fountain of youth.

On the thirteenth day out we sighted Cape Mary's, and stood all day along the southern coast of Newfoundland. Small fishing-schooners were numerous, noticeable for their black sails, dyed in oil and tar to make them durable, which entirely ruins the picturesque appearance usual to fishing craft, and aids to give a melancholy aspect to a shore that is already sufficiently barren and dismal. No other signs of life were visible from dawn until nightfall, except two or three fishing huts, and the light-houses on Cape Pine and Cape Race. Having a leading wind, and no fog, we passed within half a mile of the latter, so famous for its ship-

CAPE RAY.—TELEGRAPH HOUSE.

wrecks. It is altogether a very cheerful spot, invested with the most agreeable associations. In Trepassy Bay, close at hand, for example, four ocean steamers have been lost, two within a year, with all on board; and just beyond, scarce a mile north of the cape, is the graveyard on the cliff, where those are buried whose bodies were recovered by divers from the *Anglo-Saxon*, which struck in a fog, and went down at the foot of the beetling crags. The *City of Philadelphia* was wrecked not far from the same spot, as well as many other ill-fated vessels.

Under press of sail we glided up the eastern coast of the island, which welcomed us with a succession of chilling squalls from the high land, which, with but one or two exceptions, is the formation of this part of Newfoundland. There was nothing inviting in the prospect. The rocky shore was like a huge wall falling sheer down most forbiddingly, seamed here and there by deep gulches, at the bottom of which two or three fishermen's huts might be discerned at long intervals. Midway between Cape Race and St. Johns we passed Cape Broyle, a forbidding headland, which is pierced by a cavity called the Spout. In easterly gales the rush of the sea forces the water up like a whale-spout, with a sound of thunder. When we rounded Cape Spear, whose light is 370 feet above the sea, the scene only became more grand and desolate. Before us, in the north, towered Sugar Loaf, like a stupendous bastion of some sea-fortress; and as we sheered to the westward, the houses of St. Johns were visible as through a telescope at the end of a deep gulch or channel, scarce two cables'-length in width, guarded on either hand by vast perpendicular cliffs. Signal Hill, on the north side of the entrance, soars to a height of 730 feet. A wheezing little tug came out and towed us through the channel into the snuggest pocket of a harbor in the world, and laid us alongside the wharf of the United States consul, the owner of the brig.

St. Johns is a place of about 23,000 inhabitants. It straggles rather aimlessly along the water and up a slope, and is a cross between an Irish and an English seaport, and, except as it thereby represents an anomaly belonging rather to the Old than to the New World, offers nothing especially worthy of note. The streets abound with dogs almost as if it were a Turkish city, generally of mongrel breeds, and burdened by a billet of wood hung to the neck, which renders them harmless. So numerous are dogs in the habited regions, and so mischievous to the flocks, that the laws of the island permit any one to shoot them at sight. But while other curs are so common, individuals of the genuine Newfoundlandic stock are scarce, and fetch from eighty to one hundred dollars. The breed is consequently guarded with great care, but seems, nevertheless, to be dying out. No dog that is not entirely jet-black, and has not the web-foot and dew-claw, is of the unmixed Newfoundland breed.

The port of St. Johns is small, but, as before observed, well sheltered, and presents in summer-time a bustling appearance, being crowded with vessels of all nations. On entering the passage to the harbor a pungent "ancient fishy smell" informs the stranger what is the trade of the island. The energies of the islanders are devoted to the seal and cod fisheries. Early in March the seal-hunters, as the sealing-vessels are called, put to sea, cutting a way out through the ice if necessary, and strike directly for the ice-fields in the Straits of Belle Isle, where the seals congregate in great numbers. From fifty to seventy-five men go in a sealer, their bunks being ranged gallery-like along the hold. Half the proceeds go to the crew, half to the owner or planter. Thirty pounds are a fair average per man, thirty-six pounds being occasionally made in one trip; and two trips are sometimes taken in the season, which lasts until May. The sealers are usually brigantines, and are somewhat wedge-shaped in the

floor, so that when nipped by the ice, they are raised up instead of being crushed, slipping back into the water when the ice parts. Nevertheless, serious mishaps not rarely occur. Latterly a few screw-steamers, carrying 150 to 200 men, have been introduced; their crews share only a third of the receipts, but the increased rapidity of locomotion enables them to gain equal profits with the other crews.

The best seals are those called whitecaps, harps, and hoods; the latter are so named because the males, when attacked, protect their faces by a cartilaginous visor, hard as India-rubber and impenetrable to the spear. Two men are requisite to kill these—one to divert the attention of the seal, while the other thrusts the lance through the throat. The men employed in this business wear snow-spectacles, formed of blue glass, and protected on the sides by a fine net-work of wire, but even thus do not always escape a touch of snow-blindness, which is very common and painfully acute.

The cod-fisheries of Newfoundland are even more profitable than seal-catching. Not only do her fishermen resort to the Banks, but all along the shore in her spacious bays they "till the farm that pays no fee," and the stages and "flakes," or platforms, for drying the fish are to be seen at every hamlet, crossing above the street like vine trellises in Italy, bearing a fruit less fragrant and graceful, but not less useful—codfish destined for the nourishment of good Catholics the world over, so long as Tuesdays and Fridays and Lent continue sacred to cod. It is interesting, when walking in the suburbs of St. Johns of a pleasant day, to see the women and boys, who cure the fish while the men are gone to sea, driving carts into town from Quidy Vidy, Empty Basket, and other little fishing ports, drawn by diminutive ponies and laden with salt fish ready to be shipped to distant lands. In other countries the peasantry flock to the shire-town with vegetables and fruits, the product of the gardens and vineyard. In Newfoundland it is codfish that the peasantry carry to the market-town.

And yet, although the profits of the seal and cod-fisheries are large, and all on the island are in some way connected with what is virtually its sole business, poverty of the most abject character is the rule among all but a very few. This business is under the control of monopolists, and presents, by the way it is managed, an instructive example of what may result when the sense of mutual interest which should bind capital and labor is forgotten. Twelve men, most of whom reside in England, and carry on the business through agents in Newfoundland, furnish the capital on which the fisheries are conducted; consequently a large portion of the profits does not remain in the country, but is taken abroad to be distributed elsewhere. But this is a minor evil compared with the iron clutch by which these capitalists hold every fisherman, as it were, by the throat, scarcely permitting him to draw breath without their leave. The truck system, so powerfully rebuked in Parliament, and working disastrously in some of the Pennsylvania mines, is in full force in Newfoundland. The capitalists, in return for the fish, pay the fishermen in kind; that is, furnish them with all the supplies for supporting their families or carrying on their vocation, so managing as to oblige them to draw in advance of the profits of the still ungathered crops of fish or seals—a draft on the future—and contrive that the account shall always so stand as to leave the poor fisherman, already rendered improvident by this practice, always in debt, and thus always in the power of the capitalist. In addition to this, the capitalists or their agents meet in a club or Board

CLEANING FISH.

of Trade room at stated periods, and arrange among themselves the values to be placed on the supplies furnished to the fishermen in their employ, and from these prices, be they never so high, there is no appeal, nor, from the situation of affairs, is there any remedy to be provided against the repetition of the extortion. Gradually, but surely, has this tremendous tyranny gained strength on the island, and, so long as they remain under the present Government, shuts out all hope or power of improvement or progress in the condition of the islanders, or of the development of the mineral and agricultural resources which Newfoundland undoubtedly possesses in a remarkable degree.

The island has nearly the superficial area of New England, and yet with a population of only a trifle over 150,000; and these, with the exception of

St. Johns and Harbor Grace, are doled out along the singularly indented and irregular coast in little settlements of half a dozen cabins, widely separated from each other; and even this meagre civilization is confined to the seaboard. Immediately on striking inland, one comes to the primeval forests of spruce and pine, which are about as destitute of traces of the supreme Caucasian race as if Columbus had never been born. Half a century ago, one white man, with an Indian guide, crossed from the eastern to the western coast, and wrote a valuable account of his trip and of the interior wilds; but no one has followed in his track until within five or six years since, and the deer still migrate unmolested from north to south with the change of the seasons. The few Micmac Indians remaining live chiefly along the northern shore. The time is not far distant when a railroad will traverse the island from Cape Ray to Trinity Bay or St. Johns, connecting with a line of transatlantic steamers. From Cape Ray to Cape North, on Cape Breton Island, it is only forty miles, and travellers afraid of sea-sickness or pressed for time could thus reduce the distance by water between New York and Liverpool 1200 miles.

The Roman Catholics have, in former time, been in excess of the Protestants of the island, and, as elsewhere, have characteristically secured the most commanding site in St. Johns for their cathedral, which is the first object that meets the eye on entering the port, its imposing Italian architecture suggesting similar scenes in the Mediterranean, and its size and position leading a stranger to infer that opulence and numbers are monopolized by the Romanists; but the exterior is far more showy than the interior, which is cold and barn-like, finished off with crumbling stucco, and poorly ornamented with cheap copies after the Masters.

The last census, however, showed that the Protestant element is gaining, and is now in a respectable majority, chiefly of the Church of England, but including a fair proportion of Scotch Presbyterians and Wesleyans. The Anglican Bishop of Newfoundland presides over the most extraordinary diocese in Christendom. The see may almost literally be termed the *sea;* for while it is the largest in limits in the world, it is almost entirely composed of water, and the good prelate discharges his episcopal duties by much traversing of the boisterous Atlantic. Newfoundland and the "vexed Bermoothes," with all the waters wide that roll between, are comprehended in this episcopate of many miles and few souls, unless we include soles that in the sea do dwell. A schooner-yacht is owned by his reverence, who in the summer visits and confirms his Northern flocks, a third of the coast of Newfoundland being thus circumnavigated by this ghostly yachtsman once a year. The fourth summer he rests from these maritime visitations, and the winters he devotes to the spiritual necessities of the Bermudas, who evidently receive more than their share of spiritual nourishment. A suffragan bishop resides at St. Johns, and missionaries, as they may well be called, are set over the fishing hamlets. They take charge of several each, and go from one to the other in fishing-boats, faithfully and patiently doling out the scant store of religion to the poor islanders, and, as one of their number observed to me, "endeavoring to make good Christians of them, or at least good Churchmen."

It is supposed by many in the United States that Newfoundland belongs to the New Dominion, while others, better informed as to that, but, as would seem, against the best interests of our country, which already embraces all the territory we can take care of for the present, have endeavored to create a movement in favor of the annexation of that island to the "States." For Newfoundland, at least, it would doubtless prove an advance on her condition as it is now, split by rival factions and under the control of monopolists, who repress the energies of the people and prevent the improvement of the vast mineral resources of the island. There are two political parties there, strongly divided on the question of confederation with the New Dominion, a measure which could only result to the ultimate advantage of the islanders. So it is properly regarded by the best citizens, but they are unfortunately still in the minority; and such is the ignorance of the masses, that they are, of course, under the guidance of pestilent demagogues, those curses inevitably attendant on democracy in all ages, who, for the accomplishment of their selfish ends, give currency to the most amazing stories against Canada, so incredible that I refrain from repeating them here, yet not too incredible for the credulity of those for whose benefit they are manufactured. The elections are attended by much excitement and corruption, and the intelligence and integrity of the Legislature are not above suspicion. Lowell's "New Priest of Conception Bay" gives a vivid idea of certain phases of life in Newfoundland. The lower classes are generally a very rough set, especially on the southern coast, and, if we may trust the statements of some of the clergy, an infusion of practical Christianity into the morals of the people is one of the demands of the island.

There is some attempt at popular education on the part of the Government, but, judging from the intelligence of the popular mind, wisdom will not die with the Newfoundlanders. There is a reading-room at St. Johns, for the free use of which I here tender my grateful acknowledgments; but communication with the outside world is at best but scanty.

The United States press is represented in the book-stores by the most vulgar of the New York weeklies, which may account for the not unreasonable opinion expressed to me by a usually well-informed clergyman, that he supposed "the United States was governed entirely by mob law." The papers of St. Johns are of a contemptible character; the telegraphic news they contain is much garbled, and, what seems extraordinary, considering the near vicinity of Heart's Content—the terminus of the cable—is obtained by way of Boston and Halifax, several days after date! Mail communication is maintained with Halifax, and the rest of the world thereby, once or twice monthly by steam-packet. Considering how rarely the mails have to be made up and distributed, the post-office might almost seem a sinecure, and yet it will excite a smile to learn that the postal officials have been known to complain of overwork!

After all, I found it pleasant to be quiet a while, and free from the turmoil and confusion, the constant hurry of events, the swift-recurring rush of telegrams, the fever of life in the nineteenth century, and to live over a bit of "still life," somewhat as it was in some retired English seafaring town seventy years ago. And while one can hardly consider Newfoundland, with its pale sunlight and sere plains, solitary forests and infrequent mails, altogether the place to live in, yet it is well worth a visit. Its aboriginal scenery, unexplored wastes, quaint capital, curious fishing-ports, frowning coast, legendary lore, hospitable folk, and blooming lassies with eyes of brimming blue, cheeks mantling with the roses of health, plump, trim figures, and elastic step, and its unusual fishing and hunting advantages for sportsmen, present a variety of attractions adapted to interest and please the stranger, and store his memory with delightful recollections.

CHAPTER VIII.

THE BERMUDAS.

SEVEN hundred and seventy miles south-east from New York, in the latitude of Charleston, and the other side of the Gulf Stream, to which we are indebted for a variety of ill-natured weather, lies the celebrated cluster of islets called the Bermudas. Having been long desirous of seeing them, I was duly exultant when I at last held in my hand the ticket of the "Quebec and Gulf Ports Steamship Company," entitling me to a berth in the steamship *Canima*. We left the wharf on a Thursday, at 3 P.M., and made the land on Monday morning at 3 A.M. Steering around the southern side of the islands, we entered the narrow channel north of St. George's, and, passing inside of the reefs, meandered among islets and hidden shelves until we came to Hamilton, by one of the most tortuous and difficult channels ever attempted by a vessel.

Once within the basin forming the port of Hamilton, we found our-

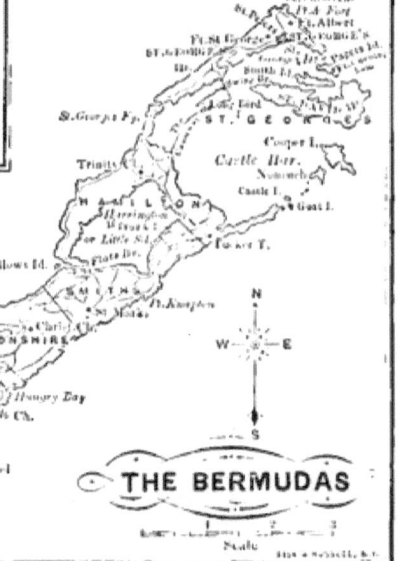

selves in a lovely, landlocked lake, girt with a diadem of miniature isles, and the white-roofed and latticed cottages and palms of the little capital straggling dreamily to the water's edge at the bottom of a fairy-like bay. Dropping an anchor and mooring to it, the *Canima* was gradually warped to some forty feet from the quay, which she could not reach on account of a shallow, that might be dredged out with a moderate sum and a trifling amount of enterprise. The great events in life at Hamilton, aside from the yacht-races and paper-hunts, are the arrivals and departures of

the New York packet. Accordingly, the pier was thronged with people, black and white, showing on the glaring, calcareous soil like pawns huddled in disorder on a chess-board. There they stood, aristocrats and plebeians, with a sprinkling of redcoats and jolly men-of-war's-men, chattering and chaffing, while we on board also leaned expectant on the bulwarks, wondering how we were to get on shore. To land in boats when we were but a dozen yards off seemed preposterous; but no other visible means of getting to land with dry feet seemed to offer. A bustle in the crowd soon indicated a solution of the problem. Ropes flung from the ship were caught on shore and made fast to the outer end of long timbers, which were now pushed out into space by ebony 'longshoremen, until by means of the ropes the oscillating ends were drawn on board, thus causing the timbers to rest one end on shore, the other on board. Immediately a swarm of shining blacks, grinning and yelling, bestrode these beams, holding crossbars, which they lashed to the underside of the timbers. It was a novel sight, the double row of lithe, half-clad darkies, clinging with bare feet to the logs fifteen feet above the water. When the frame had been properly lashed together, planks were laid over it, and thus we passed from deck to land. A crane, by which a bridge could be lowered, or such a bridge on wheels as we use in New York, would be perfectly feasible, and perhaps less costly in the end; but, were any such innovation to be introduced, a riot might result, to which the *émeute* excited by Demetrius the coppersmith would be trifling, the negroes who put up and take down this rude bridge bawling with "damnable iteration," "This our craft is in danger to be set at naught!"

I never witnessed a more thoroughly laughable and ridiculous incident than a palaver between a half-breed and a full-blooded Congo on Hamilton Quay, about a cur which the latter had pushed into the water on a certain steamer-day. Such grandiloquent language, perpetually mispronounced, such mock dignity and high sense of personal honor, such absurd gestures and rolling of the eyes, such barbaric eloquence about nothing, would bring tears of laughter to the eyes of the Cardiff Giant.

The Bermudas received their name from Juan Bermudez, who, when driving past in a gale of wind, first sighted them in 1503; but no attempt to profit by the discovery seems to have been made until 1552, when Philip II. concluded to assume formal possession of the group, and Ferdinand Camelo sailed for Bermuda with a band of colonists. A rock bearing the initials of Camelo, the date of landing, and a cross, still stands near the centre of the island. No other relics of this Latin colony exist; but Henry May, an English

HAMILTON, BERMUDAS.

seaman, wrecked there in 1593, relates that he found an abundance of wild-hogs, a relic of this colony, which have long since been exterminated. In 1609, Sir George Somers was on the voyage to Virginia, and was wrecked on the Bermudas, where he died in 1611, and the group is sometimes called after him. At some earlier period, the ubiquitous Captain John Smith, who turns up in all the American colonies at intervals, landed at the Bermudas, and made some startling statements regarding the aboriginal spiders he found there. In the words of an old chronicler: "They could not find by any observations that they [the spiders] were at all pernicious; yet they are of a very large size, but withal beautifully colored, and look as if they were adorned with pearl and gold. Their webs are in color and substance a perfect raw silk, and so strongly woven that, running from tree to tree, like so many snares, small birds are sometimes caught in them. This Captain Smith reports, upon whose credit as great an improbability as this may be ventured to be related." No such magnificent spiders now inhabit Bermuda, and we must say Captain Smith's testimony on the subject is hardly sufficient to satisfy the scepticism of this faithless and unbelieving generation. But some large-sized, although harmless, spiders are there still, which have an uncivil habit of entering one's bedroom without leave and dropping down on the pillow from the ceiling after the light has been blown out for the night.

Representative government was organized in Bermuda in 1620, the year the Pilgrims landed at Plymouth. As the first permanent settlers of the islands were Puritans, impelled thither in search of an asylum for religious freedom, the coincidence is rather remarkable, and worthy of more attention than it has received from the historians. These settlers were for a while great sufferers from a memorable plague of rats as numerous as the swarm which devoured Bishop Hatto on the Rhine. They were everywhere, and destroyed everything, even swimming from one island to another. Cats and dogs were of little use in combating the vermin, which finally disappeared almost as mysteriously as they had come. The cats naturally began to pine after that, and they do not seem to have got over it yet, for a more woe-begone, rough-haired, angular, crop-eared, and bob-tailed set of quadrupeds than these felines is not to be found out of Bermuda.

But, while having nominally a government of their own, with a miniature legislature chosen from a few property-holders out of a total population of 12,000, the Bermudas are in reality a naval station of Great Britain, under the charge of a military governor appointed by the crown. A garrison of two regiments is permanently settled there, and the most advantageous points bristle with fortifications. On Ireland Island an artificial port has been created by a breakwater, and an extensive arsenal exists for repairing ships-of-war. There is to be seen the famous floating-dock, towed from England in 1869. It is 381 feet in length over all.

The reputation of Bermuda is owing largely to the circumstance that no similar group of islands has been visited and sung by so many writers of note. Influenced, perhaps, by the narratives of Captain Smith and Henry May, Shakspeare laid the scene of "The Tempest" on a desert island, and gave a birthplace to Ariel in the "still vexed Bermoothes."

FLOATING-DOCK.

Later, Edmund Waller came to Bermuda with the Earl of Warwick, in order to get over his disappointment regarding the Lady Dorothy Sidney. He wrote a spirited poem, entitled "The Battle of the Summer Islands," describing a combat between the Bermudians and certain whales. Amidst

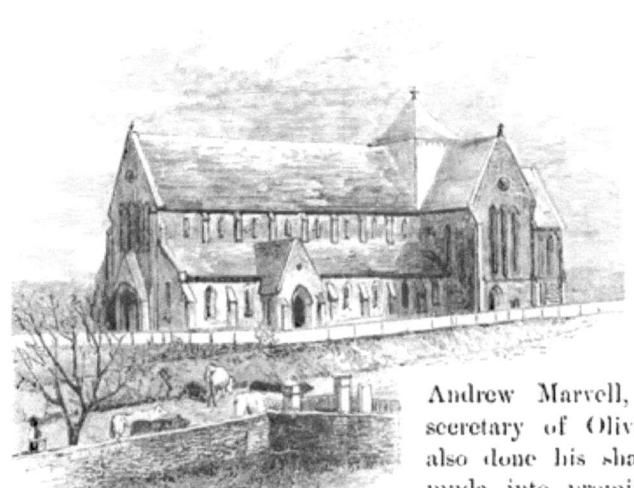

TRINITY CHURCH, HAMILTON.

considerable bombast there are a few good lines in the poem; but the poet gave rein to his imagination, and pictured scenes whose like can only be found amidst the rank growth of tropical vegetation. Andrew Marvell, the well-known secretary of Oliver Cromwell, has also done his share to bring Bermuda into prominence by his exquisite lines, "The Emigrants in Bermudas," which show that the Puritans were able to compose admirable poetry as well as give "apostolic blows and knocks." In this century, Tom Moore, the jolly bard who translated Anacreon, drifted over to these isles with a commission to the Vice-admiralty Court in his pocket. There was nothing Puritanic about Moore. As soon as he landed, he went to making love and weaving amatory couplets, which were probably no more sincere than most of his verses; for, his poetry to the contrary notwithstanding, he records in his prose that he found the ladies more susceptible than beautiful, while the husbands also came in for a share of unfavorable criticism. He adds, "The philosopher who held that in the next life men are transformed into mules and women into turtles might see this very nearly accomplished at Bermuda." The house where Moore lived, the dripping cavern he frequented, and the ragged calabash-tree under which he composed his verses, continue to be objects of rational curiosity.

Without making comparisons, which are said on good authority to be odious, it may be truthfully affirmed that the scenery of Bermuda, although never overcoming one with enthusiasm, is, however, always pleasing, and, like a choice work of art or a quiet but thoughtful piece of music, has the inestimable quality of improving on acquaintance. Its charms are so subtile that, before one is aware, it has stolen an enduring place in one's affections. I have seen islands far more striking and magnificent, which have gained scarcely so strong a hold upon my memory, or seemed to invite the stranger to return with such singular magnetism. The pomegranate grows abundantly, and its brilliant green foliage, starred with the flame-like splendor of scarlet blossoms, forms one of the most characteristic features in a Bermuda landscape. The same may be said of the fiddle-tree and the geranium; while the oleander, growing in lofty groves, and festooned with wonderful masses of crimson-and-white flowers, often imparts regal beauty to the rural roadside. Variety is also given to the flora by the interweaving of the tamarind, the red cedar, the century-plant, the Surinam cherry, the grape-fruit, the banana, and, waving majestically over all, the queenly palm, a bronze-like shaft lithely swaying in the sea-wind and crowned by an undulating crest of emerald plumes. The mangrove is abundant in the coral coves, its snake-like

MOORE'S CALABASH-TREE.

branches twisted together most inextricably over the water, and forming green coves, where the dreamer may suppose sea-fairies dwell, if he be so minded.

The scientist would probably tell us that there are no such things as fairies, that this scenery and these trees have higher uses than to please, and would direct us rather to turn to a serious consideration of the interesting geological phenomena of the islands; and, as he has got us by the

VIEW FROM LIGHT-HOUSE.

button-hole, and, like the Ancient Mariner, is bound to repeat his story, we must listen a few minutes while he tells us that the soil is very thin, and of a red color; that it is already overworked, and constantly demands fertilizers; and that it is but a sparse stratum, deposited in the course of long ages on a limestone basis. The most noteworthy characteristic of the Bermudas, in the opinion of the aforesaid scientist, is their formation. Originally they were nothing but reefs of coral. Gradually the central portions arose above the sea, and then the surf, beating on the outer coral ledges, wore them into sand, which was washed up on the higher parts. Exposure to the weather of an ocean celebrated for the inhospitable treatment it extends to those who court its acquaintance had a hardening tendency, such as the human character undergoes when lashed by oft-repeated, long-continued adversity; and these heaps of loose sand became indurated into limestone. Nor is the process yet complete; it is still going on along the southern coast, where limestone in the various stages of formation may be seen, from hard rock to softer masses like cheese, and mere shifting hills composed of the disintegrated coral washed up by the latest storm.

These islets number one hundred, with a large flock of nameless rocks. The main group forms a chain shaped like a fish-hook, from St. George's Island to Ireland Island, and connected by causeways. On the northern side they are hedged in by a remarkable coralline reef extending in a semicircle completely across, subtending the arc of the bay lying between these two islands, a distance of twenty-five miles. It is worthy of remark that the Bermudas are in the highest latitude in which coral insects build in the form of rocks. In heavy weather this immense barrier is cruelly terrible, beaten by an unbroken mass of raging breakers. As there is but one passage by which it can be entered, it serves as an impenetrable *che-*

COTTAGE AND GARDEN IN HAMILTON.

val-de-frise against all ships of the enemy. There is a fine light-house on Gibbs Hill, 362 feet above the sea, and visible twenty-five miles. They need another one, and came to that conclusion a long time ago. But as time is the cheapest thing going in a place like Bermuda, it is well to employ a good supply of it in everything that is undertaken there. It costs

A STREET SCENE IN HAMILTON—THE WHARF.

nothing, while hurry, money, labor—these things cost; and therefore this additional light-house will not be erected, probably, before the year 1900.

The islands, in a direct line, are but fifteen miles in length, and never over two miles broad, and generally very much narrower, and excessively cut up with creeks and bays; and yet they give an impression of a much larger area—to such a degree as almost to come within the definition of an illusion. The surface, nowhere over 250 feet high, is always undulating; and thus one will often find himself in a little sylvan hollow surrounded by hills so steep as to give the impression of considerable elevation; they are clothed with cedar groves. On the intervening meadow-lands lies perchance a little pool surrounded by attractive farm-houses and gardens, and a church-spire. One could easily imagine himself in some New England vale hundreds of miles from the sea, when a turn in the road reveals the ocean only a few score yards away; and the illusion is heightened by the numerous admirable roads running in every direction. A penal settlement existed until recently in Bermuda, and the convicts were employed to hew out of the rock 120 miles of carriage-roads. The question is, "If these men had not sinned, would these roads have been constructed; and what would the islands be without these roads?" "Whatever is, is right," says Pope. Not a bit of it! But in Bermuda let us throw casuistry and physic alike to the dogs.

Hamilton is a charming little town, doing its best to emulate other English colonies by maintaining an insular aristocracy, and feels as important as if it had twelve hundred thousand instead of twelve hundred souls. Better than all, there is a poetic element, a narcotic property, in the air which invests it, that makes one forget that New York is so near at hand, struggling under the burdens of the nineteenth century. The pretty cottages in the neighborhood, embowered in flowers, are very inviting, and seem to offer a nearly perfect combination of rural and domestic attractions.

Of St. George's I cannot speak so favorably. It seems to present the decay without the picturesqueness, the decrepitude without the respectability of old age, and the neighboring shores are less inviting. On St. David's Island, in the port, people are still found who have never been

A STREET SCENE IN ST. GEORGE'S.

off that little islet, and have never seen a horse except in a picture! Donkeys they have seen, for the good reason that dwarf donkeys are found everywhere in Bermuda, trotting in front of miniature carts. St. George's was a noted rendezvous for blockade-runners during our civil war, and the depression into which it has fallen is proportioned to the feverish pros-

THE DEVIL'S HOLE.

perity of that period. It may be added here that the oft-repeated story of the enterprising hero who made several trips from Charleston to Bermuda, carrying a ton of cotton across each voyage in an open boat, has no foundation in fact.

The two pleasantest spots in Bermuda are Harrington Sound and Fairy-land. The former is a salt-water lake, or estuary, surrounded by cavernous shores, and over its delicate green water hovers the poetic pintail, reflecting on its downy white breast the emerald tint of the sea. The Walsingham and Joyce caves in the vicinity are well worth visiting, although the beautiful pendant stalactites hanging from the Gothic vaults are gradually falling before the blows of visitors, and blackened by the smoke of the bushes burned to light up the gloom of the interior. The Devil's Hole is also a spot where, for an extravagant fee, one may have his curiosity relieved by looking into a pit filled with sea-water through a subterranean channel. It is surrounded by a high stone wall, carefully protected by a vast quantity of broken glass, although it is difficult to imagine any one so infatuated by curiosity as to try to scale a high wall in order to look into a pool. But there is no glass wasted in Bermuda. The walls are everywhere so plentifully guarded by a frightfully jagged edge of broken bottles as to lead the stranger to think it must be a very insecure place to live in. It must be admitted that the color of the water at the Devil's Hole is of the most exquisite cobalt hue, shading off into emerald and brown in the shadows, and the azure angel-fish it contains are equally beautiful.

Fairy-land is topographically the most attractive spot in Bermuda, and should therefore be visited last. Art has done little for it, and Nature a great deal. The main island is here cut up most marvellously into cove and bay, isthmus and peninsula, like the bits of a puzzle-map, and the coves are in turn studded with green islets, reposing in magical beauty on a summer sea. I know of no country villa more admirably situated than the residence of Mrs. Stowe, who courteously allows visitors to walk over her grounds. Near Fairy-land is Spanish Point, a picturesque rock, with a very fine bit of marine foreground, complete and lovely of its kind; and beyond this point is a sea-cave reserved as a bathing-house for the ladies of the governor's family. It seems hollowed out on purpose for Amphitrite and her Nereids.

CAVES ON THE COAST.

The admirable facilities for boating at Bermuda naturally cause great interest in yachting. There is a yacht-club, and the Bermuda yachts have more than a local reputation. The boats are, however, built on principles that have been exploded by the latest practice. They are a curious combination of some of the opposite qualities of English and American yachts

RAVINE ON SOUTH SHORE, BERMUDA.

at the time of the famous international race in 1851. They have great beam, but it is forward of the centre; and great draught, but it is aft; and the keel runs up toward the stem. At the same time they depend altogether upon ballast for stability, and are so heavily sparred that they have to be loaded down with a great weight. The mast is also set so far in the eyes, and has such a rake, that it buries the bow in running, and even when close-hauled, thus checking the speed. The only quality in which they seem to me to excel is in going to windward. It is affirmed that some of them can look up within three points and a half of the wind; but our best sloop-yachts can do the same thing. They are built entirely of red cedar, scraped and varnished, and certainly look very coquettish and saucy when under press of canvas. The main-sail is triangular, and boats in racing-trim set masts twice the length of the deck, and carry bowsprits little short of the length of the keel. They have an absurd rule in racing that the main-sail shall be laced to the mast, and, blow high or blow low, that sail shall not be reduced. As many craft actually go better sometimes in a sea by a judicious reef or two, even if they can bear more canvas, this system makes racing in Bermuda chiefly a question of foolhardiness, rather than of judgment founded on a knowledge of what each yacht can do under given circumstances.

I saw a race in the Great Sound. It had been announced for a long time. The two semiannual yacht-races are great events, and my expectations were proportionately elevated, especially as the Bermuda Yacht Club is under the distinguished patronage of his Royal Highness the Duke of Edinburgh, and the vice patronage of the governor, four major-generals, two admirals, and a vice-admiral. It seemed, therefore, rather a coming down to find that, although every craft that could float was on hand, and almost every one in the town turned out to see the sport and picnic on the islands, there was to be nothing in the race measuring over ten tons, and only seven entries for the first and second races, while only five yachts actually competed, and two of these were but sixteen-feet length of keel. As usual, also, in Bermuda, there was so little punctuality shown in getting on the ground, or rather on the water, selected for the race, although there was a fresh and favorable breeze, that the second race had to be postponed.

PITTS BAY.

The quay of Hamilton looked very lively as party after party came down to the water, followed by negro attendants bearing baskets of provisions and suspicious-looking bottles, to embark in the jaunty boats waiting impatiently, with streamers flying and main-sails set, chafing like spirited steeds. One by one the boats received their live freight, the jibs were hoisted, and heeling over to a spanking breeze out of the west, they shot down the bay, their swelling sails gleaming snow-like on the purple sea as they threaded the tortuous channels among the islands, like a long procession of swans. The racing yachts really looked like things of life, newly scraped and varnished, spreading a cloud of new canvas, and burying their lee-rails as they started off with a bone in the mouth. They were, however, not sailed by the owners, but by negro skippers and crews, the owners looking on from other boats, which seemed to me very much like dancing in the Orient, the dancers being professionals hired for the occasion, while the host and his guests look on, instead of dancing themselves. After the racers had started, all the other boats landed their parties on the neighboring islands to dine. A more lovely day or a more charming scene could hardly be imagined. The sea-wind inspirited one like an elixir, and, as we sat under the trees taking our luncheon, listening to the musical play of the surf on the beach, and the breeze in the leaves overhead, and gazing on the reach of lovely azure sea beyond, and the sails dotting the distance, we did not in the least envy the lotos-eaters. When the racers were on the home-stretch to the stake-boat, every one turned out again to see them come in. The scene, as they gibed and rounded the goal, was very exciting; for there was a stiff breeze, the shifting ballast had to be carried over very rapidly, and the danger of capsizing with such a press of canvas was very considerable. The third yacht yielded to the sudden pressure, as she took the wind on the starboard quarter, and gracefully but rapidly lurching, filled and went down like lead, with six men on board. But one by one they bobbed up again like burnt corks, and, grappling with other boats, were soon out of danger of waves and sharks.

Many varieties of birds frequent the Bermudas, generally such as are found in our woods—the cat-bird, the robin, the bluebird, the scarlet tanager, and the brown thrush. The beautiful Virginia cardinal-bird is also very common. The variety and number of singing-birds is indeed one of the most pleasing characteristics of the island. But game-birds, or game of any sort, are too scarce for mention. The sport-loving Englishman finds this a hardship which he overcomes by artificial means. The reader may remember Hughes's description of the game of hare-and-hounds in his "School-days at Rugby." Something of this sort is the fashion in Bermuda, and is called a "paper-hunt." Hurdles, intended to be very formidable, are laid here and there in the otherwise smooth fields and slopes, and men are sent in advance to scatter a trail of bits of paper. The ladies and gentlemen privileged to belong to what may be called the Bermuda Hunt assemble at a concerted rendezvous, mounted on steeds which are certainly not excelling in the points of a thorough-bred, and then, hurry-skurry over hurdles and hedges, dash the hunters, following the paper trail, until they all finally meet at a selected spot, where a grand banquet is served to finish up the bloodless sport. Miss Lefroy, the daughter of the governor, is the Di Vernon of Bermuda.

The question of meat and drink is one which absorbs even more attention at the islands than it does elsewhere. People must have liquids;

INDIA-RUBBER-TREE.

but, as there are neither streams, wells, nor springs there, fresh water must be caught from the skies; and every roof in Bermuda is, therefore, enlisted into the service by being tiled with limestone and whitewashed, and the rain-water runs from them into ample cisterns. The houses are constructed of the soft limestone of the islands, which can be readily cut into blocks with a handsaw when first quarried, but hardens after a few weeks of exposure to the air. Beer is largely imported from England, and once a serious calamity seemed to overhang the devoted islands, when long head-winds kept back a cargo of malt liquors. Daily, with long faces, the care-worn Bermudians came down to the quay to inquire anxiously if the *Sarah Jane* had arrived yet. A while since, a universal remedy at the islands for all the ills that flesh is heir to was brandy and salt; but it is more than suspected that the salt too often came out of the sugar-bowl.

Bermuda potatoes have a wide reputation with us; but if the visitor to Bermuda wishes to eat them there, he must carry a barrel of them with him from New York, for they are all exported to that city and Philadelphia, and sold at high prices as early potatoes, while others are imported from New York at a lower price. Meat is also imported from our continent, and when the transport loaded with beeves arrives it is a novel sight to see her land them. Mooring opposite the cattle-yards some little distance from the shore, an inclined plank-way is placed on the deck reaching to the bulwarks. One by one the oxen are let out from the stalls on deck, or hoisted from the hold, and permitted to walk up this inclined plank. With immense satisfaction that gives almost a human expression to the bovine eye, the poor animal looks out once more on green fields, with curiosity toned by placid content, when suddenly a rope is tightened behind him so violently that, *nolens volens*, and without the slightest chance of resistance, he is hurled into the sea. When he comes up at last, almost suffocated with the salt-water he has swallowed, he is towed on shore by two men in a skiff. Some would call it an entertaining spectacle to see a couple of hundred oxen treated in this way. It would be very amusing if we could only be sure that they do not suffer, or that they are destined to some compensation for the torture which they endure in this world, under the operation of the inscrutable laws of the infinite wisdom.

I returned to New York in the *Bermuda* steamer. We encountered very heavy weather, and one morning four men were washed off the main-boom when reefing the main-sail. Almost by a miracle they all contrived to grasp hold of some rope or spar, and were saved. The steamer was loaded with tomatoes and onions; and as the skylights and companion-way had to be tightly closed, the smell of the onions became almost overpowering, and it was therefore with unwonted relief that I hailed the sight of land.

CHAPTER IX.

BELLEISLE-EN-MER.

BELLEISLE-EN-MER is so called, probably, in order to distinguish it from a village in the interior of Brittany, which, for some strange reason, is called Belleisle-en-Terre. Very few besides Frenchmen have heard of this little island, and fewer still know much about it, which is sufficient cause for giving a chapter to it here. It is an islet about ten miles long, off the coast of Brittany, and my attention was drawn to it when I was at Auray. Every one said to me that I ought by all means to visit Belleisle, and as this advice tallied exactly with my passion for islands, it required only about five minutes' deliberation to decide to go there.

A miniature steamer of forty tons plies daily between Auray and Belle-isle, winds and weather permitting, which is a very important proviso on that bleak, rock-bound, fog-hidden, and tempestuous coast, and, considering the extreme violence of the sea sometimes, especially in the winter season, which was exactly the time when I took my trip. It was a gray, sad morning as the boat left

FISH-WOMEN OF THE MORBIHAN.

the pier at Auray, which is surrounded by groups of exceedingly picturesque old buildings. We glided down the Auray River into the Sea of Morbihan, a large landlocked bay, which receives the broad estuaries of Auray and Vannes, and is studded with barren, but picturesque and legendary isles. The scenery on the river-banks pleased me more than any landscape I saw in Brittany. Oak woods, mossy and venerable, and untouched by the axe, gave a bit of antique forest-land quite unusual in Northern France. It was entertaining to see the fishing and market boats rowed and sailed by women, rough, stout, and rosy, sometimes a little touched with liquor, and proportionately jolly, and with only one man at most on board.

I may mention here that throughout Brittany, owing to the conscription, the exodus of young men to Paris, or other causes, the women may be seen in the majority everywhere, and in almost all departments of trade. What we call women's rights have been practically adopted in France for centuries, the constant wars having drained the supply of men. The result has been not so much what it is claimed it would be

CÆSAR'S TABLE, OR TABLE OF THE MERCHANTS, LOCMARIAQUER.

if women should obtain what some are pleased to call their rights—that is, the general refinement and improvement of society—but rather the reverse. I do not blame women for having to labor in the fields, or fishing and digging for oysters, or pursuing any honest means for gaining a livelihood; but I always feel sorry for them when they are forced to adopt vocations purely masculine, which destroy the natural refinement and beauty that are the peculiar traits of womanhood.

We passed by Locmariaquer, where some of the most stupendous remains of the Druids still exist, remarkable even in a country which abounds with them like Brittany. One of the largest of these is a dolmen called Cæsar's Table, or Dol-ar-Marc'hadourien, which means the Table of the Merchants in Celtic. After passing out of the Sea of Morbihan, we encountered a stiff sou'-west wind, but for some distance were protected by the long, narrow peninsular spit called Quiberon, and the adjoining islets of Honât and Hedic. Quiberon extends into the Atlantic like a breakwater, and is exposed to the full brunt of all the gales which beset that melancholy coast. It has acquired a terrible celebrity for the events of which it was the scene during the French Revolution. There, June 27th, 1795, an English fleet landed a corps of *émigrés* composed of the best blood of France, spared thus far by the guillotine. They were commanded by D'Hervilly, and latterly by Sombreuil, who was the brother of her who quaffed a goblet of human blood during the massacre of the 2d of September in order to save her father's life. Sombreuil arrived with re-enforcements toward the close of the ill-fated expedition, in season to take command, and sacrifice his life for a cause and an army already doomed. The *chouans*, or peasantry, flocked to the royal standard, and a force of ten or twelve thousand men was soon collected, which would have swelled to a large army but for the incompetency of D'Hervilly. Much precious time was wasted, and when the royalists were at last ready to move, Hoche, the ablest general of the Revolution, appeared, and, by a series of masterly movements, hemmed in the invading army, and forced them back on Quiberon, where they were caught as in a trap. The failure of concerted movements, caused partially by lack of confidence in the royalist general, resulted in the defeat of the *émigrés* near Fort Penthièvre, after heroic efforts. Treachery did the rest. Fort Penthièvre, the key to Quiberon, was given up by traitors. A heavy gale was blowing when Hoche made the final attack, which drove the ill-fated royalists to the extremity of the peninsula, and while some were able to escape to the English fleet, many perished, dashed against the rocks, in that fearful night when nature seemed to combine with man to increase the horrors of fratricidal war. Nothing was left but to surrender or fight to the last man. Sombreuil, who was in command after the fall of D'Hervilly and the dastardly flight of Puisaye, the next in command, advanced beyond the lines and held a parley with Hoche. A surrender was agreed upon.

Tallien, the member of the Assembly who had been detailed by the Government to be present to give his sanction to the proceedings at the expected surrender, then returned to Paris with General Hoche, after having given his acquiescence to counsels of mercy. But there the courage of both these men gave way in face of rumors concerning their lukewarmness or infidelity to the cause. With a perfidy which is but partially palliated by the state of affairs, when to be suspected was to be condemned, they both abandoned the prisoners of Quiberon to the tender mercies of the Jacobins, Tallien even descending so low as to suppress an appeal he had made in favor of mercy, and to urge the execution of the whole number. The Assembly sent orders that all over sixteen years of age should be shot. The executions were superintended by a tiger named Lamoine, and took place simultaneously at Vannes, Auray, and Quiberon. Every day at noon, for thirty days, the unfortunate captives were taken out by thirties and by forties, ranged facing a deep trench, and shot, and as they fell in the trench they were left, whether alive or dead, and the dogs were allowed to pick their bones. Many atrocities accompanied these wholesale executions. The number murdered is not certainly known, but it was not less than three thousand, and by some it has been placed much higher.

On getting abreast of the Teignouse Light, in the channel between the rocks on which it is perched, and the reefs which skirt the little islands

LE PALAIS, BELLEISLE.

of Houat and Hedic, we encountered a most tremendous and irregular sea, for which this spot is noted when the tide, undertow, and sea-waves conflict with each other. A very stiff breeze was blowing, and the little steamer, although buoyant, buried herself in a way astonishing to behold. They made sail on her as soon as possible to keep her steady, and stood away to the eastward, taking the sea more abeam, until we got under the lee of Belleisle, when we came to on our course, and arrived at Le Palais, the chief place, toward night. I stepped ashore with the proud consciousness of being, so far as I could learn, the first American traveller who ever landed on the island.

When I reached the Hôtel de France, I was charmed to find a neat, cheerful hostel, and that an excellent dinner was on the point of being served. The landlord, a man of fair average intelligence, but ignorant, like most Frenchmen, of any other country besides his own, gave me a cordial reception, and said to me,

"Are you an Englishman?"

"No," I replied, "I am an American."

"Ah, indeed! And how did you come from America? Did you come by rail?"

"No, the railroad is not yet built," I answered; "so I had to come by steamer."

He did not seem at all abashed by my reply, feeling probably, like many of his countrymen, that what he did not know was not worth knowing; in fact, he did not seem at all aware what an absurd question he had asked. Nor was I surprised that he should ask it, as it is the most common thing in the world to find astonishing ignorance among Europeans regarding America, even on the part of educated people.

Le Palais is situated on a long, narrow port, protected by a mole, and inaccessible at half tide; but the inner port is always provided by floodgates with water for vessels of moderate size. The entrance and the whole land side of the town are admirably fortified by massive walls and bastions, designed by Vauban. Ships of any size can ride in the roads in the heaviest weather. Le Palais is entirely a modern town, having been built chiefly during or since the time of Louis XIII. But the island has a history dating back to the earliest periods. It was originally covered with forests, and governed by the Druids, who left important monuments, most of which have been destroyed. At one time Belleisle was an appanage of Fouquet, the famous prime minister of Louis XIV.

The chief business of the island has always been the fishery of sardines. During the season, which is in summer, many fishermen from the main-land flock to the island, and near a thousand boats, large and small, are engaged in laying the nets. The fish are, for the most part, cured at Le Palais. Besides these boats, a number of extremely picturesque *chasses-marées*, or two-masted luggers, admirably effective, whether on the gray-green sea of the Bay of Biscay or in a marine painting, are owned at Belleisle, and are engaged all the year round in dragging for turbot and lobsters. The ship-yard at the head of the port, where these luggers are built, is attractively picturesque, under a hill, and shaded by a grove of lindens, leading to a public promenade.

Everything here is in miniature, and there is little of the very striking or impressive character belonging to many of the Atlantic isles. In a week one can see it all, and yet there is a certain nameless charm about it which is both novel and piquant, while the cliffs on the southern coast are often very wild and grand. The climate in winter and spring is milder even than that of the main-land of Brittany, besides being more free from fogs, more sunny, more bland. For an invalid nothing can be imagined more agreeable or soothing than some of the cheerful sunny days of charming little Belleisle during two or three seasons of the year. The prevalence of easterly or land winds and absence of shade in summer make it rather warmer than is generally the case on islands, although quite bearable in that latitude, while the fine beaches on the north-eastern coast afford excellent bathing-places, much resorted to by those from France whose means or tastes lead them to avoid Boulogne or Biarritz.

The island is divided into four parishes: Le Palais, Port Philippe, Bangor, and Locmaria. Each of the three country parishes has a nucleus where the parish church stands, and collects around it the peasantry on fête-days and Sundays. Besides this nucleus, the houses of each parish are scattered in little knots, or hamlets, of five to ten houses, a quarter to half a mile apart; I counted at one time fourteen within a radius of a mile and a half. Port Philippe alone numbers thirty-five of these miniature villages. At this place is a harbor with a mole and light-house. A beautiful valley continues across the island from this little port to Point Stervrose, a small peninsula, with a narrow bay on one side, called the Port Vieux Château, where the largest ships can ride at any tide, but evidently more impracticable in our day than in the time of the Roman conquest, owing, possibly, to a change in the prevailing winds. The plateau of this peninsula has from very early times been called the "Camp of the Romans." Before the invention of cannon it could afford an impregnable position for 5000 or 6000 men—say, a legion. On the sea side the cliffs fall vertically over 100 feet everywhere, while the land side is protected by a rampart and trench extending entirely across, perhaps 200 yards; it is excellently preserved, and there is little question of its Roman origin. The coast-line from Point des Paulins westward to Locmaria on the east is very impressive, generally perpendicular, presenting some very remarkable rocks and cliffs, and a notable *soufflense* near Vieux Château. The islanders graphically call the south-western shore, where the surf breaks all the year round on the cliffs, "La Mer Sauvage." Mr. Ruskin has somewhere inveighed very severely against such artists as have dared to present a precipice as actually vertical, or sometimes overhanging, asserting, in his usual dogmatical and vehement manner, that such cliffs never occur, and are impossible in nature. Those who know his style can easily imagine to what depths of infamy he consigns the artist who has been thus guilty of what this critic considers falsehood. Often have I thought of this passage in my wanderings, when I have seen instances which prove that in this case, as sometimes in others, Mr. Ruskin's statement must be taken as having more rhetoric than truth in it. With a perpendicular line for comparison, I have repeatedly proved that it is possible for cliffs to be both vertical and overhanging. At Belleisle I saw the head of a sea precipice overhanging its base in several places, notably at the Port Vieux Château.

In Bangor, near the edge of the cliffs, stands a light-house, soaring 165 feet from the ground and 302 feet above the sea, constructed in the most massive and careful manner, and lighted by a Fresnel-light of the first class. The lantern is finished on the interior with polished slabs of variegated marble. It is worth a visit to Belleisle to see this light-house, which is probably the finest in existence, unless we except, perhaps, the one at Cordouan, at the mouth of the Gironde, built by Henry IV., if I remember rightly. The French coast is everywhere very finely lighted.

The largest and most elegant homestead on the island is owned by M. Trochu, brother of General Trochu, whom he strongly resembles. They are both natives of Belleisle. The house stands a little out of the town, surrounded by a picturesque wood of evergreens. The courteous and hospitable proprietor is interested in agricultural progress, and devotes his energies to raising early market crops.

My rambles about this choice little isle were chiefly in a rather primitive two-wheeled carriage, accompanied by a chatty, good-natured driver, who seemed to know every one we met, and was able to call them by name. The peddler, with his leather leggings and pack of cloths and trinkets suited to the wants and tastes of the country women, seemed to be ubiquitous. I met him on the highway, or by the shore, or in the cabaret, and found him, like peddlers generally, garrulous, long-winded, and not likely to die for lack of cheek. When unfolding his goods to a bevy of rosy, black-eyed girls, his unlimited flow of words was often seasoned with flattering remarks and jokes just broad enough to make them blush and giggle in the most entertaining manner. I met him once when I stepped into an *auberge* in Bangor to snatch a bit of lunch. The landlady, a buxom widow, had two daughters, whose intense black eyes, raven tresses, and warm brunette complexions, tinged with red, would set an artist raving. They were all having a very merry time of it, bantering over the goods contained in the peddler's pack. He was rolling out his grandiloquent periods and fluent falsehoods with extraordinary volubility; but when I called for a bottle of wine and the necessary adjuncts of a "pennyworth of bread" and meat, he developed a sudden and remarkable interest in me. While the widow was spreading the table, he left his goods and came and sat himself down opposite me at the table.

"Monsieur, if I mistake not, is a traveller in our fair little island?"

"So it seems," I replied, distantly.

"An Englishman, perhaps, who, having the leisure and the means denied to so many, wisely devotes his intelligent observation to travel?"

PEASANT-GIRL, BELLEISLE.

I shrugged my shoulders, as much as to say, "Have it so if you like."

"Now, if you are looking about Belleisle, monsieur, allow me to assure you that I am your man if you wish a competent guide, who knows every legend, and every nook and cranny from one end to the other of the island."

"I am already provided with a guide. Jean, the driver, knows all I want to know about Belleisle, and he does not talk too much; he is un brave garçon."

Not abashed by this rebuff, he fetched a glass unasked, and tasted of my wine. "That is very fair for a vin ordinaire," he said. "I was afraid madame might not have given you her best wine."

Finding I could not very well get rid of a varlet who had made up his mind to lunch at my expense, without causing "a coldness in the meeting," and rather enjoying his impudence, and willing to please the hostess, who seemed to be kindly and polite, I called for another bottle of wine and a plate for the peddler, and soon the conversation became general and very entertaining, the widow and her daughters and my driver joining in the gossip, and a peasant or two who were going by, sitting on the doorstep or looking in at the window, and contributing their share to the palaver. I noticed in them all, as in the peasantry of Europe generally, simplicity and cunning, gross ignorance, and a quaint, crafty shrewdness clashing, and curiously contrasted. One thing I feel quite certain of, and that is, that country folk are not as such more honest than other people, although honesty and rusticity are often thought to be interchangeable terms.

But the day came which I had set to leave Belleisle-en-mer. I was called before dawn. It cost me a struggle to keep to my resolution, for it was storming furiously out of the south-west. The wind was howling over the roofs of the little town, and the rain was pelting the window-panes; nor did the prospect seem more cheerful as I went down to the quay in the dripping dimness of the early morning. Two steamers and several ships were lying in the roads, having run in there to ride out the storm under the lee of the island. Our little steamer was at the mouth of the port. It was not for her to consult winds and weather, when the wind at least was fair, for she carried the mails. We rowed out to her in a small boat, and were soon under way, and the little island was rapidly hidden from us in a dense curtain of gray mist. And now we had a race with the tide. The sea was running from the south-west, and, so long as the tide went with it, was comparatively regular, although high; but just so soon as the tide should turn, the sea would become tumultuous and dangerous, especially in the narrow passage by the Teignouse Light, where numerous reefs and islets tend to make the waves more broken. We crowded on all sail and steam, and passed the Teignouse a few minutes before the tide turned. The tremendous breakers, rolling just under our lee on the savage, bristling reefs, or dashing, high and ghostly, up the sides of the light-house, were terrible and sublime; but once inside of the rocky barrier, we found the water comparatively smooth, and glided rapidly toward Auray.

CHAPTER X.

PRINCE EDWARD ISLAND.

THE *Caroll* packet steamed away from Tea Wharf, Boston Harbor, one glorious noon-time in August, bound to Charlottetown, Prince Edward Island. Having paid ten dollars in gold to the International Steamship Company, the writer was graciously permitted to occupy a state-room in the after-cabin. Board, which was "fair to middling," was extra — a wise provision in favor of sea-sick passengers, but a doubtful economy in my case, as I never yet lost a meal at sea. Early on the second day we sighted and passed near to Sambro' Head, a cruel, iron-gray mass of granite off the entrance to Halifax, crowned by a light-house which is celebrated in naval annals. The port of Halifax is very spacious, being really the widening of an estuary, which, after winding some twenty miles, loses itself in the woods of Nova Scotia. This is a noble sheet of water, admirably situated for yachting, to which some attention is given by local yachtsmen. The view of the harbor from the fort behind the city is both extensive and beautiful; and from the opposite village of

SAMBRO' LIGHT — ENTRANCE TO HALIFAX HARBOR.

Dartmouth, Halifax presents an effective and pleasing picture, as seen in profile on a hill-side sloping to the water. But a close inspection of the city does not add to the visitor's interest in Halifax. It is one of those places which residents assure us improve on acquaintance; but it certainly does not leave a very favorable impression on the stranger. Judging from my own experience, he who has seen it once never wants to see it

ENTRANCE TO STRAIT OF CANSO.

again; and he whom a mysterious Providence has directed hither a second time, wonders what sin may have caused him twice to realize the meaning of the amiable exclamation, "Go to Halifax!"

In the afternoon we steamed out again, and headed eastward for Canso. Down the savage, reefy coast of Nova Scotia we scudded before a sou'-westerly gale, accompanied with lightning, and passed through the river-like strait of Canso on a fine breezy morning, that enabled us to see to best advantage a really beautiful sheet of water. We touched at Port Hawkesbury a few moments—a village of small houses, generally devoid of paint and destitute of verdure, and scattered about the naked hill-sides without order. Cape Porcupine, on the left, is a bold headland of considerable height. After passing this, we came out on the broad blue waters of the St. Lawrence, arriving at Pictou at noon-time of the third day out. A lovely bay is the bay of Pictou. As one enters, Prince Edward Island skirts the northern horizon, a low, pale line; nearer rises Pictou Isle, red-cliffed and wood-tufted. On the left is the spit lying in front of the port, sustaining a striped light-house. In the distance, gray and dreamy, a mile or two down the bay, are the spires of Pictou topping the slope of a range of hills. From the summit of these hills the traveller who climbs them is rewarded by one of the most beautiful and extensive water views on the continent: the broad bay of Pictou, invading the land with many steel-hued winding arms and creeks, and studded, in turn, with islets; the flashing surf on the bar; the green rolling land fading in a golden haze illimitably toward the setting sun; the dark-purple Gulf of St. Lawrence spreading as illimitably toward the east, with roseate cliffs skirting the offing like phantom islands — all contribute to compose a picture inexhaustible in its variety and the satisfying character of its attractions.

Picton is the seat of coal-mines, and large quantities of the mineral are exported. Here our steamer coaled for the trip. A tunnel of iron

HALIFAX, FROM THE CITADEL.

plates was fitted to the forward hatchway, and a platform was lowered over the hold. The cars were run out on this, and through a trap-door in the bottom of the car the coal was dropped into the vessel. In a few hours we had taken a hundred tons of coal on board, and about three in the morning left Picton for Charlottetown. At sunrise we lay in Hillsborough Bay in a dead calm. A light, low fog hovered on the water directly across the entrance to the port, and we were forced to wait for the sun to dispel it. We were surrounded by the red cliffs of Governor's, St. Peter's, and Prince Edward islands, mirrored on the glassy surface of the bay with absolute fidelity, or half lifted in the air by a partial mirage. Here and there a schooner lay idly over the quivering reflection of its own spars and sails. Overhead, the sky was cloudless azure, specked only by flocks of wild-fowl, and no sound disturbed the magical stillness of this peaceful scene but the far-reaching, quavering cry of the loon throbbing over the water.

On the clearing away of the fog we glided by the light-house on Rocky Point and the wreck which lies close thereby, and Charlottetown, with the broad estuaries that branch away from it for many miles in three directions, under the names of North, East, and West rivers, was revealed to us in the sheen of the morning sun. Charlottetown, in Queens County, the capital of the island, is a city of 9000 inhabitants, on a tongue of land between North and East rivers. The city was founded about 1765, on a regular plan. The streets are of great width, and are laid out at right angles to each other on parallel lines. The houses are generally small and unpretentious in their appearance, but neat; while in some parts of the city, along the esplanade and inland, past the Government buildings, dwellings of considerable taste and elegance, and embowered in shrubbery, are growing more numerous every year. The residence of the governor is a neat building, admirably situated at the head of a close-shaven lawn, which slopes down to the water, and flanked by the sighing pines of the primeval forest. The present occupant, Sir William Hodgson, is the first native governor placed over the island. He is a hale old gentleman of eighty-six—genial, courteous, and capable. The other Government offices are situated on Queen's Square, in the centre of the town, and surprise the visitor by the completeness and elegance of their construction and arrangement. They consist of a state-house, in which are included the halls for the Upper and Lower Houses of the Legislature, and other offices; of a court-house, just completed; and of a post-office which will compare favorably with many of the post-offices in our larger cities. Of the management of the postal department, I cannot speak in the same terms. I found the clerks at all the island offices unnecessarily inquisitive, and capable of incredible blunders. There is also inexcusable laxness in the forwarding and care of letters and mail-bags, insomuch that I never felt sure of receiving letters addressed to me, at least not for long after they were due, or that mine would reach their destination after I had posted them.

LIGHT-HOUSE.—ENTRANCE TO PICTOU PORT.

That this was not my own experience alone was evidenced by the frequent complaints against the department constantly appearing in the local papers. This defect in the administration of the Government supervision is one of serious and increasing importance, and demands immediate reform. It is said that, until within a very few years, such was the highhanded authority assumed by the self-styled upper classes of Prince Edward Island that it was by no means uncommon for letters to be seized

GOVERNMENT HOUSE, CHARLOTTETOWN.

and examined by them with no other right than that of the strongest. Under the modifying influences of the Dominion and increasing intercourse with the United States, many customs suggested by a colonial state of things are gradually passing away as obsolete; but the divisions of caste, so strong in England, and preserved with so much more intensity in all her colonies, are still maintained in Charlottetown with a rigor that, if it were not pernicious and prejudicial to true social progress, would be ridiculous; for whatever palliation there may be for it elsewhere, there is none in a place where the richest are but moderately well off, where intellectual culture is at a low ebb, where no men of such superior ability have yet arisen as to found even the only aristocracy for which there is any plausible excuse, the nobility of moral and mental supremacy.

The market, in Queen's Square, is a noteworthy building. On market-days—Wednesdays and Fridays—the farmers come in from the country with provisions of every sort: provender for cattle, fish from the rivers and the sea, homespun goods, game, confectionery, and the like. These are arranged in stalls in the interior, and the towns-people assemble to purchase a stock of food to keep them alive until the next market-day. Around the building wagons and carts are collected, loaded with hay or lobsters. It is quite a lively and interesting scene, deriving picturesqueness from the ruddy complexions and flaxen or coal-black tresses of the buxom Scotch and French country lassies, and the tawny, unkempt Indian squaws from Rocky Point.

The churches of Charlottetown have little to boast of. The ritualists have begun a chapel with a slant to the roof so excessively steep as to come within the term "loud." The zeal of the congregation is in excess of their funds, and the building is at present like a chapter to a serial story whose author is at a loss to furnish material for the next chapter. The Kirk are erecting a neat, commodious edifice to replace the present sanctuary, which, it is pleasant to report, is too small for their enlarged congregation. The Methodists have the handsomest church in the city, and are in a flourishing condition. The Roman Catholics worship in a large, barn-like structure of wood. They are active, and are spurred on to increased architectural efforts by the bishop, who, considering that appearances have great weight with a large portion of unreflecting mortals, has devoted his episcopal labors to the increase of the brick and mortar owned by the Church. A costly residence for the bishop of that communion and extensive buildings for convents and schools have also been erected recently at Tignish and Charlottetown, and one is to be reared soon at Souris. The population of the island is 94,021, of whom about 42,000 are in Queens County. The number of Roman Catholics is 40,765. The average increase in Protestants during the last seven years has been 18.8 per cent.; the increase in Roman Catholics has been 13.7 per cent. The present free-education act was passed in 1852; a Board of Education exists, and the entire cost of public instruction is defrayed out of the general revenue.

METHODIST CHURCH AND PART OF CHARLOTTETOWN—EAST RIVER IN THE DISTANCE.

A subject which has seriously agitated the island for nearly a century is the land question. The island, which is 140 miles in length and 34 miles wide, was discovered by Cabot, who called it St. John; and it still retains that name among the French to this day. As the English failed to take possession of it at the time of discovery, Verazain claimed both the discovery and possession of it for the French in 1523, and it was granted by them to the Sieur Daubet, who, with a company of adventurers, established several fishing stations there. When the Acadians emigrated from Nova Scotia, in 1713, many of them settled on the Isle St. Jean, and a garrison was stationed at Port la Joie, now Charlottetown. By the Treaty of Fontainebleau, in 1763, the island was ceded to Great Britain, and received its present name. The victorious Government immediately decreed a careful survey of the island, and various plans for settling and dividing the lands were proposed. Lord Egmont, then First Lord of the Admiralty, devised a Utopian scheme to this end, which was supported by powerful influences. It was based on the theory that the perils from the Indians and other foes were much more formidable than they actually were. His memorial prayed for a grant of the whole island, holding the same as a fief to the crown forever.

AVENUE LEADING TO GOVERNMENT HOUSE.

The two million acres, more or less, which the island was estimated to contain, were to be divided into fifty parts, called baronies or hundreds, forty of these to be granted to as many men with the title of Lords of Hundreds, owing feudal allegiance to him as Lord Paramount. These baronies were in turn to be subdivided into manors of two thousand acres each. Five hundred acres from each barony were to be set apart for a township. Fairs were to be held in each barony four times yearly, and market twice weekly. Many other feudal regulations relating to the judiciary, and the building of numerous castles and other matters, were included in this extraordinary memorial, which was intended to transfer to this side of the Atlantic a system better suited to the state of affairs in the times of King Alfred and William the Conqueror, on the supposition that the island was a place "where the settler can scarce straggle from his habitation five hundred yards, even in times of peace, without risk of being intercepted, scalped, and murdered;" the fact being that the Micmacs, never very numerous, were quite inoffensive, and it is doubtful if a white man ever lost his hair on the island, except in the natural way.

Lord Egmont's plan failed of acceptance; but another scheme for dividing the lands, which was adopted, was also open to grave objections, as proved by subsequent results. The island, with some reservations for fortifications, churches, and other public purposes, was divided into sixty-six lots. One lot was reserved for the crown; the remainder were in one day awarded by ballot to as many grantees, who had merited reward for military or political services. Quit-rents were reserved on all these lots, payable at the end of ten years, it being also stipulated that each township should be settled within that period by at least one person for every two hundred acres, and, failing fulfilment of the conditions by the grantees, the land to be forfeited. On a petition by the proprietors, the colony was granted a local government of its own; but the governor was appointed by the king. Captain Walter Patterson was the first governor, and the quit-rents were made payable at the end of twenty years.

The conditions accepted by the grantees, or those to whom they sold their rights and grants, were in many cases unfulfilled, and they thus lawfully escheated to the crown. The acts of Governor Patterson under the circumstances, the action of the home government, the long struggle, resulting in a drawn battle between all concerned, form an intricate story,

MARKET BUILDING, CHARLOTTETOWN.

too long for repetition in these pages. But long since the recall of Patterson, during the present generation, new difficulties have arisen, resembling the famous anti-rent wars of New York. Those whom the planters have invited or permitted to settle on their lands for certain rentals have, in many cases, claimed that the rents were in excess of the value of the lands, or that they had already paid enough to entitle them to hold the lands they occupy as freeholds. The problem was partially solved by the purchase of some of the territory under dispute by the colonial Government, and selling it over to the farmers under more favorable conditions. Since the island entered the Dominion, on the 1st of July, 1873, the question has again come up, and a royal commission was appointed for the appraisal and purchase of the large estates still remaining in the families of the original owners, the sum of $800,000 having been appropriated for this purpose by the Dominion as one of the conditions on which the island joined the confederation. Thus far the appraisals seem to have been fair and impartial, although, from the nature of the case, inevitably giving rise to considerable discontent and hardship in some instances. It is one of those questions on which much may be said for each side, and with regard to which the public good would appear to require an act of seeming bad faith on the part of the Government. The best good of the largest number is a right to be exercised with great caution, and the moral question involved in the consideration of the rights of the minority is not often regarded with sufficient attention by a ruling majority.

Since Prince Edward Island joined the Dominion, it has taken a fresh start in the march of improvement, and evidences of this are everywhere seen in its increasing commerce, the growing value of the fisheries, the many new buildings going up in Charlottetown and the environs, and the new railroad, measuring 167 miles in length, and completed in the year 1875. It is run on a gauge so narrow that only three persons can sit in the cars abreast, the seats being for one and for two persons alternately on each side of the car. The rolling stock was made on the island, and is very creditable. The car windows are not washed quite often enough, however. Ship-building is also in a very thriving condition. In the various ship-yards of Mount Stewart, Summerside, and Souris, I counted sixteen vessels going up, from seventy-five to twelve hundred tons in size, and I heard of others building at Fortune Bay and elsewhere at the same time. The new tonnage built for export for the fiscal year of 1874–'75 amounted to $632,440 in value. The total value of the exports during the same period was $1,940,901, of which lumber was $105,407; agricultural products, $787,070; live stock, $94,047; and fisheries, $308,637. Of the last item the United States took $272,620, and the total exports to the States of the products of the island for the year reached $365,352. It is worthy of mention that the fisheries of the island and the commerce in the same are chiefly in the hands of two enterprising Americans, Messrs. Churchill and Hall. For the same period the total value of the imports of Prince Edward Island amounted to $1,973,222, the balance of trade showing an increasing demand for foreign goods. It should be added that the foregoing data are given on a gold basis.

But one who has been in Charlottetown a week or two is not satisfied only with the evidences of insular prosperity furnished at the Government offices by the courteous and efficient servants of Her Majesty, or by the pleasant glimpses of farm, and river, and sea gained from window and roof. These very charming bits of nature only serve to tempt the visitor to sally forth, and, in carriage or boat or by rail, to view for himself the exquisite beauty of the island, and the proofs offered on every hand of its thriving condition, as well as the manifold attractions it offers to the tourist and invalid—in summer and fall, should be added with emphasis. In winter, which begins with November and lasts until May sometimes, Prince Edward offers special inducements to those who enjoy six months of snow, and unlimited opportunities for sitting by the fireside o' stormy nights and listening to the furious din of sleet and hail beating against the ringing panes. Northumberland Strait, which separates the island from the main-land, is frozen over from December to April, or, rather, it is filled with floating ice, which sometimes freezes together in a compact mass. Where the strait is but nine miles wide, the mail is carried across

CARRYING THE MAILS ACROSS NORTHUMBERLAND STRAIT IN WINTER.

every day on the ice, sometimes at great hazard. A boat on runners is used to carry the bags, serving, as the case may require, either as boat or sledge. The labor of going over the ice-hummocks is often excessively laborious. Travel is, of course, almost entirely stopped for the season. I heard of one lady who went across on the ice to attend by the bed of her dying son. But in summer the weather is moderate and equable—more equable than that of the adjacent continent. Vegetation springs forward

SCENE ON HUNTER RIVER.

rapidly after the winter has fairly passed away; and the verdure on the fields, including wild flowers, continues later than in the New England States. Fogs, which are common in the Gulf of St. Lawrence and on the Atlantic coast of Nova Scotia, are very rare on and around Prince Edward Island; and hay fever, that distressing complaint, avoidable only by change of locality, is unknown on that lovely isle.

Steamers ply up the East and West rivers, and an afternoon spent on each of these takes one through beautiful scenery, and gives a fair idea of the characteristic beauty of the island. Never over five hundred feet high, the landscape is rarely monotonous, for in the interior it is much broken and undulating, while it falls away toward the sea and the bays into gentle slopes which terminate in abrupt red cliffs fifty to seventy feet high. The brilliant tints—vivid orange and Indian red—of the new red sandstone, still in a formative state, harmonize admirably with the rich ultramarine of the water and the white trunks of the birch woods, or the emerald of the natural lawns which gradually slope to the water, in front of neat, cosy farm-houses, kept in good condition, and sheltered from the winter gales by clumps of primeval fir, pine, and spruce. Nowhere very striking, the scenery of these rivers is charmingly rural and picturesque, everywhere pleasing, and offering quiet little bits that the artistic eye might transfer effectively to canvas. On Rocky Point, opposite Charlottetown, is a settlement of Micmac Indians, who live by fishing, hunting, and barter. They are inoffensive and indolent. But the largest settlement of Micmacs, the only tribe now on the island, is at Lennox Island, in Richmond Bay, which is reserved for them, and there they hold their annual powwows. Their number is gradually decreasing, and does not now exceed three hundred and five. They are in charge of a special commissioner.

A delightful excursion may be made to Rustico from Charlottetown. Going by rail to Hunter River Station, one finds himself at once in a beautiful region among hills, and glens, and wooded streams. Thence a carriage carries the traveller over farming country resembling some of the most beautiful portions of old England, by way of Wheatley River to Rustico Bay. On the road I passed a country school-house at recess-

FISH-HOUSE AND STAGE, AND FISHING-BOATS, RUSTICO.

time. The children were playing in the road, but when they saw the carriage approaching they ranged themselves in a row, and as I went by the girls courtesied low, and the lads bowed in the most respectful manner.

It was a quaint and pleasing sight, and might be imitated by our school-children with advantage. Passing by the French settlement and Roman Catholic church at Rustico, we jogged along to the end of a peninsula that

FISHING-BOATS BEATING INTO RUSTICO HARBOR, BETWEEN THE BAR AND THE SPIT: BATHING-HOUSE IN THE FORE-GROUND.

is near the mouth of the bay. The last part of the way was over a kelp-strewn beach which is covered at high tide. There, on a bluff, I found the Rustico House, admirably situated on the edge of the spruce woods. Facing the bay, like a breakwater, lies a sand-spit tufted with long salt grass. Opposite the hotel is the entrance into the bay. The flashing rollers of the St. Lawrence Gulf break on a bar across the mouth, and between the bar and the shore is a narrow, shallow channel. Through this, twice daily during the season, the little fishing-schooners of the port pass out to fish for shore mackerel and herring. It is a very pretty sight to watch a fleet of these white-sailed fishermen dodging in and out about the bar. The fish are landed on stages built out over the water inside the port. Outside of the spit, on the sandy beach, there is excellent surf bathing, and bathing-houses are also furnished to visitors, who enjoy, in addition, good boating facilities; and, of course, capital sport is afforded for those who love the rod and the line. The mackerel fishing outside is exciting and novel, while the Hunter and Wheatley rivers in the immediate vicinity offer numerous attractions to sportsmen, especially in sea-trout fishing. The sea trout is a fish peculiar to the waters of Prince Edward Island, living in rivers or arms of the sea which, influenced by the tides, are alternately salt and fresh. It is the size of the lake trout, with silvery skin, and pink flesh like that of the salmon. It is caught with the fly, and is game for the best sportsmen. The season for this fish is chiefly during June and July, and East River, near Charlottetown, Dunk, Morell, Winter, Hunter, and Trout rivers are the streams in which it is most abundant. Salmon is also common in these streams; but shad is scarce. All the rivers of the island were restocked in 1876, and the Dominion fishing laws enforced. Lobsters are very abundant, and large canning factories have been established at Alberton and Souris. Duck, snipe, teal, plover, quail, and other game are sufficiently abundant to make hunting attractive, and dogs trained for sport are common. Wolves and deer, formerly plenty, are now all but extinct; but a few beaver and otter are still found: and in the tangled depths of the primeval forests, which still exist here and there, black bears are quite numerous, hibernating undisturbed in winter, and creeping forth sometimes in summer to try a fat slice out

FISHING PARTY.

of a tender young heifer. Oysters of the finest quality abound in the bays of Prince Edward Island. They are not as large as our largest, but they make up for size in flavor and lusciousness. Bedeque oysters from

Richmond Bay are already famous, and are shipped in large quantities to Great Britain and other parts of the Dominion.

The agricultural products of the island are of less relative importance than those of its waters, yet they are noteworthy. The woodlands, consisting of beech, birch, maple, spruce, and fir chiefly, are gradually thinning out, while the product of grain, and hay, and vegetables, especially potatoes, is increasing. Fruits are in a backward state, and must always remain more or less so, owing to the lateness of the summers. The apples are hard and sour at best. Apple-pies there must be made according to a receipt furnished by a sprightly young lady of the island: "Put in sugar as long as your conscience will allow; then shut your eyes and throw it in by handfuls." Rich pasture is seen everywhere, and the landscape is dotted in all directions with cattle and horses. As one rides along the roads and sees the beautiful horses and colts galloping or grazing on every farm, he is reminded of the Homeric period when Thessaly was famed for its steeds, and the heroes of the Trojan war were styled owners or tamers of fast horses.

Returning to Hunter River Station over the highest land on the island by the very charming road through New Glasgow, the tourist can take the cars to Souris, at the north-eastern end of the island. The railroad in this direction passes through a more level country, but more savage and melancholy, because less inhabited, and presenting waste moorlands abandoned to the rabbit, the grouse, and the bear. At Mount Stewart a branch of the road turns off to Georgetown, on Cardigan Bay, a sleepy, aristocratic, unenterprising town. Souris is quite the reverse. Originally a French settlement, and receiving its name from a swarm of field-mice which once invaded it, the little place, since the railroad has reached it, has sprung into a new existence. Houses are rising in every direction, and its ship-yards ring with the merry, tumultuous din of calkers' mallets. The port is exposed to southerly gales. Some years ago twenty-three schooners went ashore there in one day. But the Dominion has appropriated $60,000 to continue the breakwater across part of it, and this will give a fresh impetus to the prosperity of one of the most thriving towns I have seen in the Dominion. The neighborhood of Souris is very attractive. The drives are of the most pleasing character, the landscape quiet, home-like, and yet stimulating to the imagination. At Gowan Brae, the late residence of John MacGowan, Esq., is a hillock which bears unmistakable evidences of being artificial, and it is most probably the funeral mound of an Indian chief of other days.

Malpeque, or Richmond Bay, near the west end of Prince Edward

Island, is a large and beautiful sheet of water. The island is here but three miles wide, for Bedeque Bay makes a deep indentation on the southern shore. On the latter lies Summerside, a town which scarcely had an existence twenty years ago. It has not grown quite as rapidly as Chicago; but within five years it has greatly gained in commercial importance, and in that respect appears to be in advance of any other town on the island, except Charlottetown. The steamer which connects Prince Edward with the railroad on the main-land plies daily between Summerside and Shediac, thirty-five miles distant, on the opposite side of the strait. On each side the cars run out on a jetty to meet the boat. This, of course, adds greatly to the business activity of Summerside. In the bay, a mile from the town, and at the mouth of the Dunk River, is Indian Island, on which Mr. Holman, one of the enterprising men of Summerside, has erected a hotel called the Island Park Hotel. This islet is just one mile in circumference, and is overgrown with picturesque primeval woods. These have been very judiciously intersected by rural drives and walks. The building itself, which is after the American plan, faces the harbor and the town; and bath-houses, billiard-tables, bowling-alleys, and other decoys to attract the traveller in search of health or pleasure, are provided. At low tide the strait on the south side can be easily forded, and the drives on that part of Prince Edward Island are charming.

Of the people, so far as personal observation goes, I can speak favorably. Among them are many descendants of loyalists of our Revolution, who are generally more opposed to the United States than others. The general feeling toward our country is, however, apparently friendly, and, until quite recently, the desire for a reciprocity treaty was very strong. But underneath is, I am convinced, an undercurrent strongly English, notwithstanding that the people are really more like Yankees than Englishmen in their habits and language. There is just difference enough between their ships, their houses, their vehicles or agricultural tools, their papers and their colloquial diction, for a careful observer to note that he is not in the United States; but often the difference is nearly imperceptible. It is in their value of time that I discovered the greatest dissimilarity. The phrase "Time is money" is certainly not true on Prince Edward Island, however true it may be with us. No one is on hand when he should be. Everything is done with a leisure that would imply longevity rivalling that of Methuselah. Punctuality in the hours of meals at the hotels is a thing not dreamed of, resulting in great waste of time and cold food. Nor did I see any evidence anywhere or in the character of any one that indicated that the word has any meaning on Prince Edward Island. This taking life easy is a very delightful thing under some circumstances, but it will not do in this age and in the Western World, in the wholesale manner in which it is practised on that beautiful island, for those who desire to rise in the world. And herein seems to be partly the reason why the British Provinces of North America have not progressed as rapidly as their neighbors south of the Great Lakes.

Of the hospitality of the islanders I can speak in high terms; and to Mr. Campbell, author of a forth-coming history of the island, and many others, the writer is indebted for numerous acts of courtesy, which aided to render the pursuit of knowledge in the Gulf of St. Lawrence a fascinating pleasure excursion. I returned by way of Summerside, Shediac, and St. John, New Brunswick, arriving at the latter place in ten hours from the island. From St. John, Portland can be reached by rail or steamboat, and the tourist who does not like travelling by water can thus go to Prince Edward Island entirely by land, excepting the thirty-five miles in a strong boat across Northumberland Strait.

CHAPTER XI.

ISLES OF SHOALS.

ABOUT seven miles from the coast of New Hampshire lie the Isles of Shoals. Their situation is admirably planned with a view to harmonizing the sometimes conflicting wants of guests and landlords, of tourists and invalids, and of the proprietors of hotels. They seem to be a

SHAG AND MINGO ROCKS, DUCK ISLAND.

cluster of nuggets conveniently dropped off our coast where they can be turned into current coin by enterprising hotel-keepers, artists, poets, and scribblers of a thrifty turn.

Often had I passed by these islets, in all times and weathers, and welcomed the gleam of the friendly light on White Island, which warns the mariner to give them a wide berth in heavy weather. But the first time I ever landed there was on a yachting cruise a year or two ago. Once before had I started for the "Shoals" in my little sloop, the *Zephyr*, but we so loitered on the way, fascinated by the many curious attractive nooks along the coast, that when we at last stood across toward the islands we were overtaken by a gale of wind and forced to put into Newburyport, and sailed thence directly for home. But at length it was destined that I should reach the islands, having been invited to make one of a party in a small sloop-yacht, and assist in navigating her.

It was a charming morning in July. Various express wagons brought

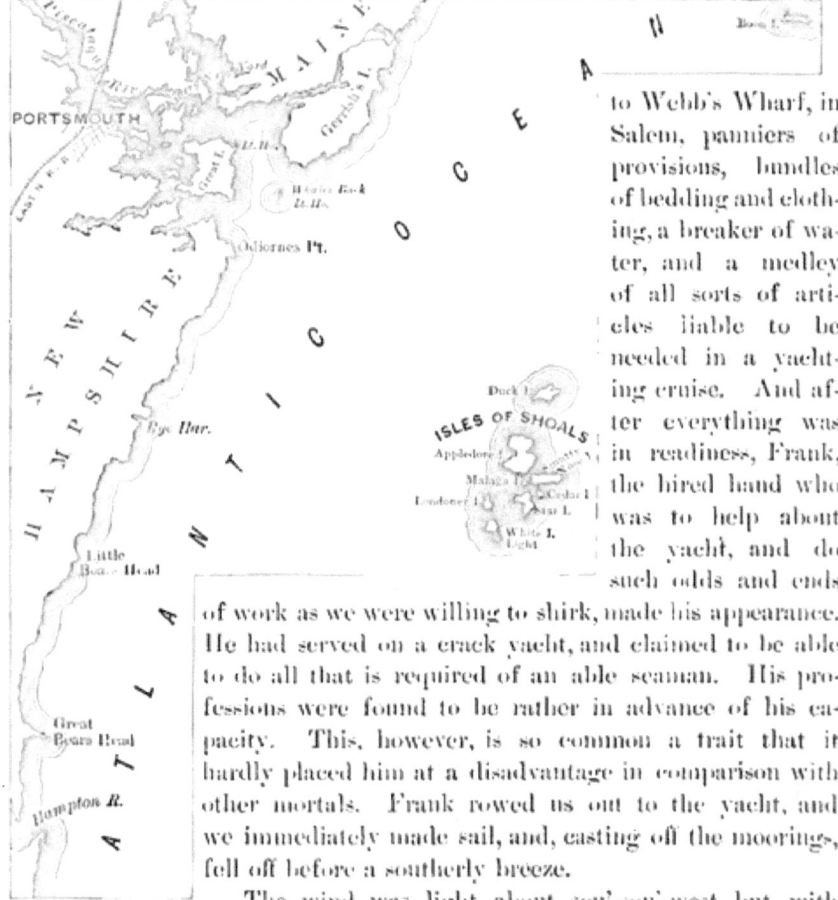

to Webb's Wharf, in Salem, panniers of provisions, bundles of bedding and clothing, a breaker of water, and a medley of all sorts of articles liable to be needed in a yachting cruise. And after everything was in readiness, Frank, the hired hand who was to help about the yacht, and do such odds and ends of work as we were willing to shirk, made his appearance. He had served on a crack yacht, and claimed to be able to do all that is required of an able seaman. His professions were found to be rather in advance of his capacity. This, however, is so common a trait that it hardly placed him at a disadvantage in comparison with other mortals. Frank rowed us out to the yacht, and we immediately made sail, and, casting off the moorings, fell off before a southerly breeze.

The wind was light, about sou'-sou'-west, but with the aid of the gaff-topsail and jib-topsail we fanned along slowly. After passing Kettle Cove the breeze began to freshen, and when we came abreast of Gloucester the "kites" were taken in. Standing out past Cape Ann and Milk Island, we sailed around Thatcher's Island, whose twin light-houses, towering one hundred and thirty feet, seem placed there like giant sentinels to guard the approach to the coast. The wind, as the day wore on, became very stiff, with quite a "lump of a sea;" but as the yacht was fairly "skooting" like a frightened steed, we hoped that we should be able to reach the Shoals before the wind should grow much stronger. The probability was that it was only a summer breeze, which might shift to the westward with a thunder squall, as it often does on the North Atlantic, and go down with the sun. If that proved to be the case, we could run for Portsmouth or Newburyport, for these shifts of the wind are generally well announced to the experienced eye.

When we were about half-way between Cape Ann and the Shoals, we all went below to take some refreshments, leaving Frank in charge of the helm. Nearly the whole of the centre-board was up, and the sloop steered a little wildly; but with a safe hand, there was no reason why she could not be left to his care alone, unless the wind should freshen. Notwithstanding the breeze, the day was warm, and it was wisely decided to prepare a mild brew suited to the occasion, and largely flavored with the pure juice of the lemon.

"Now, this is what I call jolly," said Varney, with enthusiasm, reclining on the cushion and affectionately regarding his glass.

"It reminds me," said Bent, "of what Mohammed, father of the late Sultan, used to say when he quaffed lemonade in the gilded halls of the Seraglio. Holding up his jewelled goblet, brimming with lemonade cooled with the snows of Olympus, he would exclaim, 'As I am the King of kings, so this is the king of drinks!'"

"Well, he knew what's good, that's evident," said Jim.

"It reminds me," said Varney, "of when I was in the army. It was a blistering hot day; we'd had a brush with the enemy the day before, and a rather lively time of it, as you may guess, for my horse was shot under me, and I had a ball through my hat that grazed my hair. Well, that's neither here nor there. What I was going to say was, that the colonel said to me, 'Varney, what do you say now to—'"

Varney did not finish his sentence, for on the instant the yacht, without the slightest warning, gave a tremendous lurch to starboard, lying over almost on her beam ends, the sea boiling furiously on deck, and pouring through the open dead-light of the trunk into the cuddy. Down went glasses, plates, and, in fact, everything movable in the cabin, in a broken and confused mess to leeward; while Varney, with outstretched arms, pitched headlong into Joe's stomach and nearly squeezed the breath out of his body, Jim plunging in turn, with all his huge size and weight, on the three others.

As soon as this crushed, mauled, and puffing pile of humanity could return to its individual parts, I scrambled to the companion-way, and, in the mildest terms that the circumstances would allow, demanded of Frank what he was trying to do with the yacht.

"Oh, nothin'; I just thought I'd let her jibe, that's all," he answered, sulkily.

WHALE'S-BACK LIGHT.

"You just thought you'd let her jibe, did you? You mean that you were not minding your business; that's what's the matter. Any lubber could tell you that to jibe a sloop like this under such canvas, in such a breeze and such a sea, is just the way to carry away your main-boom or capsize the sloop."

"If you think you can steer her any better, just you take the helm yourself!" Frank retorted, rising surlily and going forward. He was too conscious that it was sheer carelessness that had brought us so near a serious accident to say anything more in his defense.

The Isles of Shoals were now rising rapidly, blue and beautiful, in the north. Another hour brought us close to them, and, rounding a reef on which the sea was breaking with vast masses of flashing foam, we stood in for the cove between Appledore and Star Island, where a number of yachts were lying. We also would have gladly selected a berth and come to anchor, for it looked very inviting on the islands. But the sky to windward was now very threatening. A grim thunder-storm was rolling up in the west, and all the yachts at the "Shoals" were making sail to run for a safe harbor at Portsmouth. Our yacht was therefore brought around on the port tack, and headed in the same direction, with the wind just abeam. It was a lively sight as we approached Whale's-back Light, sail after sail converging toward the mouth of the Piscataqua, and the black, scowling mass of clouds from the westward, streaked with lightning and muttering deep thunders, overarching the whole sky. The tide and current, both running out against the southerly sea, made quite a high, abrupt, and irregular chop; but the yacht, still under whole main-sail and jib, behaved beautifully. She was fairly under the lee of the land when a blinding flash and a deafening peal broke overhead, while a pelting sheet of rain and a powerful squall of wind struck the fleet of yachts. We were just in time; letting go the halyards, we rounded to and dropped anchor in a snug cove, in the midst of a crowd of small craft, and then ran below to escape the deluge which poured down. In half an hour the squall had gone off to leeward, the setting sun came out brilliantly, and a noble rainbow spanned the gloom of the retreating storm.

On the following day the barometer foretold a gale of wind; and so, with the other yachts, we concluded to run farther up to Portsmouth, where we should find more to entertain us while waiting for good weather. The sloop easily stemmed the tortuous, eddying, rushing waters of the Piscataqua, and, successfully passing Pull-and-be-damned Point, where the currents and eddies are peculiarly trying to an unsanctified temper, we anchored in Portsmouth harbor, opposite the Navy-yard at Kittery.

Some sixty or seventy yachts, many of them among the finest craft afloat, were clustered there, and it was a very brilliant sight, a spectacle full of inexhaustible interest, to one who has a passion for naval architecture, and is smitten with the yachting fever—a passion which is born with a man, and leaves him only when he goes to a world where yachts and yachting are unknown. The ancient, storied, little city swarmed with yachtsmen in characteristic rig, and the coming race was a topic which afforded a common ground on which all could meet and talk until the wee sma' hours. To your true sailor, a love for ships and the sea affords a common bond of union not unlike that of freemasonry. The subject he has at heart is Sanscrit to the landsman, and the sea terms he uses are but unintelligible gibberish to all out of the guild.

The gale of wind lasted two days, and was followed by a mild westerly breeze, and as fair a summer's day as ever shone on New England's shore. Nearly one hundred and forty yachts, large and small, collected at the Shoals, many of them drawn thither to witness the race which came off during the day. Of course, the Islands were thronged with vis-

DUCK ISLAND, FROM APPLEDORE.

itors, and it was indeed a gala-day at sea. One may well say "at sea," speaking of this cluster of islets, for they are all so small, the effect to one who lives on them is quite that of being "at sea," in the ordinary sense of the term. They are all mere rocks, none of them rising exactly to the dignity of islands, but they are generally placed so near together that several of them give the impression of forming one island. Were they more isolated and distinct, their minute dimensions would be more apparent. Their total area is less than one square mile.

These islets were first discovered by Champlain, and later by Gosnold. Probably the first white man who visited them was Captain John Smith, who called them Smith's Isles, and so they appeared on the old charts for a while. Although much cannot be said in favor of the beauty of the name, it seems a pity that this indefatigable wanderer and explorer should not have had the satisfaction of attaching his name permanently on some one of the many spots he visited during his romantic career. The present name of the islands seems, in the absence of any definite information on the subject, to have been suggested by the clustering of so many rocks together, like a shoal or school of fish.

Appledore, the largest of the group, is perhaps two-thirds of a mile long. It is divided into two portions by a valley and two inlets. There is one tree on the isle, a venerable elm, attached to the piazza of the hotel. But although destitute of trees, like all the neighboring islets, Appledore is overgrown with the tangled meshes of blackberry, raspberry, and blueberry vines; and many richly tinted lichens clothe the rocks, while the sweet-scented bay breathes its fragrance on the summer air. The shores, as in all of these isles, are bare, composed of red granitic and trap rocks, beautifully harmonizing with the vivid hues of sea and sky on a clear day. Nature, however brilliant her colors, never allows her effects to be out of tone. Her magical atmosphere scumbles and glazes every object into unison with the landscape in which it appears. Although never very high, the cliffs of Appledore are often bold and uncompromising in the aspect which they present to the surges of easterly gales. South Gorge is a very striking bit of rock scenery, whose trap cliffs, eaten away by the battering surf of untold ages, actually overhang the sea.

LAIGHTON'S GRAVE.

North of Appledore is Duck Island, perhaps a mile distant. It is a low, uninhabited isle, surrounded by the Shag and Mingo rocks, and a net-work of reefs which seem laid to entrap unlucky vessels sailing by. Duck Island, Appledore, and the three adjoining islets belong to Maine, while the four southern isles form part of New Hampshire. This seems to be an absurd and unnecessary geographical division.

Appledore was the first to be settled, and until the close of the seventeenth century was occupied by a flourishing hamlet, including a church, and an academy of wide repute. But of all this nothing now remains but the site of a few houses and a cemetery. The old settlement had long passed away when the Hon. Henry B. Laighton, once a member of the Legislature of New Hampshire, became weary of the haunts of men, and disgusted with his race. He sought and obtained the office of keeper of the light-house on White Island. After remaining there six years, he removed to Appledore, and there built himself a house, where he remained until his death. For twenty-five years this modern Timon gazed on the

SOUTH-EAST END OF APPLEDORE, LOOKING SOUTH.

main-land, but a few miles off, but never stepped foot on it again. He is buried on a knoll a few yards from the hotel which gradually grew up under his charge. From offering a shelter to the occasional visitors who sometimes sought the islands, he gradually became the proprietor of a large and fashionable hotel, thronged by hundreds of guests. This hotel is now under the charge of his two sons. His daughter, Mrs. Celia Thaxter, the well-known poetess and historian of the Isles of Shoals, resides in a house adjoining the hotel.

Small as are these isles, they have already given rise to a literature of their own. Captain Smith and Cotton Mather have considerable to say about them in quaint and vigorous English. The town records of Gosport, on Star Island, are entertaining, both as local history and specimens of English undefiled by the learning of the schools. Mr. Jenness and Mr. Chadwick, the poet, have both written capital historical and descriptive sketches of the islands. The ballads founded on the romantic scenes that have occurred on the Isles of Shoals have given Mrs. Thaxter a well-known position as a writer of picturesque verse, and have done much to invest the Isles of Shoals with that delicate veil of romance and legend, that air of sentiment and human interest, which add an indescribable charm to the attractions of natural scenery. It is not so much the actual man as the memory of his existence in a rural or sea solitude which enhances the interest of a landscape.

Smutty Nose, now called Haley's Island, is next in size to Appledore, which it adjoins. Its first name was derived from a dark-hued ledge that still bears the name. The rocks called Malaga and Cedar Isles are close to it, and, together with the breakwater between Haley's and Cedar, form the harbor of the Shoals, a commodious and tolerably safe port, except in gales from south-west to north-west. Haley's was named after Mr. Samuel Haley, one of the former inhabitants, who found, even on this minute theatre of action, room for the development of the noble

HALEY'S DOCK AND HOMESTEAD.
(In the third house from the left the Wagner murder was committed.)

qualities which mark the upright and public-spirited citizen. He built windmills to grind the grain, which grew more liberally on Haley's Island than on the other isles, and laid out a rope-walk. He was also a sheep and cattle grazer on a somewhat limited territory. But his memory is chiefly to be cherished because of his solicitude for the storm-tossed sailor. For many years a light shone in his window at night to warn the passing

LEDGE OF ROCKS, HALEY'S ISLAND.

ship away from those cruel rocks. He also built the breakwater with the proceeds of three bars of silver which he found under a cliff, doubtless washed ashore from some hapless wreck, and he afterward added a wharf, which, although now in a dilapidated condition, affords a safe shelter for boats. Near his grave are the graves of the Spanish sailors of the ship *Sagunto*, which was wrecked in a winter snow-storm. Those who live on that bleak coast, and have often seen the terrible gloom and severity of a north-easterly storm in December, know well what must have been the sufferings of that ill-fated crew. Their nameless gravestones were erected by the sympathetic kindness of Mr. Haley, who now lies in turn at their side; for to all mankind there is a common lot. Whether at sea or in port, all are wrecked at last.

Haley's Island has acquired a melancholy celebrity within a few years by the awful tragedy of March, 1873. Louis Wagner had an idea that he should find money in the house of a Swedish family then living there. He rowed in the moonlight from Portsmouth, and stole unnoticed on the sleeping inmates, who suspected no danger in the quiet little isle, where only the seas seemed savage. Marie Christianson he murdered in the house. Annetta, her sister-in-law, who had escaped, half awake, through the window, was standing there, stupefied with horror, when he stealthily crept up behind her, and, with one blow of an axe, completed the bloody tragedy. Marie Hontvet, flying to the water, and waving her arms with frantic appeals, was seen by Ingebertsen, who flew to the rescue.

But Wagner escaped, and returned to Portsmouth. He rowed eighteen miles in a small boat between midnight and mid-day, murdered two women, and tried to slaughter a third, and earned for all his trouble only sixteen dollars and the rope by which he was hanged.

About the year 1700, Star Island became the seat of the capital of the Isles of Shoals, if we may so designate the village which arose there after the decay of the hamlet on Appledore. The new townlet was called Gosport, and fishing was carried on by the quarter of a thousand inhabitants with such brisk enterprise, that by 1750 ships came to its little harbor from the Mediterranean ports, to load salt fish for Lenten days in foreign lands. Like the first Greeks and Romans, the founders of Gosport were patterns of virtuous integrity, and the local code was severe, and was administered without regard to rank or sex. Joanne Ford received nine stripes, delivered with impartial vigor, in the presence of the municipal authorities in council assembled, because, as it is recorded, she had called the constable "horn-headed rogue, and cow-headed rogue." It is quite possible he had justly earned a right to these titles, and had not unlikely given her severe provocation; but the law and its officers must, of course, be above insult. The success and wealth which attended the fisheries of Gosport seem, however, to have had the same effect on the *jeunesse dorée* of this populous seaport that prosperity usually produces in all large cities.

SMUTTY NOSE.

Riotous living became too common; the Decalogue, as a guide for practice, fell into disuse; and, what seemed quite as bad at that time, the inhabitants were proved guilty of giving aid and comfort to the British and the Tories at the outbreak of the Revolution. They were ordered to leave the islands, and the census of Gosport fell suddenly from 284 to 44 individuals.

The proprietors of the large hotel which now occupies the former site of Gosport bought out the few remaining inhabitants, and their cottages

OLD CHURCH, STAR ISLAND.

have been turned into tenement houses, which are leased to visitors when their number is too large to find accommodation in the hotel. On the barren, broken, rock-strewn hill, the culminating point of Star Island, stands the old church of Gosport, a stone structure thirty-six feet by twenty-four on the outside; the walls are two feet thick. A vane crowns the steeple, which was considered elaborately ornamental and costly by those who put it there. It was also used as a storehouse for salt fish on week-days; sometimes it was left there during the hours of service.

Gosport was like other towns, large and small, in one respect. They all have their graveyards. Gosport is now one of the towns that have ceased to be, and the place where it stood knoweth it no more. But there, on the western side of Star Island, facing the setting sun, and washed by the moaning sea, its lonely graves remain to tell of those who, ages ago, lived and toiled, and loved, and suffered, and sinned, or triumphed over sin, on Star Island. And there they may yet repose for centuries to come, if the sacrilegious visitor, or the grasping money-seeker, does not invade that little cemetery, which seems to have been left in trust to the generations yet to be.

Near the eastern end of Star Island stands a monument erected to

Captain "John Smith, the Discoverer of these Isles," as the inscription runs. It was placed there by the islanders, and cannot be justly considered either classical or graceful in design. Three steps are surmounted by a pedestal that supports a triangular marble column, which is in turn crowned by three Turks' heads, or, rather, three heads were once there; but wind, weather, and vandalism have made sad work of two of them. Captain Smith was justly proud of his exploit in shearing off the heads of three Turks in his Hungary campaign, and this monument is a tribute to the lively satisfaction with which he regarded that pleasant incident in his varied career.

The annals of the Isles of Shoals include two other names of local note, the Rev. Mr. Tucke and the Rev. Mr. Brock, both good Puritans. Mather has somewhat to say of the latter, who seems to have been a strong, quaint, sincere, decided character, well adapted to deal with the weather-worn fishermen and broad-shouldered fish-wives of his insular parish. In the "Magnalia" we read that one of the fishermen, who had often ferried the people across the cove to church, lost his boat in a

CAPTAIN JOHN SMITH'S MONUMENT, STAR ISLAND.

storm. When he informed Mr. Brock of his misfortune, he suggested that an overruling Providence did not seem to have taken his pious services into sufficient consideration, or he would not have been repaid by the loss of his boat. "Go home contented, good sir," said Mr. Brock; "I'll mention it to the Lord. You may expect to find your boat to-morrow."

GORGE, STAR ISLAND.

The next day the boat floated to the surface, brought up by the fluke of a ship's anchor. The angel delegated to recover the boat may have gone down and fixed the point of the anchor-fluke inside of the gunwale, just

WHITE ISLAND LIGHT.

as they catch the mutton-fish in the West Indies, which is said to be so sluggish that divers descend and put the hook into its mouth.

The frequent wrecks on the Isles of Shoals have naturally caused more or less treasure to be washed up on the rocks. Even as early as the time of Captain Smith coins had begun to be found occasionally, sometimes in the mouths of fish; and the Indians told as exaggerated stories about it as the Indians farther south related to Columbus about the gold in the West

CLIFFS, WHITE ISLAND.

Indies. The following exquisite passage from the worthy captain's journal will match what he said about the spiders of Bermuda:

"And is it not a pretty sport to pull up twopence, sixpence, and twelvepence as fast as one can bate or veare a line? The salvages compare the store in the sea to the hairs upon their heads; and surely there is an incredible abundance of them upon the coast."

The scenery of Star Island—if one may apply that term to an islet scarce half a mile long—is broken and rugged, and rising at each end.

COVERED WALK AND LIGHT-HOUSE, WHITE ISLAND.

The most remarkable spot in its warm gray cliffs is the Gorge, formed by untold ages of breakers thundering against it before ever man appeared on the wild New England shore. The magnificent picture, entitled "The Breaking up of a Storm on Star Island," painted by Mr. M. F. H. de Haas, is a grand representation of the rocks of this island in a roaring northeaster.

Due east from Star Island, half a mile distant, is Londoner, a low, bare, uninhabited rock; the ruins of one small dwelling still remain upon it. At the north-western end lies a most cruel reef, over which the surf rolls with terrific grandeur.

A quarter of a mile south of Londoner is White Island. The northern part of it is called Seavey's Island, because a high tide sometimes overflows the neck which joins them. White Island proper is a grim, stubborn rock, sturdily breasting the Atlantic surges, and is by no means the least interesting of the group. Its rugged, abrupt, deeply furrowed form, and the perpendicular face it shows to the south, give to it a savage wildness and grandeur out of proportion with its actual dimensions. On the summit of its highest point, eighty feet above the water, stands the light-house which has been rendered famous by the graphic muse of Mrs. Thaxter, whose girlhood was spent on White Island. It is a solid stone structure, picturesquely harmonizing with the scene of which it is the central object. The lamp is a Fresnel light of the first class, and cost thirty thousand dollars. The violence of the sea when it bursts on White Island may be judged from the fact that the heavy covered walk, over a hundred feet long, was once washed completely away, and, rushing down the gorge, was crushed and swept out to sea.

The Isles of Shoals entirely merit the reputation they have acquired. In a space under six hundred acres they offer manifold attractions to the invalid, the artist, or the pleasure-seeker. A residence there possesses the tonic qualities of a sea-voyage; and as for hay fever, the unhappy victim who has vainly sought freedom from an affliction which has destroyed so many a fair summer's sport may calmly sit on the piazza at Appledore or Star Island, and, while he smokes his cigar with serene exultation, can laugh to scorn the relentless demon who watches on the opposite coast, unable to cross the sea, but waiting to seize him again when he once more leaves the Isles of Shoals.

LONDONER, FROM STAR ISLAND.

CHAPTER XII.

CAPE BRETON ISLAND.

IT was late in October that I arrived on the coast of Cape Breton, in the good bark *Ethan Allen*, from Madeira. The exceptionally favorable winds we had enjoyed now left us, and it was only after battling with heavy squalls, and gales, and adverse currents for several days, at the entrance of the Gulf of St. Lawrence, that we succeeded in making the port for which we were bound, and we were quite able after that to realize why insurance premiums are doubled after October sets in on all vessels sailing for that inhospitable coast. It took all day to beat up the long, narrow entrance to Sydney harbor, and we passed a steamer which had gone on the bar in a storm which had forced us to stand out to sea two days before. The prospect was rendered somewhat dismal by a crowd of damaged vessels which had been wholly or partially wrecked in the appalling hurricane of the previous August. Of Sydney little can be said that is inviting. The lay of the land is very much that of our own New England, but vegetation is more sparse, and the general appearance of the landscape more sad and sere. The bay is spacious and well protected, affording several excellent harbors for ordinary weather; but the town presents a singular blending of squalor and thrift, the former being the first feature to impress the stranger on landing. Shanties and groggeries, disreputable to a degree, abound, and lead one to think he has fallen on some maritime Laramie or Cheyenne; while to the westward new houses, glorying in the tawdriness of white paint, green shutters, and flimsy verandas, indicate that the place is not altogether going to the dogs. Coal is the chief stock in trade, and the supply is apparently inexhaustible; the whole island is, in fact, intersected by seams of the black mineral. The veins run under the harbor at Sydney, and are worked to a considerable depth. The population is, consequently, mining, combined with a large floating class of fishermen and seamen, ever ready to "splice the main-brace" and chuck the rosy girls of Cape Breton under the chin. It must be added that they do not always stop there, and street brawls, as may be easily imagined, are not uncommon. It is difficult to fancy any one lying awake o' nights sighing for Sydney.

This port has of late years become a great resort for our mackerel fishermen. It is not far from Cape North, one of the fishing-grounds, and the fish are also found toward the close of the season off the harbor. Seventy of our schooners made Sydney a rendezvous during the previous

FISHERMEN CRUISING.

summer, and it is indeed a stirring and beautiful spectacle to see the graceful little craft dodging up and down the long entrance to the harbor, or darting hither and thither in white groups, like sea-fowl, in search of schools of mackerel. So fascinated was I by the sight of these schooners, that, on finding my bark was not going to return to Boston, I at once decided to get passage in one of the schooners, if possible, in preference to the steamer. Fortune seemed to favor me. The skipper of the *Anna Maria* came aboard to bring us some fresh mackerel, and told us he was to start the following morning for home, going, for the first time, by way of the Bras d'Or, which I had long wished to see. He kindly offered me a bunk, and a share of grub for myself and dog. I jumped at the proposal, and early the next day took my traps aboard; we peaked the mainsail, tripped the anchor, and stood out to sea. The *Anna Maria* was twenty-four years old, forty-one tons burden, and had a small forecastle and a diminutive trunk-cabin aft; five men slept forward, and there were six of us, or seven, including a dog, in the cuddy. The deck was lumbered up with a quantity of fish-barrels and tubs, and the whole vessel was in an unmentionable state of dirtiness, resulting from twelve weeks of fishing.

There are two entrances to the remarkable sea-lake called the Bras d'Or, which separates Cape Breton Island into two nearly equal portions. Within a short time a canal, scarcely half a mile long, has been cut through the isthmus, permitting the passage of vessels of small burden. It is about sixty miles from the canal to the two eastern straits or entrances. The southern entrance is impassable except for steamers and boats. We struck for the northern passage, called the Great Bras d'Or, having a leading wind, without which it is impossible for a sailing vessel to pass in. The navigable channel is very narrow, the tide runs through it like a mill-race, and, for the first few miles, any vessel getting ashore there is exposed to the full sweep of easterly gales.

There were seven schooners in company with us, all keeping so closely together that the bowsprit of one would almost overhang the taffrail of the next one; sometimes one would becalm another, and thus shoot by. Finally, one of the schooners got slued aside on a bank, and had to be left behind, to get off as she could. Happily for the rest, a pilot appeared at this juncture in a dory, and agreed to pilot the little fleet. He carried us as far as Kelly's Cove, when, fog and twilight both coming on, we all dropped anchor, and the pilot proceeded to levy toll before leaving us for the night. He was a curious specimen of the genus *Bretoniensis*. Keeping his eyes always down, while he hung on to the side of the vessel, he rattled away with great volubility, which was evidently increased by the bad whiskey he had taken before coming off to us. "I don't care for any bluidy silver. A little bluidy pork or beef, a little bluidy salt or bluidy jigs, you don't want any more, my hearties, or any other bluidy thing will do me jist exactly as well. I should be only too glad to take such a pretty schooner through them narrows for nothink, but don't ye sees, we can't do nothink for nothink in Cape Breton no more than nowheres else? And that's the truth. That'll do, that'll do. I don't want ye to rob yourselves. Fish-bait? no, got enough of the bluidy thing. There's no need of my coming off to ye the mornin': all ye've got to do is jist to keep that p'int close aboard, and ye'll be all right; and remember them two spar-buoys on the starboard beam, and one on the port, and there ain't no other bluidy thing in the channel that the likes o' ye need to be afeard of; and I'm

TALL FISHING.

very much obleeged to ye, gintlemen, and I wish ye a pleasant v'yage;" and off he went to repeat the farce at the next schooner.

We found ourselves anchored for the night in Kelly's Cove, under Kelly's Mountain, the highest land on the Bras d'Or. It is an isolated ridge, which I estimated to be about twelve hundred feet high, but so bold as to resemble a wall, and give an impression of greater height. Evidences of the tremendous hurricane of the previous September were everywhere visible. The wind had felled the largest forest trees in ranks mile after mile, or, where the squalls had been most violent, had cut swaths through the woods as the scythe of the mower lays the grass. This was the case all through the Bras d'Or. Many houses and barns were felled or injured; at Arichat sixty houses were blown down. Vessels were everywhere destroyed; all through the trip we came across wrecks on shore.

The boat was lowered, and skipper and I went ashore on a foraging expedition among the farm-houses. We found the people generally were "Heelanders," as they called themselves, among whom Gaelic is still the vernacular, some actually being unable to converse in English. They were mostly Roman Catholics. We finally brought up at a small house, where we spent a couple of hours chatting before an old-fashioned ingleside, over whose bright blaze the kettle was singing. A dance at a farm-house farther on was proposed, and skipper offered to bring off the schooner's fiddler to stimulate the heels and quicken the hearts of the lads and lassies; but, owing to the lateness of the hour, the plan unfortunately fell through. A brace of geese and a pail of milk were the results of our expedition. It was so dark that the buxom hostess snatched a brand from the hearth, and gave it to us by way of lantern, and we thus reached the boat without spilling the milk.

We were again under way the next morning, but the wind was so light we made but little progress. The good weather was improved to clear the deck and clean the vessel. We passed some plaster-cliffs, which furnish material for many of the best ceilings in our cities, and add a striking feature to the scenery. We also had a fine view up the Little Bras d'Or, and left the shire town of Baddeck on our right, at the bottom of a deep bay. At night we again anchored, at Grand Narrows, and skipper and I repeated our foraging expedition. We were lucky enough to come across some very nice people, bearing the famous names of McNiel and McDonald. The next morning, just after we hove up anchor, a boat overtook us, bringing a supply of milk and eggs from our friends of the previous evening, which very materially added to the slender stock of pork, beans, and molasses, that constituted the commissariat of the *Anno Maria*. But generally the people are a pretty rough set, with a decided talent for brawling and drinking. When we were going aboard at night, we came across three sturdy fellows, well braced with gin, and altogether too willing to fire off the guns they carried to make them pleasant companions, especially as they seemed inclined to pick a quarrel. But evading them in the dark, we were the first to reach the boat, beached under cover of some rushes, and shoved off for the schooner.

After leaving Grand Narrows, the passage widened into a broad lake some twenty miles across at the widest, deeply indented with bays, and studded with large islands. Fish and game abound there. While we were becalmed, signs of mackerel appeared, and all hands got out their lines, and each man took his allotted place by the side of the vessel; but, after a few minutes of spirited sport, the fish left us, and a breeze sprung

RIDING OUT A NORTH-EASTER.

up and fanned us along through the afternoon. To the sportsman, few places offer greater attractions than the Bras d'Or, in summer and early autumn. At sundown the fleet was becalmed in the middle of the lake, which was glowing and magnificent beyond description, under the splendor of a sunset of extraordinary beauty and variety of tint and hue. As I gazed, entranced, on that spectacle, I did not wonder that they called that sea strait, so rarely combining lake and river, the Bras d'Or. Golden was the autumnal glory of its shores, golden were its waters, and golden the tranquil sky which overhung and imparted to it half its wealth of beauty.

The shooting-stars and the night-breeze came together, and we watch-

THE MICMAC INDIANS.

ed the one and glided gently along before the other, until at midnight we again neared dangerous navigation, and came to an anchor. On the following day we passed a noted Indian settlement, where there is a large church with some wigwams. The Indians of this region assemble in spring and summer on their island, and attempt to keep up the dances and other ceremonies peculiar to their ancestors.

The scenery now became exceedingly romantic and beautiful, often resembling the Thousand Islands, and the region is so little inhabited as scarcely to seem a country that has been settled for two hundred years. Islands of all sizes, sometimes mere knolls tufted with birches and pines, divide the lake into numerous winding channels for a long distance. The ship-channel is often so narrow and tortuous that it was with great difficulty that even our short schooners, capable of turning within their own lengths, could be worked without going ashore. One of them here ran her nose into a mud-bank, on which we also touched, and so firmly that she lay there several days.

Just before evening the *Anna Maria*, heading the fleet, reached the canal at St. Peter's. In an hour she was again on the Atlantic; but so difficult is the way out into the harbor, that we grounded on a rock in a dangerous situation.

While we were getting her off, a party of Indians landed close under our lee, and in a very few minutes they had put up several bark wigwams, and the dusky shades of evening were rendered picturesque by the smoky gleams of their fires. The little cove where we were lying, the forests on one side and the wigwams and strange forms moving before the light and reflected in the water; the last lingering rays of sunset on the other side, vividly outlining the rakish spars of the pinks rocking in the port; the splash and swing of warps in the water; the quick movement of boats here and there, with phosphorescent drops twinkling on the oars; the shadow of the spars, and the tread of feet on the deck, as schooner after schooner warped past us in the starry gloom—presented a singular and effective scene.

Early the next morning we worked out of St. Peter's by Madame Isl-

ONE OF THE FISHERMAN'S PERILS.

and. The threatening character of the weather inclined us to go into Arichat, but a land-breeze sprung up after sunset. All night we flew before it under press of sail, and by next morning had run one hundred and forty miles, and were abreast of Halifax. On the following day our good weather came to an end. A gale was coming on, and, after pounding against a heavy sea several hours and starting a leak, we were just able to work into Shelburne, where we lay three days. Shelburne possesses the finest harbor in Nova Scotia. What is also in its favor is, that it is easy of access, and is often made a harbor of refuge. The settlement is, however, but a wretched makeshift for a town, like many places in the Eastern provinces, but has considerable ship-building, which gives it some appearance of thrift. It also abounds with herring, which are eaten in such quantities by the Bluenoses, that it is said of them they cannot pull off their shirts in spring because of the fish-bones sticking through their skin! The weather was still dubious when we put to sea in company with fifteen sail, all bound to the westward, but we hoped the easterly wind would hold to take us across the Bay of Fundy, the worst bit of navigation, owing to its fogs, rips, reefs, tides, and currents, to be found anywhere on the coast of North America. But, in fact, nowhere does a close inspection of the ledges along the Nova Scotia shore inspire one with agreeable sensations, nor are such names as Ironbound or Ragged Harbor pleasingly suggestive. I never can pass that forbidding coast without thinking of some grim monster showing his teeth, ready to crunch the bones of hapless victims. The vigor with which the new Dominion has assumed the reins of government is nowhere more evident than in the increased attention bestowed on light-houses, which have hitherto been infamously scarce, considering the character of the coast, and have been badly kept and lighted.

During the day we passed a large ship, high and dry on a reef, going to pieces. The wind freshened at night, and we stood across the Bay of Fundy in fine style. The next morning it was thick and nasty, blowing a gale of wind, with a heavy following sea. Wing and wing we "kihooted" before it under a press of sail such as only our fishermen indulge in. The least carelessness of the steersman might have sent us to the bottom. "A man must have his life insured who sails on the *Anna Maria* to-day," said one to me. At noon a violent squall obliged us to take in sail. With some difficulty, we took in the mainsail, and, jibing the foresail, brought the lively little craft around just in time to get control of her, laying her half under water as she came up to the wind. We ran till night under close-reefed foresail, and then hove to near Cashe's Ledge till morning. Then the wind shifted into south-west, and finally came howling out of the north-west, and, as the skipper forcibly expressed it, "it everlastingly screeched." We had but one suit of sails; they were old and worn, and the foresail split and gave us some trouble; our stock of provisions was running low, and there was some reason to fear we should be blown to the eastward again. Generally, our fishermen fare very well, frequently laying in fresh provisions at the ports they visit. One of the crew is usually chosen as cook, and receives, like the captain, a double share of the catch. But the staple article of diet is pork and beans—a very savory dish if properly cooked. This gave rise to the story of a fishing-schooner, which was sighted flying a flag of distress by a ship standing out to sea. They ran down, and hailed her. The skipper replied that the schooner was still one day's sail from port, and had only one barrel of beans on board.

During all these days the spinning of yarns went on without intermission fore and aft, and I gained new ideas of the constant and almost incredible perils to which our fishermen are exposed, especially on the Georges and off the Magdalen Islands. Many a hair-breadth escape from being run down in the fog, or from foundering, was narrated. One of our crew had been on board a schooner which turned completely bottom up, and righted on the other side, when riding out a gale on the Georges Shoals. He was on the lookout, and, seeing an immense wave coming, pulled the slide over the companion-way and rushed below. Almost impossible as it seems, it is recorded as a true story in the fishing annals of Cape Ann. Euchre and checkers, which were played on a board carved on the top of a locker, and the whittling of knick-knacks, went on along with the spinning of yarns. It was interesting to see how, through it all, these hardy fellows managed to retain characteristics purely human; for example, the habit of croaking, and of finding fault with those on whom the responsibility devolved. Did the skipper carry sail hard, they said he did not know when to take it in; did he prudently seek to spare the only suit of canvas we had, or avoid running on the land in the fog, they said, "The worst fault a master of a ship can have is to take sail in too soon." Like unwhipped school-boys, they thought they knew everything, and, like sailors in general, exercised little foresight or prevision for contingencies. Of course, on a vessel where all sailed on shares, any regular discipline was out of the question, the authority of the skipper being nearly nominal, the man making it rather than receiving it from the office.

Our skipper was a man of the most imperturbable good-humor, but a good seaman, shrewdly adapting himself to the unruly spirits he had to deal with, and generally exercising control without appearing to do so. "Come on, bullies, let's take a turn on the main sheet," was the usual form of an order; or, "Keep her off a little mite, Uncle Mike!"

The watch usually consisted of two men, one at the wheel, and the other acting as lookout, and oscillating between the stove in the cabin and the bows, with a strong gravitation toward the former. The clock forward was half an hour ahead of the one aft; I don't know whether the fact was generally known, but I think it was known to some: I observed that some of the watches were shorter than others.

One night, two of the leading faultfinders were directed to tack ship in their watch, there being a heavy sea running at the time. Three times these self-sufficient fellows tried to bring the schooner about; three times they failed, mouthing enormous imprecations, and with such frequent mention of hell that I fancied I could smell brimstone. The skipper, meantime, quietly lay in his bunk, and enjoyed the discomfiture of his defamers. At last he put his head up the companion-way and said, "Your jib is eased off too much; haul down the jib, and she'll come around all right!" They obeyed, and the schooner was off on the other tack at once. He said nothing more, but an hour after went on deck himself, and tacked ship with the ease of a man who knows what he is about. The men could say not a word.

TAKING A SPELL.

Another curious trait among sailors, especially noticeable among those so little under discipline as our fishermen, is the way they act in emergencies. The vessel, perhaps, is threatened by a heavy squall, and sail must be taken off at once, or the gravest consequences may ensue in a moment. One would suppose, therefore, that when the lives of all on board, including the crew themselves, are imperilled, and the quick orders of the captain summon all hands on deck without delay, they would need no further urging. Not a bit of it. The first thing they do is to grumble. "D-- the weather! what the devil does he want to hurry a fellow out of his bunk for?" Then they will not stir till they have arranged their oil-suit, as if it were a dress suit for a ball; after that, some of them must fill and light their pipes! If the captain puts his head down and repeats the order, "Come out of there, and don't be all day about it!" they mutter, "D—d if I will before I'm ready!" This does not result from superior courage or recklessness so much as from a species of pigheadedness or habit; for the same men will be as much appalled as other men by danger when they fairly realize it, or if it be in a form to which they are unaccustomed.

We managed, in the teeth of a violent wind, to beat up as far as Cape Elizabeth, where we found the water a little smoother. But we should have kept on and made a harbor in the Sheepscot River, if the wind had not moderated after sunset, so as to enable us to work down to the Isles of Shoals, which we passed at daybreak. As we neared the destined port, razors and blacking-brushes were brought out of hidden corners, and a general burnishing followed. Those who had "boiled shirts" actually went through a transformation, when they put them on in exchange for their heavy blue or red woollen shirts. It took us the rest of the day to beat into Gloucester under a press of canvas, with a foot of water in our lee scuppers, and carrying away the maintopmast-staysail as we came abreast of Norman's Woe.

The good old *Anna Maria* laid her bones on Newburyport bar two years after, in 1877, and poor Captain Jewett has met the fisherman's fate on the Grand Banks.

CHAPTER XIII.

THE ISLE OF WIGHT.

AN evening in an enchanted region, gliding over an enchanted sea toward an enchanted isle, was the fair night when first I approached the far-famed isle of beauty which lies on the South of England's shore. The stately line of battle-ships of other days, their long tiers of port-holes lit up and reflected in the still waters of Portsmouth, lent magic to the scene. Out of the starry gloom beyond, ghost-like yachts, one by one,

silently stole by, fanned by the low sea-wind. The strains of martial music floated out to sea, now rising, now falling, in harmonious cadences, and, as we glided across Spithead strait, a calcium-light suddenly burst at intervals across the night, like a noiseless explosion of a powder-magazine, revealing the secrets of the darkness, and as suddenly concealing them again. The lights of the island we were approaching constantly grew more and more distinct, wavering on the glassy floor of the still water, and the dark outlines of woods and hills became less spectral and mysterious, until, almost before we were aware, we were making fast to a pier, and stepping ashore on the Isle of Wight.

By the Romans the island was called "Vectis," by the Saxons "Wihtea," by the Celts "Gwyth," which means channel; and thus reduced to its original sense, the name literally means the Channel Island. By seamen it is called "the Wight." Well, after much wandering among other isles of the sea, I had at last arrived at "the Wight," and fortunately, as I found when daylight came, had been first introduced to it at Ryde, which is a fitting vestibule through which to enter the island. In former years, before the building of the pier, Ryde was accessible from the sea scarce twelve hours out of the twenty-four, owing to the long stretch of

RYDE.

muddy flats which lie more or less exposed at low water. Passengers often had to be landed, like poor Fielding, the inimitable author of "Tom Jones," on the backs of sailors. Later, a cart was substituted; and, finally, a pier was built. This, proving too short, was eventually carried out into deep water to a distance of half a mile. There it terminates in a covered platform, from which an extensive and satisfying prospect is obtained of the northern coast of the island, from Seaview Point to Cowes, of which the central object is Ryde itself, reposing on a gentle slope embowered in civilized masses of patrician verdure. To the northward and eastward lie the shores of the main-land, and the ships and roofs of Portsmouth. Around this pier-end the prettiest, sauciest, most bewitching of yachts collect during the season, so in love with their own beauty that of a calm, pleasant morning they, swan-like, gaze at themselves reflected in the burnished mirror of the bay. There, too, full-cheeked musicians blow magical strains beneath the silent moon, and the fairest dames and damsels, and the most high-mettled aristocrats of Rotten Row, in the jauntiest of summer or yachting rigs, collect in enraptured pairs to repeat the old story which Jessica and Lorenzo rehearsed in Venice ages ago. Amidst this romantic throng may be detected sometimes the thoroughly prosaic form of your genuine cockney, and the stocky, broad-collared, and wide-trousered figure of an old tarpaulin gazing knowingly to seaward, or elbowing the crowd with the rolling movement of a heavy-laden ship running before a gale of wind.

Ryde Pier is one of the rarest spots in Old England. Ryde town is also a charming place of residence, presenting lanes hidden in shrubbery and flowers, and cosy, often elegant, cottages at every turn. It also possesses a yacht-club building and an art academy. A certain rustic, primitive simplicity seemed to me, however, to cling to it still when I heard the town-crier going about the streets in a dog-cart, ringing a bell, and shouting, "A large and valuable collection of water-color paintings will be sold to-day, at No. —— —— Street." But Ryde is fast losing its insular rusticity, and is, I fear, degenerating more and more into a vast congeries of boarding-houses and hotels, with placards in every window, and fees from a ha'penny upward, payable to every one of whom you may happen to ask a simple question. There is a museum at Ryde worth visiting. It contains local antiquities and relics, including the ossuary remains of the monks and founders of Quarr Abbey, which once stood a couple of miles west of Ryde. It was a wealthy corporation, owning lands in most parts of the island. The inmates waxed fat on the revenues, were noted for their sharp practices, and for disturbing the domestic peace of the neighborhood by a lax interpretation of the seventh commandment. At any rate, the reputation of the abbey was not savory. Founded by Redvers de Baldwin, lord of the isle in 1132, it was abolished by Henry VIII. Little now remains to mark the site of Quarr Abbey; but stone coffins have from time to time been revealed, and the spot is still haunted by certain characteristic legends. It is claimed that a wood near the abbey, called Eleanor's Grove, after the queen of Henry II., was often visited by her during her imprisonment at Quarr. After her death she was buried there in a coffin of gold, which is guarded from the cupidity of an unregenerate generation by the potent spell of a magician.

The Isle of Wight is divided into two grand geological divisions—the tertiary eocene, and the cretaceous, or chalk, formation. The former includes the northern half of the island, the latter the southern half. On the southern coast are also two narrow, isolated strips of wealden strata. In point of scenery, the southern portion is by far the grandest and most various in its aspects, and toward that, therefore, I first directed my steps on leaving Ryde. In former years, the stage-coach was the only and the all-sufficient public conveyance for the traveller who did not care to see this fair isle on foot. But the vast and constantly increasing number of tourists who overrun the island has caused the construction of two miniature railways, soon to be succeeded by others, until ultimately an iron network shall weave its meshes over the idyllic vales of Wight. But the pedestrian will always find the old charming lanes and stiles, and prefer thus to see some of the choicest nooks of the island. It is a pleasant morning stroll to Brading, passing by the spot where were laid the bodies raised from the *Royal George*.

GRAVE OF THE YOUNG COTTAGER.

Midway between Portsmouth and the Isle of Wight, not a century ago, the brave old line-of-battle ship heeled over in a breeze, and went down at her anchorage with twice five hundred souls on board. Kempenfelt, the admiral, was lost, with his flag-ship; and Cowper gave immortality to this tragedy of the sea in a few famous lines. A buoy now marks the spot where the *Royal George* lies—the sands of the sea choking up her port-holes, and the monsters of the deep toying with her mighty skeleton.

Brading, a quaint little town, lies at the head of Brading Haven, a lake-like cove, embayed among lovely hills and groves—a most charming scene, except at low water. A stone-cased well in the centre of the port shows that it was once dry land. To the outside world Brading is known chiefly as the home of little Jane, the Young Cottager, whose simple and pious life was described by the Rev. Legh Richmond. Her rustic cottage still stands in a green lane at the bottom of Brading Down, and her grave, in the south-east corner of the village church-yard, has been visited by scores of thousands. Legh Richmond, who was pastor here in the early part of this century, not only achieved a wide fame by his pathetic rural narratives, entitled "The Annals of the Poor," but also wrought an influence for good hardly equalled by any other religious writer since the time of John Bunyan.

But Brading has other points of interest. The church, which has recently been most carefully restored, is undoubtedly of very ancient date. It is known that a church existed here as early as 704, in which Bishop

LEGH RICHMOND.

Wilfrid baptized the first Christian convert of the island; and there seems nothing to disprove the fact that the present building either contains certain portions of that primitive chapel, or was erected on its site at a remote period. Half-way down the long street of Brading is an open space where bull-baiting was formerly enjoyed by the island swains; the ring to which the bull was made fast is still fixed in the centre of the spot. A well-worn pair of stocks are yet shown in front of the venerable town-hall, and some of the diamond-casemented cottages exhibit the rings to which tapestries were suspended on festal days of yore.

South of Brading, on the Ventnor Railway, is Sandown, which gives its name to the most beautiful bay in the whole island. As a residence, it is chiefly attractive for its sands, admirably adapted for bathing. But to the lover of nature they are sadly marred by the inevitable rows of bathing-machines, which largely neutralize the effect of the coast scenery at most of the English and French watering-places. The Culver Cliffs, perpendicular walls of chalk washed by the blue sea, add majesty to the lovely sweep of Sandown Bay. That notoriously eccentric demagogue of the last century, John Wilkes, owned a "villakin," as he sportively called it, at Sandown, where he spent the last years of his life. The grounds were curiously decorated with grotesque pavilions and imitations of classic tombs, inscribed to those he most admired—not excluding himself. A pillar, embowered in shrubbery, bore the epitaph, "*Carolo Churchill, divino poeta, amico jucundo, civi optime de patria merito*—To Charles Churchill, the divine poet, the genial friend, the citizen who has deserved well of his country."

But Shanklin, reputed the loveliest of the lovely villages of the isle, drew me by its fame from Sandown—Shanklin, sung by poets and haunted by artists. Keats says, "Shanklin is a most beautiful place; sloping wood and meadow ground reach round the Chine, which is a cleft between the cliffs, of the depth of nearly three hundred feet." The site of the town is deeply undulating, presenting many quiet nooks and dells, wherein nestle the most charming of leafy cottages, surrounded by dense hedges and espaliers tapestried with masses of flowers—fuchsias, geraniums, sweet-peas, heliotropes, and roses, deftly interwoven by nature and art combined. On the sea-side the village everywhere terminates in bold precipices, whose brow is parapeted with turf, and furnished here and there with rustic seats. On the sands, at the base, fishermen's rude huts, fishing-boats, lobster-baskets, and fishing-nets are picturesquely grouped, and, I regret to add, rows of the inevitable bathing-machines. It is but small compensating consolation to the artistic eye to be assured that the sandy floor is here the finest on the island. From the lofty slopes of Dunnose the prospect over Sandown Bay offers one of the loveliest sea-views to be found on any coast, when the skies are blue, flecked and barred by the faint tracery of fleecy, moveless summer clouds, the shining

JOHN WILKES.

cliffs assuming a tender roseate hue in the mellow afternoon glow, and the amethystine sea enclosing the isle with a line of silver foam, and itself enclosed in the distance by the dreamy coast of Old England, and lit up by the sails of trim yachts or clippers fading away toward unseen lands.

But to most people the great attraction of Shanklin is the Chine. The word *chine* is a local name applied to deep grooves or clefts worn into the sides of the sea-cliffs, in the course of long ages, by streams seeking to merge their brief current of life with the eternity of ocean. Many have been the enthusiastic lovers of nature who have visited Shanklin Chine, and have lived poetic hours or composed living verse in this romantic ravine. The steep, closely opposing sides are densely hung with verdure, and it is certainly a very attractive spot. But I confess to disappointment when I saw Shanklin Chine. The stream is generally exceedingly meagre—a mere insignificant thread dribbling down the side of a low precipice, and slipping with proper humility over a succession of narrow steps or ledges toward the sea, close at hand. It did not add to my interest to find that in some places artificial, squarely cut slabs had replaced the natural bed where it had been worn away. The dampness of the place, even in midsummer, is quite repelling; and if poor Keats spent much time there when he was trying to recruit his health at Shanklin, it must have added to the intensity of the fatal disease which brought him to an early grave. I have seen scores of places of the sort, but much less known, which quite surpass Shanklin Chine in beauty and impressiveness.

SHANKLIN CHINE.

It was with a certain sneaking feeling of recreancy to my principles that I stole into Ventnor from Shanklin by the railway. It was an evening of surpassing loveliness, the western sky lit by the hyaline amber and gold of warmer climes, and the crescent forming a silvery cleft in the twilight —fortunately over my right shoulder—when suddenly, with a diabolical shriek from the engine, we were whisked out of the glimpses of the moon into the Plutonian darkness of a long and most unromantic tunnel. When we at length emerged, and found ourselves in Ventnor, and I entered the hotel coach, the extraordinary steepness of the streets suggested the hope that the steeds were not of a frolicsome nature, or we might bring up on the edge of a precipice, and take a plunge of several hundred feet into the sea. But we stopped safe and sound at the Crab and Lobster, of which I can speak in the most hearty terms of commendation. Years ago, ere Ventnor had arrived at its present importance, the Crab and Lobster was a wee bit of a hostel nestling under the cliffs, noted for its good cheer and a thorough respectability which rendered it inaccessible to all but respectable guests. But times changed; visitors increased in such degree that at last a larger building was added on to the old inn, which, covered with ivy, clings to the newer and more pretentious dwelling. To make room for the latter, the steep rock-sides were hewn away. Even now the Crab and Lobster is of moderate proportions, thus offering accommodation to a limited few, an immense advantage to the visitor, and, in the way it is kept, it is truly a model English inn. From the heights immediately in the rear, reached by steep winding paths, where seats, shaded by flowering shrubbery, are provided, a most delightful prospect is obtained over isle and sea.

Ventnor is situated on the undercliff, a narrow, broken strip of land,

VENTNOR, FROM PULPIT ROCK.

half a mile wide and seven miles long, from Luccombe Chine, in the east, to Blackgang Chine, in the west. On the north it is bounded by the steep, lofty wall of Boniface Down and St. Catherine's Hill, springing to a height of over eight hundred feet. On the south it terminates in precipitous cliffs, washed by the ocean surges. Such is a general plan of the undercliff, which was formed ages ago by the breaking away of the slopes, undermined, perhaps, by streams and rains. In dire confusion, the sliding mass rushed toward the sea, and the undercliff was the result. But neither pen nor pencil can adequately portray the limitless variety of forms, the exquisite and suggestive beauty, which render the undercliff the most enchanting spot in the island. It is as if some vast capital of the giants of old had been overthrown, and its palaces and towers mingled and heaped in indiscriminate ruin, and then overgrown and beautified with the rank vegetation which time throws like a green shroud over the remains of dead cities. The illusion is heightened by the cliffs from which this landslip was detached. In many places the jagged and vertical rocks, sometimes actually overhanging the road, bear the closest resemblance in form and color to ancient fortifications of stupendous dimensions.

So far, Nature has done her part in beautifying this part of the Isle of Wight; while man, with the best intentions in the world, is doing his best to subtract from these attractions. A few cottages and country-seats, such as the English know how to create to perfection, did no harm to the undercliff; they, perhaps, added to its beauty by the introduction of here and there a lovely garden, a Tudor casement peeping out of viny trellises, a few rosy-cheeked children playing by the road-side, or some peerless English girl reclining on a green bank, or blending her evening song with the warbling of the nightingale. But alas for the truism, "One may have too much of a good thing!" for that is exactly the trouble with Ventnor just now. From a humble hamlet, reposing in the sweetest spot of Old England's loveliest isle, it has reached a population of six thousand, which is rapidly increasing, with newspapers, shops, hotels, and all the other appurtenances of a highly popular watering-place. The rapidly rising houses are fast hiding some of the characteristic features of the undercliff, and every pretty drive is disfigured by such advertisements as the following: "This fine lot of two acres to let for 999 years;" or, "This noble estate to let for 2000 years; inquire of Find and Fleecem, Cheatem St., London." Why a piece of land that is to let for twenty centuries should not be sold outright, it is difficult to understand. Imagine the bother of now collecting rent from an estate on a lease made before Julius Cæsar was born. The two thousand years since that event are not yet up. Besides, if titles and contracts can be made available for such a period, it is rather sharp practice to try the process at the undercliff, for some of the estates so leased there have, in all probability, but a short tenure of life. The overhanging cliffs are sure to tumble on the estate before the two thousand years are out. A landslip in 1810 destroyed thirty acres; one, in 1799, hurled one hundred acres seaward, and several similar convulsions have occurred more recently. Those who would see the charms of the undercliff before it has been further defaced by man should, therefore, not delay their visit to the Isle of Wight.

But, after all, one cannot blame the good people who flock to Ventnor during the summer and winter for pleasure or health. He has only himself to blame if, when he goes to commune with Nature in her happiest moods and aspects, he allows his reflections to be constantly disturbed by the hundreds and thousands of chattering tourists, swarming over cliff and vale like flies over a bowl of sugar, or geologists and mineralogists chipping the rocks with their hammers, indifferent artists sketching in every choice nook, and photographers introducing their instruments in the most impressive spots. As to invalids, if they must go to the Isle of Wight for their health, Ventnor is, of course, the only place for them there, after the autumn sets in, with its southern exposure and protection from northerly winds. An asylum for consumptives, entitled the National Cottage Hospital for Consumptives, has been established at Ventnor, consisting of a central church, and eight pairs of cottages on each side; it also includes a hall for concerts and social entertainments. The object of this institution is to furnish comfortable lodgings, with the best medical attendance, to invalids unable to go to better health resorts, or who cannot afford the expenses of good boarding-houses or hotels. It seems to have been attended with a fair degree of success since its foundation in 1868. The manager's report for 1876 curiously sums up the net gain of the year as represented by a ton of flesh. A ton of flesh is not bad. If not strictly elegant, it is expressive, and saves the bewildered mind from floundering among the

THE NATURAL ENEMY.

minute details of most sanitary reports. Is not the hint worth following in other social statistics? In municipal reports, or a national census, in-

BONCHURCH.

stead of summing up the number of dead and born, or the gains in population, why not simply and effectively set down the net result in tons of flesh?

To the eastward, and immediately adjoining Ventnor, which has grown up to it, is the lovely hamlet of Bonchurch. In Monk's Bay, by which it lies, St. Boniface landed, in A.D. 755, and Bonchurch is said to be a corruption of Bonecerce—the Church of St. Boniface. There is a well called after and dedicated to the saint by a certain bishop, who, on a dark night in the nights long ago, lost his way on the steep side of Boniface Down. His horse, and, in fact, the whole of creation, seemed slipping from under him as he sped down the declivity, when the horse's hoofs were caught in the cavity of the spring, which gave the bishop breathing-time to vow an acre of ground to the saint if he would carry him safely to the bottom. The saint was so pleased to become a land-owner that he closed with the terms, and the bishop lived to keep his promise. The well, on the day of St. Boniface, was formerly resorted to by the village maidens, who hung garlands there. Divers superstitions and much love-making and junketing—all common features of holy wells—were also associated with this spot.

There are various other attractions connected with the idyllic charms of Bonchurch, but the choicest, sweetest spot within its bounds is its little church and church-yard. This quaint little chapel, built four or five centuries ago, is scarce thirty feet long, but contains two minute galleries, and is not a bad specimen of the Norman style. A curious painting of the Last Judgment adorns the wall. The little graveyard, overlooking the sea, and overhung by ivied elms, seems, in its quiet beauty, to rob death of some of its bitterness. Here lie the remains of the Rev. William Adams, author of "The Shadow of the Cross." John Sterling sleeps close by, poet, prose-writer, novelist, and conversationalist, who died aged thirty-eight, according to the tombstone, and in his day was highly appreciated by certain cultivated minds—not so much, it would seem, for anything he actually achieved as for the general sum of his powers and the

THE WELL OF ST. LAWRENCE.

impression of possible greatness. A grave of more recent and melancholy interest is that of Emily Cowper-Coles, who died in 1876. She was the widow of Captain Cowper-Coles, who, on a wild night off the coast of Portugal, went down with five hundred souls in the famous, ill-fated iron-clad *Captain*, of which he was the builder.

To describe all the delightfully rural walks and coignes of vantage which offer pleasing views in the neighborhood of Bonchurch and Ventnor would be a tedious task—they are so numerous. But by keeping on to the westward along the undercliff, one comes to the miniature chapel of St. Lawrence, said to be the smallest in Great Britain, and a well dedicated to the same lazy saint. Thence it is a pleasant stroll to St. Catherine's Point—how the saints do abound in the Isle of Wight! On this headland is a handsome light-house, whose lantern is 174 feet above the ocean.

A CRAB-NITONER.

Niton, or Crab Niton, just beyond, noted for its crustacea, is attractive for its charming country-seats, and is also the scene of an interesting historical incident. Admiral Hopson, who was born at Bonchurch, was apprenticed to a tailor at Niton, when an English squadron was seen manœuvring off the coast. The Anglo-Saxon love of the sea suddenly smote his heart. He rushed to the beach, sprung into a boat, rowed off to the fleet, and was taken on board. An engagement with the French soon after occurring, the lad is said to have achieved distinction, and hastened the defeat of their fleet by springing from the main-yard into the enemy's rigging, and, under cover of the smoke, tearing down their colors. Whatever be the truth of this not impossible feat, it is quite true that he was promoted early, and eventually reached the highest rank in the British navy by his courage and skill.

Beyond Niton, we come to the Black Gang Chine, a grim abyss, over whose frowning edge a stream spills its wavering torrent into the surging vortex below, where the restless ocean forever foams and thunders. From here, by coach or on foot, sometimes by the margin of lofty sea-cliffs, sometimes by the most home-like and tidy farm-houses and hamlets imaginable, we come to Brixton. Frequently, in the green lanes, one meets groups of flaxen-haired, plump-cheeked, and rosy urchins and girlikins, such as Birket Foster delights to paint—the future hope and strength of the land of Shakspeare and Cromwell.

Brixton, or Brightstone, has within its bounds a typical English village church in good preservation. The low, square, turreted tower, with its peaked roof, is singularly picturesque. The original Norman arcade has recently been restored. In this little church once ministered those two good men, Thomas Ken, the religious poet, and Bishop of Bath and Wells, in the seventeenth century, and Samuel Wilberforce, late Bishop of Winchester.

Passing by Brooke, the parish of Freshwater is reached, which, within its brief limits, contains some of the grandest coast scenery in Great Britain. Freshwater is a small peninsula formed by the Yar River, which takes its rise within a few rods of the southern shore, and runs north into the Solent, where lies Yarmouth town. This little peninsula trends off to a point which terminates with the famous Needles. On the south is Freshwater Bay, a little bight, with a gray beach enclosed at either end by rugged cliffs and some bold rocks. One of these, rising hugely out of the surf, is pierced by a Gothic-like arch. Here, also, is the delightfully rural village of Freshwater, which is, however, fast losing its primitive quiet and

BLACK GANG CHINE.

beauty before the invasion of a horde of tourists, and the jejune rawness of the frequent new houses of a rapidly growing population. Faringford, Tennyson's famous residence, is here; but it is no cause for wonder that the poet has at last fled from a spot which has lost the sea-side seclusion which gave it such attractiveness. Ere long there will be a railroad between this place and Newport.

Beyond Freshwater Bay is Scratchell's Bay, a cove at the extreme west-

FARINGFORD, THE RESIDENCE OF ALFRED TENNYSON.

ern end of the Isle of Wight. The chalk cliffs here soar to over six hundred feet above the sea, bidding defiance to the ocean with aspect austere and sublime. A cave or arch, three hundred feet high, at the base of this stupendous wall, adds to the grandeur of this magnificent scene, which is fitly terminated by the immense savage rocks called the Needles. They are five in number, but only three of them are conspicuous. On the outermost stands a lofty light-house, built to supersede an older structure which stands on the higher cliffs, but was found to be too often enveloped in mists to be of service to the mariner. These cliffs are haunted by innumerable sea-birds, and some of the adventurous islanders swing themselves over the edge by ropes, and, dangling in mid-air, search the crannies for eggs, which are accounted a delicacy. A cool head and a strong grip are the requisites in a business which must continue a monopoly for some ages to come. The pursuit is not likely to suffer from competition, that blessing of the consumer, and bane of the producer.

Passing around the Needles, we enter Alum Bay, which is encircled by tremendous precipices ranged with a sort of artificial regularity, like the segment of an amphitheatre. But the severe sublimity of the scene is relieved by the surprising variety of colors in the cliffs. By a singular geological freak, the pearly-gray monotony of chalk is relieved by vertical strata of sand, clays, or marls, inlaid, mosaic-like, on the stupendous mass in narrow but distinct stripes of red, black, white, blue, green, or yellow.

These tints are harmoniously blended by the soft light of evening into a picture of extraordinary beauty.

Going from Freshwater to Newport, by rolling downs, overgrown with swaying harvests, one passes, by an easy transition, from the grander aspects of nature to the alluring charms of a shire town reposing in a happy valley, by a tranquil river, and hallowed by the historic associations of other times. The wooded coast of Hampshire is visible on the left, under the setting sun, as one crosses the Yar River, and Hurst Castle on the end of a spit, which, like a breakwater, lies across the mouth of the Solent, and reduces the channel to scarce half a mile in width. Newport lies near the centre of the island, where the Medina River, a brief little stream, becomes an estuary, subject to the tides, and navigable to small craft. A Roman origin is claimed for Newport, with some plausibility. That the Romans once held and dwelt in the place is beyond question—the tessellated floor of a Roman villa still exists in the vicinity—but that they were

SCRATCHELL'S BAY.

the original founders admits of doubt. In such misty problems as this, why not follow the bold example of the Dutch chronicler who began a history of Holland by saying, "Noah was the first Dutchman?"

Newport is a thriving place, more intent on the present than the past, presenting a bustling appearance on Saturdays, when a market or fair is held, to which the neighboring farmers flock. The chief objects which the fair left on my memory were buxom girls selling chapbooks, rustics swollen with overmuch small-beer, and proportionately pugnacious, strapping redcoats elbowing the crowd, restive cobs put through their paces before customers incredulous of their good points, and lastly, but not leastly, a pig determined to make a noise in the world, whose erratic obstinacy aroused the mirth of even the most stolid countryman. Newport is the birthplace of Sir Thomas Fleming, who was Lord Chief-Justice of England under James I. Until 1853 there was a very interesting parish church there, dedicated to St. Thomas à Becket. But in that year the decay of the venerable building made it necessary to demolish it, and another edifice was erected on the old site, after the early English decorated style. In the new building several interesting monuments were retained that had been in the church it replaced, including a very curious pulpit, carved by Thomas Caper, in 1630, who has hieroglyphically placed his name upon it in the form of an antic goat supposed to symbolize the word *caper*. The pulpit is divided into a double row of emblematical figures in bas-relief, and on the sounding-board is wrought the gilded inscription, "Cry aloud and spare not; lift up the voice like a trumpet."

Another deeply interesting object in this church is Marochetti's beautiful monument to the Princess Elizabeth. It was erected at the expense of the Queen. The princess is represented in the position in which she died, reclining on her side, resting her cheek on the Bible given to her by her royal father at the last interview before his execution. The likeness is from a portrait still existing. The inscription runs as follows: "To the memory of the Princess Elizabeth, daughter of Charles I., who died at Carisbrooke Castle, on Sunday, September 8th, 1650, and is interred beneath the chancel of this church, this monument is erected—a token of respect for her virtues and of sympathy for her misfortunes—by Victoria R., 1856."

The princess died at Carisbrooke Castle, where the last weeks of her young life were passed. A few days after her arrival there she was overtaken by a sudden shower when playing at bowls; a rapid illness followed, of which she died in a fortnight, at the age of thirteen years. She seems to have been a very amiable character. She left a simple but affecting account of her royal father's last farewell.

Carisbrooke Castle is but a short mile from Newport, on the edge of the village of Carisbrooke. The fortifications crown the crest of a steep hill, which seems as if it had been formed expressly for such a picturesque pile. By a winding, leafy foot-path, one approaches the imposing entrance, a lofty archway bearing the initials of Queen Elizabeth, and the date 1598. The turf-carpeted moat is crossed by a massive stone bridge, leading to the noble barbacan erected by Antony Woodville. It is composed of two ponderous but elegant round towers, pierced with machicolations. The curtain which joins them is grooved for two portcullises, and bears the rose of the house of York and the Woodville escutcheon. Passing through this stately and venerable gate-way, one enters the spacious court-yard of the castle, and finds himself surrounded by an unbroken circuit of brown, mouldering walls, profusely draped with ivy. On the left are the apartments occupied by Charles I. The roof has fallen in, but the fireplaces are still distinctly visible, and the divisions which marked his dining-hall and bedchamber. The window out of which he tried to escape is filled up with masonry, but the original

TOMB OF THE PRINCESS ELIZABETH.

outline remains. Climbing up to the summit of the barbican, the long, narrow walk along the ramparts leads one to the keep, on the north-east angle of the castle, said to stand on an artificial mound. It is an exceedingly venerable pile, erected by the Normans. They have seemingly wrought into it their sturdy and determined character. Like a sentinel who steadfastly remains at his post when all his comrades are gone, it towers above the land, grim and immovable, to guard the trophies of a race that long since passed away to the halls of oblivion. A light-house on a stormy coast, it braves alone the surges of ages, while from winter to winter wreck after wreck sweeps by. Its own turn must come at last.

A flight of seventy-four marble steps, excessively steep, narrow, and worn, leads to the platform, which is guarded by a gate grooved for a portcullis. From thence is obtained one of the most extensive and beautiful prospects in the Isle of Wight. In former years the landscape was

CARISBROOKE CASTLE.

so covered with forests, that it was said a squirrel could go from Carisbrooke to Gurnard Bay without touching ground; but now much of the larger portion of the island is bare, here and there embossed with clumps of massive elms and limes, but generally devoted to agriculture and pasturage. Immediately below the keep, and entirely surrounding the ancient mural fortifications of Carisbrooke, are the works thrown up at the time of the Spanish Armada, modelled on the plan of those erected at Antwerp by Italian engineers. They have undergone little modification since, but are well turfed and neatly kept. It is not to the credit of the English Government that the original castle is in such a dilapidated condition. To be sure, it is thus more picturesque; but unless more care of this majestic and interesting relic of past ages is better guarded in future from the gnawing tooth of time, coming generations will have just right to murmur at a parsimony which allows one of the most impressive and instructive monuments in Europe to slip into annihilation.

The remains of the chapel are worth noticing, although they do not date back of the last century, having been erected on the site of a much older structure. It is not uncommon to see picnic parties taking tea under the trees which overtop the roofless fane. The building formerly occupied by the governor of the castle is very old, including within its walls the chapel of Isabella de Fortibus. But it has been so repaired, altered, and restored from time to time as hardly to be in keeping with the antique ruins by which it is surrounded. There are two wells of great depth in the castle; the one in the donjon is fabulously deep, but being choked up with stones, one must be content to accept the current statements without question. The other well is 144 feet deep—quite sufficient, one would think; but the visitor is liable to be informed that it is 300 feet. It is covered by a room, in one side of which is a very large tread-wheel. A venerable donkey is introduced on the scene; he walks into the wheel with deliberation, and, the while inquisitively eying the by-standers, draws up the bucket. No sooner does it reach the curb than he makes an abortive attempt to bray; but old age has impaired his once tuneful throat. He has been employed at this not severely intellectual occupation for thirty-three years. Several donkeys have served before him—one for thirty years, and two others for over forty years each. Rotation in office does not seem to be common at Carisbrooke. Office-seekers will therefore find it useless to apply.

Many interesting historical incidents are associated with Carisbrooke Castle, but none more interesting than the imprisonment of Charles I. within its walls. Contrary to the general opinion, that unfortunate monarch was not sent to Carisbrooke by Parliament, but went there of his own accord, as to a safe asylum from his enforced confinement at Hampton Court. Restive under restraint, and perhaps apprehending assassination from poison or the dagger, King Charles contrived to elude his guard, and fled to Titchfield House, near the southern coast, where he was hospitably received and concealed. Thence he despatched messengers to Colonel Hammond, the governor of the Isle of Wight, in whose well-known character for kindliness, and moderation, and honor he placed reliance. Hammond returned with them to Titchfield House, and the king concluded then to place himself under his protection, trusting for his favorable interposition between Parliament and its captive. Accordingly he crossed the Solent, and entered the stern walls of Carisbrooke. But the Parliamentary leaders, having the king once more within their grip, were not minded to release him, and Colonel Hammond received strict orders, which made him answerable for the possession of Charles. However, he treated the king with much kindness, allowing him large liberty, even to hunting in the neighboring forests. But after the king's first attempt to escape, he was brought under much closer surveillance. Henry Firebrace, a faithful adherent of the king's household, devised a plan for escape by entering into communication with Captain Titus, one of the wardens, who was secretly a royalist. A system of correspondence was contrived, and it was finally decided that on a concerted night Charles should let himself down from the window of his chamber. Horses would be in waiting to carry him to the coast. He was advised to cut the bars of the window with aquafortis and a file, but maintained that where his head could pass his body could follow. All was in readiness when the appointed hour arrived, and Firebrace, by a concerted signal, flung a stone against the window. The king was to descend, seated on a crossbar attached to the end of a rope, and he now proceeded to pass out of the window; but his shoulders stuck fast, and for some moments he was in a very painful position. Had it not been for the precaution he had taken of fastening a cord to a staple within, he would have been unable to withdraw himself from this awkward situation. Firebrace heard him groan, and soon after Charles put a candle in the window, indicating the failure of the scheme. One need not necessarily be a royalist or an Episcopalian in order to sympathize deeply with this ill-fated but heroic monarch in his misfortunes. By a mysterious law of Providence, it was his destiny to expiate the crimes of his predecessors by being placed in a false position, with which he was incapable of coping successfully. He was made the scape-goat for the sins of Edward IV., Henry VIII., Mary, Elizabeth, and James I. His public errors were the results of education or incapacity to deal with a great crisis. In private life and character, he surpassed his predecessors and most of his successors.

OSBORNE.

A pleasant stroll of three or four miles from Newport takes one to the peaceful vale and village of Arreton, the scene of a simpler, yet not less instructive, drama than that of Carisbrooke. There still stands the picturesque cottage of Elizabeth Walbridge, the "Dairyman's Daughter," whose story is so beautifully told by Legh Richmond. Her grave is in the village church-yard, from which her cottage is somewhat over a mile distant; the headstone bears a beautiful tribute to her memory.

After seeing Newport and Carisbrooke, one naturally and rightfully concludes that to linger long at Cowes, at the mouth of the Medina, is of little advantage, unless he is of a yachting turn. West Cowes Castle, built by Henry VIII. out of the ruins of Beaulieu Priory, was, in 1651, the prison of Davenant, the father of English opera. In 1856 it was sold to the Royal Yacht Club, who employ its battery for firing yachting salutes. The Royal Yacht Club has its rendezvous at Cowes, and includes over one hundred and fifty crack yachts on its rolls. The annual regatta occurs in the third week in August, and the plate is given by Her Majesty. East Cowes, on the highlands, on the right bank of the Medina River, is the seat of some handsome villas. Here, too, is Osborne, one of the favorite residences of the Queen, an elegant and imposing edifice after the Palladian style. Connected with the extensive grounds is the model farm which was one of the hobbies of the late Prince Consort. But the public is never admitted to the palace or gardens, and one can only speak of Osborne from hearsay.

At the north of the Isle of Wight the waters of the Solent and Spithead unite in what is called Southampton Water, the beautiful channel which leads up to Southampton. It was on a charming day, after gazing for many hours at the graceful yachts lying at Cowes, drying their canvas or gliding from point to point, that I reluctantly took the steamer, and landed at Southampton, thirteen miles away.

APPENDIX.

I.

ON THE ADVANTAGES OF SMALL ISLANDS, ESPECIALLY ATLANTIC ISLANDS.

The advantages of islands, especially small ones, for purposes of health or pleasure, were not as yet clearly perceived in the time of Sancho Panza. But with the good sense and shrewdness which were so often apparent through his rustic simplicity and clownish ignorance, he early displayed an admirable perception of the value of islands as playing an important part in the economy of human affairs. To be sure, the island of which he eventually became the governor was not exactly the sort of island included as such under the ordinary acceptation of the term; but Sancho was correct in his apprehension of the principle involved. It was for an island, and not for a continent, that he sighed. And he was abetted in his insular aspirations by no less a traveller, adventurer, and ornament of chivalry than Don Quixote himself, through whose influence Sancho became the governor of an island so called for euphony.

I am convinced that the love for islands, and especially for small islands, is rational and improving. It enables one to gratify the roving propensity, and at the same time to combine with it the attainment of information, breadth and catholicity in judging men, and thoroughness in the pursuit of a given end. That thoroughness may be one of the results of visiting small islands is almost self-evident, but, strange to say, some may be found who doubt it; and yet is it not indubitable, for the following reasons? Every island, however small, is a distinct microcosm or community, with people, customs, climate, laws, and geographical features peculiar to itself, and separated from the rest of the world with entire distinctness by the water which isolates it. Now, we will suppose that a traveller or scientist undertakes to master the various physical, historical, and social features of France or Germany, or any other Continental country. But does he not soon find that, to acquire a broad, intelligent, and thorough knowledge of that country, he must devote to it many years, and possibly a lifetime, and will even at the last feel how much yet remains for others to discover and map out in the same inexhaustible field?

But given an island of the size of Madeira or New Providence, and while the traveller may modestly grant that, after carefully investigating it, there is still much to be learned about it, yet he can honestly claim, on the other hand, that in a few weeks or months he has been able to obtain a better general idea of it, has been able better to comprehend it as a distinct entity, than he could understand the character and institutions of Germany, or France, or Russia in a lifetime. Hence follows an incentive to thoroughness, besides a greater satisfaction in the pursuit of a subject which may be acquired with a certain rounded completeness within a reasonable period, thus enabling the traveller to turn with fresh zest to another object before he has become wearied with effort too long sustained in one direction.

Thus far as regards the advantages of small islands in general, and the attractions they offer to the tourist or the scientist. But many small islands possess still another advantage over a continent, in that they offer superior opportunities for improvement to invalids, who are obliged, on account of chronic disease, to leave their homes in search of a health resort. No one will dispute the fact that sea air is, on the whole, the most fraught with tonic qualities of any, although sometimes it needs to be warmed by a southern sun to graduate it to the wasted strength of the consumptive. Of course the best way to obtain it is on a ship at sea. But this to many is impossible, owing to sea-sickness. A small island is, therefore, the next best thing, other things being equal. And the smaller the island, the greater the advantage; for then the wind everywhere comes in a more direct manner off the sea, laden with its tonic qualities. By the same reasoning, the climate on a small island is much less liable to variations and extremes, for sea air is always more equable than land air, and the extremes of temperature are much less violent in the same latitude on the sea than on the land. If to this greater evenness of temperature is added the unchangeable, scarcely varying character imparted to a climate by the trade-winds in a latitude free from extreme heat the whole or half of the year, on a small island, we have, at last, a climate that is as nearly perfect as can be anywhere found for meeting the conditions requisite to restoration of health.

Thus we arrive at the conclusion that a small island offers, in the first place, peculiar and superior advantages to the tourist and the seeker after rational entertainment and instruction. In addition to this, and of still greater importance, we find that small islands within certain latitudes, and according to the season of the year, afford to the invalid the advantages of a tonic air and an equability of temperature superior to anything which can be obtained on a continent, even along its sea-coast. Thus, during the winter solstice the Bahamas are infinitely to be preferred to the neighboring health resorts of Florida, where a weeping sun and a capricious temperature often lead the invalid to curse the day that ever he turned toward the flowery peninsula.

We find, further, that of those islands in the North Atlantic which are free from yellow fever or endemic pests, those take the precedence which are within the beneficent influence of the trade-winds, those delicious breezes which seem by their regularity to give such an idea of permanence to life, wafting away regrets for the past and unconcern for the future, and magically luring the soul to dwell content with the dreamy days as they come and go, and simply enjoy the enormous luxury of being. It follows that those among the trade-wind islands, on which the invalid can live the year round with beneficial and permanent results, are the most desirable spots on the globe as health resorts.

We are thus able to form a distinct classification of the sanitary islands in the North Atlantic, and can state with confidence the advantages of each. First among the trade-wind islands are Teneriffe and Madeira, where the invalid can stay with the best results during the whole year. The valley of Orotava, in Teneriffe, combines more climatic advantages than any other island spot in the Atlantic, the variations of temperature being excessively slight, the influence of the main-land imperceptible, and the air dry without the parched aridity of the desert. Madeira is a little more moist, and its dampness has somewhat increased since the cultivation of the sugar-cane; but it is confined to certain localities, and can be avoided by judicious choice of lodgings. The rainfall is also greater, but is, notwithstanding, very moderate, and the variations in temperature are only a little more noticeable than at Orotava; while the social advantages, the means of locomotion, good medical attendance, and the comforts so essential to an invalid, are more abundant at Madeira than at Teneriffe. The Bahamas, while classed among the trade-wind islands, must be assigned a lower rank than Madeira and Teneriffe, because they can be advantageously used as a health resort only for part of the year—from the 1st of November to the 1st of May—while the cost of living is much more than at the islands just mentioned, without any compensating advantages. But as a sanitarium for winter alone they are, beyond all question, superior to any other health resort on the eastern coast of North America.

Leaving the trade-winds, we now come to island resorts offering less advantages than those just mentioned, but still desirable for part of the year to one who cannot go as far as the trade-wind islands. The Bermudas are the first of these in celebrity; but, charming as they are for the tourist, they cannot be safely commended to the consumptive, except in the contingency that he cannot go to any better resort. They are excessively damp, far exceeding in this respect all other sanitary islands, and the climate resembles, in boisterousness and variability, that of the adjoining continent, although, as the extremes are much less violent, it is so far a decided improvement upon that.

The Azores may be classed with Bermuda. But while the latter is wholly a winter and spring resort, the former can be advantageously visited by the invalid only from April to October. The excessive force and dampness of the wind make them very undesirable during the winter. Prince Edward Island and the Isles of Shoals are excellent resorts in summer, especially the former, which, in point of scenery, and equability, and moderation of temperature is surpassed by no other island on the American coast as a summer resort. Belleisle-en-mer is to be commended to the invalid during the winter months, at least, as a variety, in case he desires change for a few weeks, although, of course, of less value than more Southern isles.

In another class are included the Isle of Wight and the Channel Islands, which are advantageous during the whole year, although their greater dampness, more copious rains, and raw winds make them far inferior to Teneriffe and Madeira. But to the invalid who does not care to go so far, Ventnor, in the Isle of Wight, and Guernsey and Jersey can be safely recommended as superior to most resorts on the main-land, and offering excellent social advantages.

Newfoundland, Cape Breton Island, and the Magdalen Islands present superior attractions to the artist and the sportsman, but are too bleak to be of advantage to the invalid, except for two or three months in the summer to those who still have a robust constitution that is only temporarily enfeebled.

It cannot be too strongly emphasized that those who would obtain the full benefit of these resorts should go to them early. Too many make them the last resource, and go when it is too late to derive health or life from any quarter. If they then die on the islands, it is too often attributed to the climate, and not to the tardiness of the remedy. Abundant time should also be allowed for a thorough cure. Many think that they are cured as soon as they feel somewhat better, and consequently return too soon to the bleak climate from which they had fled. Chronic maladies require patience, systematic care, and time, so that the constitution may be able to readjust its disordered functions.

The patient who resorts to these islands should also distinctly understand, and constantly remember, that a few days of acclimation are generally required, during which greater caution is requisite; while prudence, and regularity of habits, and avoidance of exposure or overfatigue can at no time be dispensed with. Too many who are of convivial habits think that in such a climate they can defy ill health, and, after deriving some benefit from the change, finally neutralize it by yielding to the seductive temptations which more easily assail them while living a life of enforced idleness. The climate is then slandered, and unjustly receives the blame for the lack of cure which naturally results from vice or imprudence. This accounts for some of the pamphlets which sometimes come out against these sanitary resorts. It is well for the invalid to see a good physician soon after landing, and learn of him the regimen and regulations required, according to the climate and the nature of his disease.

II.

THE BAHAMAS.*

NASSAU, the best winter resort on the American coast, is reached by the steam line of Murray, Ferris & Co., No. 62 South Street, New York, who have entered into a contract for five years, to carry mails and passengers. One boat sails monthly throughout the year from New York to Nassau direct: fare $50—round trip, $90.

---

* The chapter on the Bahamas in this volume first appeared in *Harper's New Monthly Magazine*, together with several of the other chapters; others came out in *Scribner's Monthly*, the *Atlantic Monthly*, *Appletons' Journal*, and *Sunday Afternoon*, from which they are now republished, with considerable additional matter. The description of the Isles of Shoals has not appeared elsewhere.

From November to May, a steamer of the same company sails also from Savannah for Nassau, touching at St. Augustine; fare $21; or, from New York via the above places, $50, and the round trip $95.

The best hotel at Nassau is the Royal Victoria Hotel, a spacious, well-constructed building, erected by the Government at a cost of $150,000. It stands on an elevation, and is built of limestone, three stories high, and is surrounded by spacious verandas, commanding a noble prospect and fanned by the trade-winds. The apartments are large and airy, and well kept. The drawing-room is a most delightful apartment, and the dining-hall is very inviting. This is one of the most attractive hotels I have seen at any island resort on the western side of the Atlantic. Adjoining the hotel is a pleasant billiard-room, and the public library is close at hand. This hotel is now leased and conducted by Messrs. Mellen, Conover, & King, and opens November 1st, and closes May 15th. The terms are $3 per diem, and the average expenses are little less than those of a first-class hotel in the United States. Sail-boats and carriages are always on hand, and the numerous charming coves and lagoons, and the admirable roads, suggest various means of enjoyment to the sportsman or the invalid.

Such extravagant eulogiums have been bestowed on Nassau, that, to the appetite fed on such highly seasoned food, a more temperate estimate of its sanitary and social advantages may seem tame. But speaking as I do, without any bias, and from a wide personal experience of many island resorts, I must assign Nassau a lower place than either Madeira or Teneriffe, because it is beneficial for only part of the year, while the humidity of the evenings makes it imprudent for the confirmed invalid to expose himself to the night air; and the social advantages and the attractions of the scenery suffer decidedly by comparison with those offered by the transatlantic isles. But having made these reservations, I can heartily recommend Nassau to those who cannot cross the Atlantic as by far the best winter sanitarium within easy access of the United States.

Frost is unknown in the Bahamas. Many years ago a slight film of snow covered part of the Great Bahama Island. It was a sight never seen there before or since, and filled the simple natives with astonishment. The most careful and thorough observations, taken for successive years by the scientific men of Nassau, indicate that the temperature from November 1st to May 1st does not fall below 63°, nor rise above 82°, and rarely varies over 8° in the twenty-four hours. Once or twice in the season it may vary 12°, while oftener the change may not be over 6°. The humidity is not excessive, averaging 73.3°, but it is very marked after sunset. Yellow fever has occurred but two or three times during this century, and then was brought from Havana. There is nothing in the nature of the soil to induce that or any other epidemic, so long as the first principles of drainage are observed by the inhabitants. During the summer, however, the long-continued heat and the rains relax the system, and are weakening to invalids.

THE AZORES.

These islands are reached in the most direct manner from the United States by sailing-packets from Boston—the bark *Azorean*, John E. May & Co., the bark *Kate Williams*, J. J. Alves, and the bark *Modesta*—the latter Portuguese, and chiefly employed for the transit of the islanders emigrating to the United States. The first two can be recommended as thoroughly sea-worthy and reliable vessels, commanded by men experienced in the trade. The fare is $60, or, for the round trip, $100. The passage out averages sixteen days, and the return voyage twenty-four days. The vessel remains at the islands three to four weeks, sometimes visiting Flores and St. Michael. Ten weeks may be allowed as the time for an average trip, if one goes and returns in the same trip, making a charming summer excursion.

From England the Azores may be reached during the winter season by weekly steamers, sent by Tatham & Co., No. 35 Pudding Lane, London, from that port to St. Michael. The fare is £10, wine included. Time, about five days.

Two Portuguese steam-packets ply bimonthly between Lisbon and the islands—the *Luzo* and the *Atlantico*. The *Luzo*, leaving Lisbon on the 1st, touches at St. Michael, Terceira, and Fayal, and the *Atlantico* visits all the islands of the group except Corvo. The distance is a little over 700 miles; time to St. Michael, about three days.

The Portuguese hotel at Flores is a small affair, and cannot be highly recommended. At Fayal there is an excellent house, called the Fayal Hotel, under the courteous superintendence of Mr. and Mrs. Edwards. It overlooks the port and Pico Peak, and a large and attractive garden is attached to the hotel. The table is loaded with the game, fish, and fruits of the islands. The terms are $2 a day, and the extras are quite insignificant. The Hotel Central is also well kept, although small. Numerous meek and docile little donkeys afford the chief mode of visiting Castello Branco, the Flamengoz, and other attractive spots about the island.

At Ponta Delgada, St. Michael, is a spacious hotel near the water, managed tolerably well by Mr. Bird, an Englishman. At the Sulphur Springs, called the Furnas, there are two hotels, situated in the midst of scenery highly interesting and romantic. The best of these is very efficiently kept by Mr. Brown, an Englishman. The other is maintained indifferently well by Senhor Lerogno.

It cannot be too distinctly stated that the Azores are no place for invalids to visit during the winter season. It is true the Thermal Springs, or Furnas of St. Michael, may be visited nearly as well at that season as in summer; but the advantages they offer may be gained at some of the numerous sulphur springs of Germany or France. For those afflicted with throat or lung diseases, rheumatism or the protean forms of neuralgia, the Azores are quite too damp and boisterous in winter. The rainfall is then considerable, the winds are very violent and searching, and the houses are adapted only to those in rugged health. Not that the temperature is ever low at the Azores, the yearly mean being 62° at Fayal, and it rarely falls below

53°, although 44° has been reached; but the mean temperature of winter, while steady, rarely rises above 58°, and is raw and humid. But a marvellous change occurs after the first of May, and continues through September. The rains are reduced to a minimum, and the air becomes soft and dry. The mean temperature in July at mid-day is 73°, sometimes rising to 80°, but rarely varying over 6° in the twenty-four hours. Then is the time to visit Fayal, to breathe its delicious and invigorating air, to bask in its beautiful gardens, and enjoy the grand and beautiful scenery of those lovely isles.

THE MAGDALEN ISLANDS.

These islands are reached most easily, by one who does not mind roughing it, in a fishing-schooner. Many schooners from Gloucester make the Magdalen Islands a rendezvous for mackerel fishing, and it is not difficult to secure a passage in one of them. A less direct but more comfortable way is to go to Prince Edward Island by rail or steamer, and take the steamboat which touches at Souris, on the eastern end of that island.

At Havre Aubert, on Amherst Island, hotels or boarding-houses are kept by Mrs. Shea and Mrs. Burns. The accommodations are scant, and the fare is simple. But the rooms are clean and the food well served, and seventy-five cents a day cannot be called high for board and lodging. At the other places where the visitor may resort, he will have to depend on the hospitality of the leading families, whose charges are very moderate.

The Magdalen Islands can hardly be recommended as a sanitarium for invalids. But to the sportsman and the artist, or the searcher after an interesting spot for an invigorating and novel summer vacation, they cannot be too highly commended. As yet but little known, their wild and sublime sea scenery, the abundance of the sea-fowl, and the raciness of rambling about those wreck-strewn isles, are attractions which should not be easily set aside for resorts of a tamer character.

THE CHANNEL ISLANDS.

These islands are reached by steamers plying daily from Southampton and Weymouth. The distance is the same by each route, but the passage by water is longer from the former place—123 miles—but only 82 miles from Weymouth. The passage is often exceedingly boisterous, but the boats are strong and weatherly. There are also daily steamers plying from Jersey to Granville and St. Malo. Jersey lies 21 miles from St. Peter's Port, Guernsey, and 42 miles from St. Malo.

These islands are well supplied with hotels and lodging-houses, which generally afford comfortable quarters and a good table for a moderate sum. At the hotels 7s. to 8s. per day is the average price, and the boarding-houses charge 35s. to 45s. per week, and the extras are trifling. Gardner's Royal Hotel, on Glatney Esplanade, is one of the best at St. Peter's Port, although not very large. It overlooks the harbor. Of boarding-houses the best is Gardner's Old Government House. It occupies an elevated position, fronting a charming garden, and commanding a grand view of the town, the sea, and the adjacent isles. It is well kept, and the terms are moderate. These two establishments must not be confounded by the visitor, as the proprietor's name is the same in each. Taudevin's, Mrs. Richards's, and several other excellent boarding-houses, aid to extend a hospitable reception to the invalid or tourist resorting to Guernsey. It is not difficult to lease a pleasant cottage, and such as prefer to live in that way will find the costs of living by no means extravagant. Those proposing to winter in the Channel Islands would do well to secure lodgings at an early date. In summer the islands swarm with tourists, but they are generally only transient visitors.

At St. Heliers, the Royal Yacht Club Hotel, facing the pier, is one of the best. The Imperial, on the St. Saviour's Road, is a large and conveniently arranged hotel. Of many boarding-houses, Bree's, at Stopford Terrace, can be highly recommended as commodious, clean, the table and service good, and the charges moderate, considering the high character of the establishment. It is unfortunately situated, however, because it does not command a sea-view, which seems to be desirable in such a place; but, on the other hand, it is protected from the biting winter gales. Mrs. Treleavan's, at Mon Sejour, can also be highly recommended as moderate and thoroughly well sustained. Good lodgings can also be found in the little town of St. Aubin.

At Sark there are several hotels and boarding-houses, and lodgings are obtainable on reasonable terms in a number of private houses. Gavey's Hotel can be strongly recommended. Terms, 5s. to 6s. per diem.

At Alderney there is a good hotel, kept by Captain Scott. This island is reached by a mail-boat from Guernsey twice weekly. Sark is also in communication with St. Peter's Port by means of a small steamer during the summer. In the winter season it is reached only by the Sarkese fishing-boats, which ply between the islands in good weather. Sometimes no landing can be effected for weeks.

As regards climate, the Channel Islands have a much more equable temperature than that of the adjoining continent. The thermometer often varies only 7° or 8° in the month. They are, therefore, to be preferred to most Continental health resorts, and also to the Isle of Wight. In summer the air is exceedingly soft and balmy, and entirely free from extreme heat. An invalid who desires a change after a winter or two or three years in Madeira, might, if strengthened by his sojourn there, pass the summer in the Channel Islands with beneficial results. But they are to be recommended as a winter sanitarium only to those who cannot go to the trade-wind islands farther south; for in that season there is much dampness, occasionally a frost, and a liability to flurries of snow—at long intervals, however. But the difference between such weather and the delicious winter mildness and evenness of a winter in the trade-wind islands is great, and altogether in favor of the latter. At no season should those troubled with rheumatism or rheumatic neuralgia resort to the Channel Islands.

It is a curious fact that, although clustered so near together, the Channel Islands vary sensibly in their climatic characteristics. Guernsey is more dry and has a less rainfall than Jersey, and a more even temperature, warmer in winter, cooler in summer, and is consequently more bracing. The dews are heavy over the whole group, and dense fogs are not uncommon, especially in summer. Alderney and Sark seem to be rather more dry than Guernsey. Consumptives, in the early stages of the disease, may derive benefit at these islands, with proper care of themselves; and the air is highly tonic and invigorating for those who are simply overworked and require a temporary change.

MADEIRA.

This island is reached by several lines of sailing vessels and steamers. The firm of Fowle & Caroll, No. 31 India Wharf, Boston, forward three or four vessels during the year; fare, $70; time, about twenty-one days. It has been done repeatedly in thirteen to fifteen days, with westerly gales; the return is about twenty-six to thirty days. Yates & Porterfield, of No. 115 Wall Street, New York, send out ships touching at Teneriffe; fare, $70. From there it is but thirty-six hours to Madeira by frequent steamers; fare between the two islands, £3. Either of these routes is cheaper, and sometimes more expeditious, than *via* Liverpool. The boats of the African Steam Navigation Line and of the African Steamship Company leave Liverpool trimonthly for Madeira—time, six days; fare, 18 guineas. There is also a trimonthly line from Southampton. All these boats can be well recommended. A comfortable Portuguese steamer leaves Lisbon bimonthly for Madeira, and by taking ship direct from New York to Lisbon, time, and certainly money, might be saved. Distance from Lisbon, 500 miles; time, two days. Other steamers are constantly touching at the island, to or from Lisbon, Bordeaux, Havre, Antwerp, and Hamburg; but they are more or less irregular. Madeira has telegraphic communication with the rest of the world by cable to Lisbon and Brazil.

The accommodations for visitors to Madeira are exceptionally good. There are several very excellent boarding-houses, partaking partly of the nature of a hotel. Reid's and Miles's, in Funchal, can both be very highly recommended. The former maintains two houses, one directly on the water's edge overlooking the port, the other higher up, opposite the Church of Santa Clara, commanding an extensive land and ocean prospect. The terms average $2 per diem, which is moderate, considering the excellence of the cuisine and the efficiency of the service. Special contracts can sometimes be made by those intending to remain some time. It is well to write early for rooms if one is going in the autumn or winter. Between May and October many leave, returning again for the winter, and it is easier then to get good rooms. The extra expenses at these hotels are trifling. At Santa Cruz there is a most excellent hotel, kept by Senhor Gonsalvez, who speaks English fluently. It is charmingly situated. At Sant' Anna there is a very finely situated hotel; the host, Senhor Acciaoly, is a thorough gentleman. The terms are about $1 75, or 7s. per diem. At Ponta Delgada there is a charming little house, situated in a position of astonishing loveliness; but this may be said of most of the hotels on this matchless island. Rooms can be obtained there, and also at the inn at San Vincente, but the table and lodgings are quite simple and proportionately cheaper than in Funchal. This is fully compensated by the delicate air and the glory of the scenery. At Calheta, on the road to the Rabaçál, lodgings may be had for the night in the picturesque house of Senhor Drummond, which was once a convent.

Good horses and hammocks can be hired on moderate terms. If one is to be some time on the island, it is well to engage one or the other for the season. A *burrequiero*, or muleteer, always accompanies the horse. For an invalid no more delightful mode of locomotion can be devised than the Madeira hammock.

There is a good news-room, provided with English and American papers, at Funchal, adjoining the beach; subscription, $1 per month. There is also a good library of several thousand volumes in the next street, to which subscribers have access.

As regards the climate of Madeira, there is little to be said that is not in its favor, provided the invalid goes there in the earlier stages of the disease. It is beneficial to consumptives, and those troubled with rheumatism, neuralgia, and Bright's disease, or general exhaustion of the system. The objections brought against it have been largely due to an attempt to prop later and less-known resorts at the expense of those of established reputation; and also to the grumbling of two or three invalids of ungovernable temper, who, failing to receive the benefit which it was too late for them to receive anywhere, have reviled a resort that has done so much good to others.

The rainy season is in winter, but the rainfall is very moderate. Protracted rains are unknown. Sometimes it rains hard in the mountains, and light momentary showers are liable to occur at all times of the year. The north side of the island is cooled by the trade-winds, and the south side is fanned by a mild sea-breeze, rising in the morning and going down with the sun. Clouds temper the heat of the sun during the day.

The temperature is equable and moderate. Frost is unknown except at the summit of the mountains in winter. For eighteen years in succession the mean temperature at Funchal was 68°. It never goes below 62°, nor rises above 83° or 84°, in that city, except once or twice in the year for two or three days, when the Leste, or Harmattan (the wind off the African desert), visits the island. It is a very hot, dry, weakening wind, but is rare and of short duration. At Sant' Anna, the mercury for nearly forty years did not go below 60° nor rise above 80°. One advantage of Madeira is the large variety of resorts within the limits of the island itself. Thus, when the heat is too high and steady at Funchal, one can at once reduce it by going to Santa Cruz or Sant' Anna, or going higher up. Three hundred feet above the water it is very rarely that the glass rises above 77° at Madeira.

TENERIFFE.

The Liverpool and London boats, touching at Madeira, stop at Santa Cruz de Teneriffe also, both going and returning. The fare is 19 guineas; time, eight days. There is a Spanish steamer from Cadiz bimonthly; and French steamers from Havre, St. Nazaire, and Marseilles touch there. The ships of Yates & Porterfield, of No. 115 Wall Street, New York, stop at Teneriffe occasionally; fare, $70.

Teneriffe is poorly provided with accommodations for invalids or tourists. The Hotel Durvan, at Santa Cruz, is well kept, and those rooms which face the street are pleasant. The table is good, but not remarkable, and the terms are moderate. But the visitor should, and doubtless would, prefer the north side of Teneriffe, especially the Valley of Orotava. It is much to be regretted that better lodgings are not afforded there to strangers. Mrs. Turnbull's excellent boarding-house was admirably situated when it was at the Deheza di Ventoso. It is now nearer the water, at the Puerto d'Orotava, and the terms moderate; but the accommodations are quite limited. However, the increasing number of visitors will probably soon result in the providing of more facilities for their reception. Good houses are not difficult to find at a moderate rent, and the cost of living is not high. As the Valley of Orotava presents an ideal climate, and is easy of access, it is highly desirable that good lodging-houses should be established there without delay. Donkeys, patient and strong, are easily obtained at Orotava, and mules of doubtful character. At Santa Cruz carriages may be had on hire.

The climate of Teneriffe is remarkable for two features beyond all other regions in the Northern hemisphere—equability and freedom from humidity. Regarding the former characteristic M. Belcastel says, "The thermometer tires one with its monotony. It appears to sleep, and one can count upon breathing, when he rises, the same air and temperature as the day before." At Orotava, about three hundred feet above the sea, for five weeks in May and June, I saw the mercury rise daily in the shade to 72° about 3 p.m. At night it fell to 68°. During that period I noticed no variation from those figures. The mean temperature of Santa Cruz in January, in the shade, is 65° by day and 67° by night; ditto, for July, 79° and 78° respectively. Belcastel records the mean temperature of Orotava in January as 16.8° Réamur; ditto, for July, 24.7°. The mean annual temperature of Orotava is 20.2° Réamur, while that of Funchal is 18.8° ditto. The mean temperature is 61.6° Fahrenheit for January, and 76.6° for July. Along the coast of the island the dews are very slight, although heavy on the mountains. Rain falls at Santa Cruz and Orotava fifty to fifty-five days in the year, but somewhat oftener at Laguna.

The mortality at Puerto d'Orotava is 1 in 60; at Realejo, in the same valley, 1 in 70. That of Rome is 1 in 32. Consumption, bronchitis, asthma, neuralgia, rheumatism, and Bright's disease are all capable of amelioration, if not always absolutely curable, by a residence at Orotava the year round, or at Santa Cruz during the winter, provided the patient goes to Teneriffe before the malady has gone too far, and is resolved to use all due precautions and devote sufficient time to the rebuilding of his constitution. Dr. Perez, who has given his life to an enthusiastic study of the climatic character of Teneriffe, and has kept himself always *au courante* with the medical discoveries of the age, may be depended upon as a thoroughly capable physician.

At Teneriffe and all islands with so mild a climate and such an abundance of fruits, the visitor, whether well or sick, must not forget that unless his habits are regular and his appetites under control, especially in the fruit season, he is liable to dysentery, inflammation of the bowels, or typhoid fever.

NEWFOUNDLAND.

Newfoundland occupies an anomalous position as regards communications. It may be reached generally by steamers running monthly in winter and bimonthly in summer from Halifax, Nova Scotia. The Allan Line between Liverpool, Halifax, and Baltimore touch at St. Johns every alternate week. The boats of the Cromwell Line leave New York for St. Johns every ten days from April to November, touching at Halifax. Fare, $35; round ticket, $65. Two boats also ply between Montreal and St. Johns during the summer.

The Atlantic Hotel is a respectable house at St. Johns. Knight's Home is an excellently kept temperance boarding-house, with limited accommodations, but a good table. Mrs. Simms's lodging-house can also be recommended. At other places on the island accommodations are scarce and inferior.

Newfoundland is rather a resort for sportsmen than for invalids, although the climate during the summer is dry, and free from the extremes of heat and cold; but the summer inclines to coolness. The thermometer does not fall as low in winter as on the neighboring continent. The highest degree of heat in July is 79°; the minimum is 40°; the mean annual temperature is about 42.2°.

There is good trout-fishing in the island streams during the summer, although the enthusiastic fisherman will have to travel some distance from St. Johns to find it in perfection. The deer migrate to the south of the island in winter, but during the summer months they are not infrequent in the northern woods of Newfoundland, as well as Micmac Indians, who are familiar with the haunts of the deer. Grouse are protected by the game-laws until the 20th of August. The seal-fisheries offer many attractions to those who do not mind roughing it in every sense of the term, and aiding in the slaughter of the 150,000 to 500,000 seals annually destroyed on the ice. Much novel and wild adventure can be found in this way, and it is easy to obtain a passage to the sealing grounds in one of the numerous sealers, which go out in March or April from St. Johns and Harbor Grace.

BERMUDA.

This charming little group of miniature isles is reached in seventy to seventy-five hours from New York, by the steamers of the Quebec and Gulf Ports Steamship Company, which run bimonthly, except in May to June, when they ply weekly. The passage is more likely to be boisterous than otherwise, as it lies across the Gulf Stream, but no serious accidents have thus far been reported on this line. Steamers of this company also sail monthly from Halifax for the West Indies, and touch at Bermuda on the way.

The accommodations for travellers at these islands are various, and generally of fair quality. The Hamilton Hotel, under the charge of Mrs. I. W. Dodge, is, among a number, the best hotel in Bermuda, pleasantly situated, overlooking the town of Hamilton. The terms are $2 50 to $3 per diem. There are several respectable, moderate-priced boarding-houses, of which Mrs. Turnbull's, called the Brunswick, at Hamilton, and Mr. Peniston's, at the Flatts, can be especially recommended.

The climate of Bermuda has in times past been much noted, and for those who are strong and well it is charming, and far more agreeable than that of the neighboring continent. Bermuda is out of the range of the trade-winds, and is subject to sudden and violent fluctuations of temperature, with strong gales, attended with a heavy rainfall. It differs from the climate of the main-land not so much in kind as in degree, the extremes being less marked, and inclining toward heat rather than cold. Frost is recorded as having occurred there once—in 1840. In 1876, which is a fair average example of the Bermuda climate, the maximum rise of the thermometer in July was 94° in the shade. The lowest was 40.6°, in March. The mean for the year was 70.5°, and the range was 54.2°. The mean for the year 1874, at 9 A.M., was 72.33°. North and north-west winds prevail, and impart a rawness to the air in winter. Strange to say, very few houses have either grates or stoves, and the consumptive or rheumatic patient should always have one or the other whenever the thermometer descends below 60°. The bad drainage of the houses causes some typhoid fever; but the authorities are waking up on this important subject.

The humidity of Bermuda, especially after nightfall, exceeds anything in my experience, and is the most remarkable feature of the climate. It is so excessive that gloves and cigars, and other objects liable to mildew, are kept in air-tight glass-cases in the shops. Matches are so damp sometimes that they will not ignite, while cigars are so saturated with moisture that they will not burn. Some bromide of potassium, that I had tightly corked up in a bottle, was dissolved by the moisture it absorbed. The mean dew-point for 1875 was 63.3°, and the number of days in which rain fell was 157, the total rainfall being 44.66 inches.

Such excessive dampness is, however, less noxious in a small sea-island than on the main-land, for it is charged with a certain degree of tonic saline qualities that somewhat neutralize its ill effects. At the same time, such humidity is, under all circumstances, to be avoided if possible. For those in vigorous health, Bermuda offers a delightful but enervating climate. But invalids troubled with neuralgia and fever and ague may derive benefit from a residence there. But those who are suffering from pectoral or throat diseases cannot be recommended to go there, unless, perhaps, for the spring months. Bermuda is probably preferable to Massachusetts or Canada for the consumptive; but when there are so many resorts superior to it for such complaints, it seems strange the consumptive should continue to go there.* But whoever does go to Bermuda for his health cannot be too strongly urged to use great caution in exposing himself to the night air at all seasons, and by no means to yield so far to the seductive mildness of the air, on landing, as to throw off his flannels. I have known some, by such ill-judged imprudence, to sacrifice all the good they might have gained, while others in comparative good health who have accompanied them have contracted incipient consumption by sitting exposed to the night air. In Bermuda no one can dispense with prudence in matters of health; but with prudence one may live there a long time, and finally, as the inhabitants say, vanish in a good old age, by simply drying up and being blown away.

BELLEISLE-EN-MER.

This island is reached by daily steamers from Auray. There is also a regular line of packets between Nantes and Lorient, which touch each way at Belleisle.

The Hôtel de France, at Le Palais, can be well recommended. It is on the chief street; the rooms are cheerful, and the table is good. Carriages and wagonettes can always be procured on moderate terms.

The climate of Belleisle is more dry and sunny than that of Brittany, and travellers or invalids wintering in Brittany for their health would find it to their advantage to spend a few weeks at Belleisle. The cheerfulness of the skies, the genial warmth of the sun, the mildness of the temperature, are of a nature to aid the neuralgic or consumptive patient in the recovery of health, although a whole season there would probably be monotonous to many. In May and June the air is balmy and delicious, and the sea-bathing excellent, while the number of visitors from abroad, and the animation attending the sardine fisheries, add greatly to the interest of the little island.

---

* "The climate of Bermuda is relaxing, and, so far as I had an opportunity of observing, especially ill adapted for persons afflicted with disease of the lungs, as nearly all the cases of phthisis I have seen ran their course rapidly." Such is the testimony of Surgeon-major P. H. E. Cross, in the sanitary report of his Excellency General Lefroy, the Governor of Bermuda. Such, also, seems to be the opinion of nearly all the physicians whose opinion and experience I asked, or whose views on the subject have appeared in the official reports.

PRINCE EDWARD ISLAND.

This island is reached from Quebec by the boats of the Quebec and Gulf Steamship Company during the summer season. Navigation during the winter is closed by the ice. The International Line of steamers runs weekly, during the open season, from Boston to Charlottetown, touching at Halifax and Pictou for a few hours. The fare is $10, exclusive of meals, which are $6 to $8 more. This is a very pleasant way of reaching the island. Those who dread the sea can go entirely by rail to Shediac, New Brunswick, and cross the Straits of Northumberland, only thirty miles, in a strong boat to Summerside; or they can take the steamer running from Boston to St. John, New Brunswick, touching at Portland on the way, and go by rail from St. John to Shediac. Thus, there are many ways of reaching Prince Edward Island, all of them affording much interest and variety. The traveller would do well to go by one way and return by another.

Prince Edward Island is traversed from one end to the other by a railroad, which is tapped by another short line from Charlottetown. The carriage roads are everywhere excellent, and good horses and carriages are easily obtained.

There are many hotels on the island; Charlottetown swarms with them. They are generally of an indifferent character; but Miss Rankin's, at Charlottetown, can be very cordially recommended. It is commodious, and finely situated near the water's edge. Mr. M'Donald, who has leased the new hotel at Souris, is a most obliging landlord, and his table is well furnished with meats and game. The terms are moderate. The Seaside Hotel, at Rustico, is admirably situated on a bluff; and although the rooms are small, they are neat, cheerful, and clean, and the table is excellent. A bowling-alley and surf-bathing and fishing are close at hand. Terms, $2 to $2 50 per diem. The Island Park Hotel, at Summerside, is romantically situated on a small island in the harbor, about a mile from the town, which is reached by a steam-tender belonging to the hotel, or by crossing a ford at low water. It is the largest hotel in Prince Edward Island; the rooms are spacious, and command lovely views over land and sea. They are well furnished, and the table is served in the American style, which will please those who prefer that method in a hotel. Bath-houses, billiard-rooms, a bowling-alley, and a croquet-ground are provided; and the woods of the islet are intersected with winding paths containing rustic seats, and a carriage-road which encircles the shore. Good fishing and excellent yachting facilities also await the tourist sportsman. The terms are $2 50 per diem. At this place Prince Edward Island is so indented by bays that it is only three miles across from the southern to the northern coast of the island. Malpeque Bay, on the north side, is a large and interesting sheet of water. Boarding-houses abound, or rather farm-houses, where one can find good, wholesome, but simple fare, including pure milk, fresh eggs, and fine beef. Board and lodging of this sort can be found for $5 to $6 per week.

Prince Edward Island is wholly a summer resort, but as such it can be warmly recommended to the invalid who is suffering from general nervous exhaustion, to all those who are prostrated by overwork, to all who would fortify their constitutions against the wear and tear of the age by sensible vacations, and to sportsmen who love boat-sailing, fishing, and plover, snipe, and duck shooting, with an occasional shot at a brown bear.* Those who are already greatly reduced by lung, or bronchial, or asthmatic diseases would do better to seek a drier and warmer resort. Victims of hay fever may spend the summer at Prince Edward, and forget a torment that never worried Job, or he might not have come down to later ages as a pattern of patience.

The temperature during the summer is remarkable for its evenness and freedom from extremes or sudden changes. From the 1st of June to the middle of September the weather is very delightful, the thermometer ranging from 60° to 75°. Light showers and an occasional heavy rain occur sometimes, but equability is the general character of the summer climate there. The south-west wind, which is generally a damp wind, loses its moisture in crossing Nova Scotia, and reaches Prince Edward Island dry and deliciously soft and balmy.

ISLES OF SHOALS.

These attractive little isles are within a few miles of Portsmouth, and are reached during the season by two steamers, one running twice a day to Appledore, and the other to Star Island.

There is a large and very well-conducted hotel at Appledore, under the charge of the Messrs. Laighton, who have, by long experience, learned how to minister to the wants of their guests. On Star Island is the Oceanic Hotel, a spacious establishment formerly kept by Mr. Poore, facing the cove formed by the cluster of isles between Appledore and Star Island. Its cool verandas are very inviting. The terms are those usual at American watering-places.

The great advantage of the Isles of Shoals is that, more nearly than almost any other inhabited islands in the Western Atlantic, they realize the atmospheric conditions found in a ship at sea; for while the general temperature greatly resembles that of the neighboring coast, the extremes are tempered by the sea air, the minute size of each of the islets giving to them an atmosphere fragrant and healthy with sea qualities; and thus a residence on the islands has tonic effects very similar to those of a sea-voyage. For one trait these isles cannot be too highly recommended —the uncompromising and inflexible determination they show never to allow that strange, mysterious, summer foe, the hay fever, to make an entrance within their charmed limits.

---

* For an account of the fish of those waters and the season to catch, see p. 201.

CAPE BRETON ISLAND.

This island may be reached by rail from Halifax or New Brunswick, or by any of the routes mentioned for reaching Prince Edward Island, excepting the one *via* Shediac. The Boston and the Montreal boats touch at Port Hawkesbury, in the Straits of Canso, and passengers by rail are ferried across to the same town. From there stages proceed to Baddeck, and a steamer plies through the Bras d'Or to Sydney. The beauty of the latter route is exceptionally attractive.

Baddeck and Sydney are the chief towns. Not very much can be said in favor of their hotels; but the boarding establishments of Mrs. King and Miss Heams at Sydney are excellent. At Baddeck, the Telegraph House and the boarding-house of Mrs. Robert Jones can be recommended. The terms average $1 25 to $2 50 per diem. But the sportsman who visits Cape Breton Island will not care to spend much time at the hotels. Camping out with a tent, or cruising in a boat, with rod, rifle, and sketch-book, he will disdain a roof, and enjoy the equable air of summer and early autumn in "roughing" style. One who takes a decked boat of four or five tons to Port Hawkesbury in the steamer from Halifax or Boston, and floats it through the St. Peter's Canal into the Bras d'Or, will find few sheets of water which offer more attractions for a three or four weeks' idle cruise from cove to cove, fishing, shooting, sketching, sailing, and cultivating the acquaintance of the Highlanders and the Micmacs. Or he can hire a small schooner or sail-boat at Sydney. The climate is very even during the sporting season; and trout, salmon, snipe, woodcock, partridge, and plover abound.

ISLE OF WIGHT.

This favorite resort of pleasure-seekers and valetudinarians is so easily reached from the adjoining ports of Southampton and Portsmouth, by so many different railway and steamboat lines, that it is superfluous to go into further details on the subject.

In the matter of excellent hotels and boarding-houses, no island is better provided with the means for comfortably entertaining strangers or ministering to the comforts of invalids. They abound on every hand, and it will therefore suffice, among many, to mention favorably the Pier, the Kent, Sivier's, and the Belgrave, at Ryde. Charming cottages may also be obtained there and everywhere about the island for the season or for the year; but the terms depend so much on size or location, that the visitor intending to lease a cottage will have to look around for himself. At Brading, the Bugle Inn offers shelter to the passing tourist. At Sandown, the chief hotels are the Sandown and the Star and Garter. At Shanklin, Hollier's, Daish's, and the Madeira can be recommended among a number of excellent hotels and lodging-houses. The Clarendon is a tavern rather than a first-class hotel.

Ventnor, the choicest spot in the Isle of Wight, and the resort of invalids, abounds in hotels and boarding-houses of excellent character. The Crab and Lobster cannot be too highly recommended for the quiet order and home-like neatness and convenience of the comforts it offers to its guests. The Marine Hotel, on the cliff facing the ocean, is finely situated, and so, also, is the Esplanade Hotel. The terms at the hotels and lodging-houses of Ventnor are more moderate than the charges at Brighton or other sea-side resorts in England. The Albion and Plumbly's hotel, at Freshwater Gate, are excellent establishments. The Needles at Alum Bay, the Bugle at Newport, and the Gloucester at West Cowes, are capital hotels.

As a watering-place for summer tourists and pleasure-seekers, the attractions of the Isle of Wight are too obvious to require either praise or comment. As a sanitarium for invalids, especially those afflicted with pulmonary complaints, the advantages of this island are less certain, and have within a few years received quite as much credit as they deserve. The island, as a whole, possesses too much of the moist, raw, and variable temperature of England to make it a desirable resort for invalids. But the narrow, seven-mile-long strip of land called the Undercliff, on which Ventnor is situated, enjoys a climate that is more mild, dry, and steady than that of the rest of the island, facing the south-east, and sheltered from northerly winds by the high cliffs of Boniface Down and St. Catherine's Hill. Shanklin also rejoices in the softer climate of Ventnor, but to a less degree. The mean annual temperature of the Undercliff is $51°\ 72'$. In winter it sometimes falls much lower, but, on the whole, it is not surpassed in mildness and equability by any other health resort of the Atlantic north of the Azores. "I have counted," says the late Dr. Martin, "nearly fifty species of garden flowers blooming in the borders in December, and sweet-peas blossom on Christmas-day! The bee is on the wing when, in less favored districts of the island, a bitter frost parches all the meadows." This is the most favorable exhibit that can be allowed in praise of Ventnor. But, after every reservation, it may be frankly admitted that, for those who do not care or are unable to go to the trade-wind islands for their health, the Undercliff on the Isle of Wight offers most decided advantages and attractions which may enable them to protract for years a life that would otherwise be forfeited by a longer stay in the place where the disease was contracted. The Royal National Hospital for Consumption, notwithstanding the unwieldiness of the name, is a most beneficent institution, situated in the outskirts of Ventnor, and intended, for very moderate terms, to give a home in that charming retreat to those invalids whose means are too slender to allow them to meet the expenses generally demanded by a foreign trip for health. To such this noble institution presents remarkable advantages.

THE END.

www.ingramcontent.com/pod-product-compliance
Lightning Source LLC
Chambersburg PA
CBHW032000230426
43672CB00010B/2215